The
Revolutionary Ascetic

THE REVOLUTIONARY ASCETIC

Evolution of a Political Type

Bruce Mazlish

McGraw-Hill Book Company

New York St. Louis San Francisco Bogota Düsseldorf Madrid
Mexico Montreal Panama Paris São Paulo Tokyo Toronto

Reprinted by arrangement with
Basic Books Inc., Publishers

First McGraw-Hill Paperback edition
1234567890 MUMU 783210987

Library of Congress Cataloging in Publication Data
Mazlish, Bruce, 1923–
    The Revolutionary ascetic.
    Reprint of the ed. published by Basic Books, New York.
    Includes bibliographical references and index.
    1. Revolutionists—Psychology.   2. Revolutions—History.
    I. Title.
[D108.M34   1977]   301.6′333′09   77–6705
ISBN 0-07-041173-5

303.6409
M476r

CONTENTS

PART THREE
TWO CASE STUDIES

PREFACE

RECENT EVENTS suggest that the need to understand the revolutionary ascetic is, if anything, growing in importance: to mention a few cases, the revolution in Portugal, the struggles in the Arab Middle East, the takeover of Cambodia by the Communist insurgents, these all provide fresh aspects of revolutionary asceticism in action. In Portugal, General Otelo Saralza de Corvalho suggested at one point that the revolution could only be saved by putting thousands of its opponents in the bullring and killing them; he obviously had the temperament to do it. About former premier Vasco Conçalves a supporter said, "I could go to the theater, the ballet, the cafe, see my friends," but Conçalves "didn't go out, didn't drink or smoke." "I wonder," she concluded, whether such persons are "as much political cases as psychological cases." (*New York Times,* September 25, 1975, p. 2.) Yasir Arafat, the leader of the Palestinian guerrilla movement, said of himself, "I am married to the Palestinian people," and one commentator adds, "Certainly, he has never married anyone else, nor permitted himself any of the normal relaxations that even the most devoted politicians usually find time for . . . his life is totally political. He does not smoke or drink; he has never been linked with sexual escapades or romantic attachments with either sex." (David Holden, "Which Arafat," *New York Times Magazine,* March 23, 1975, p. 67). In Libya, Colonel Qaddafi is an even more notoriously ascetic leader of a revolution. In Cambodia, the Communist cadres are also, characteristically, imbued with revolutionary ascetic fervor.

One could go on with many other contemporary examples; let these suffice. The question then remains: What is this phenomenon I am calling revolutionary asceticism and how does it function? In the process of studying and answering this and related questions, and writing this work, I called on a number of friendly critics. Among those who helped me, though needless to say with varying degrees of agreement, I would like to thank Professors John Fairbank, Joseph Frank, Leo Lee, Richard Pipes, Gerald Platt, Lucian Pye, Benjamin Schwartz, Fred Weinstein, Roxanne Witke, and Perez Zagorin. Mr. Schofield Andrews gave grace and accuracy to some of the translations from the French. I am indebted to M.I.T. and the Department of Humanities for enabling me to receive support from the Ford Foundation Research Grant. In the department itself, Mrs. Ruth Dubois and Mrs. Ann Rourke aided me greatly in the preparation of the book. I am also grateful to Linda Zieper for preparing the index. For the rest, it is the subjects of this work—the Cromwells, Robespierres, Lenins, and Maos—to whom I am indebted.

PART ONE

THEORY AND PRACTICE

CHAPTER 1

Introduction

I

IT WOULD SEEM OBVIOUS that there is no such thing as "the revolutionary personality." Revolutions are of various kinds, and this alone would seem to demand different sorts of revolutionaries. A saintly Gandhi and a demonic Hitler must both be allowed their place in the spectrum of revolutionary leaders.

There is the possibility that underneath the saintly and the demonic qualities a common personality exists. It is this assumption that animates those who speak as if all revolutionaries were basically alike; for example, oedipal sons out to destroy their fathers in the guise of attacking established political authority. Whatever the grain of truth in this assumption, and its occasional fit with the facts, further reflection points to its grossness as a general theory and its utter simplicity in the face of the multiplicity of actual revolutions, with the resultant emergence of varied sorts of leaders and followers.

Does this mean that any effort to inquire into the personalities of revolutionaries, with the aim of establishing some sort of general theory, is foreordained to failure? In my view, it suggests only that we must proceed with great caution, with due regard for the varied nature of revolutions, and with constant attention to the actual facts.

One such "fact" seems to be the frequent appearance in revolutions and revolutionary leaders of what are loosely called "puritan" or "ascetic" qualities. These have been noticed by many observers. For example, an eminent student of revolutionary behavior, Eric Hobsbawm, remarks:

> There *is*, I am bound to note with a little regret, a persistent affinity between revolution and puritanism. I can think of no well-established organized revolutionary movement or regime which has not developed marked puritanical tendencies. . . . The libertarian, or more exactly anti-nomian, component of revolutionary movements, though sometimes strong or even dominant at the actual moment of liberation, has never been able to resist the puritan. The Robespierres always win out over the Dantons. . . . Why this is so is an important and obscure question, which cannot be answered here. Whether it is necessarily so is an even more important question.[1]

Why do Robespierres win out over Dantons? Does André Malraux hint dramatically at the answer when he reminds us of the dialogue between Robespierre and Danton in the corridors of the Assembly shortly after the latter's second marriage? "You're conspiring, Danton," Robespierre accuses his "friend." "Don't be an imbecile," Danton replies, "you can't conspire and fuck at the same time."[2] If Robespierres always triumph over Dantons, do Robespierres also inevitably appear in all revolutions? A moment's reflection on the American Revolution will dispel this supposition. Yet we are left with the conviction that, as Hobsbawm states, "puritanical tendencies" loom large in revolutions, or at least in our perception of them.[3]

Having asserted that there is no such thing as a "revolutionary personality," we now maintain, however, that there is a cluster of traits, which Hobsbawm calls "puritanical" and sees as epitomized by Robespierre, which bears investigation as possibly appearing with unusual frequency in the personality of revolutionaries. Not all revolutionaries will have these traits— one thinks immediately of a Danton or a sensual Sukarno—and not all who have them will be revolutionaries—a de Gaulle or a Nixon (who sought to model himself after the French leader) appear quite "puritanical" but are hardly revolutionaries. Thus it is those who are revolutionaries and exhibit a high quota of "puritanical tendencies" who interest us here. We shall examine them under the concept of what we shall call "revolutionary ascetics," and seek to understand what role and function, consciously and unconsciously, politically and psychologically, both for leader and led, their tendencies fulfill.[4]

I I

OUR REVOLUTIONARY ASCETIC is an ideal type to which any existing individual will only partially correspond. The ideal, however, prods us to keep a sharp eye out for the traits exhibited by a given revolutionary leader, as well as by particular revolutions. The concept of revolutionary ascetic is made up of three parts. First, the ascetic traits must be placed in the service of revolution. Since, in my view (to be spelled out a bit more shortly), revolution is itself a relatively recent social invention or means of social transformation, the problem is to trace how it becomes linked to asceticism. In any case, the term "revolutionary" is meant to set off our subject from other kinds of practitioners of asceticism, especially traditional religious ones.

The "ascetic" part of our "revolutionary ascetic" is itself made up of two components. One is the traditional cluster of traits associated with the word "ascetic": self-denial, self-discipline, no "wine, women, and song," and so on, all in an effort to reach some high spiritual state. It has been the genius of Max Weber to take such traditional religious asceticism in the West and show how, in the guise of worldly asceticism closely connected with Calvinism, it was enlisted in the service of modern capitalist, economic activity.[5] Following Weber, we shall try to show how such ascetic traits were also later put under the banner of revolutionary activity.

In addition to the traditional ascetic traits, we incorporate in our use of the term "ascetic" another element, derived from Sigmund Freud. In his essay "Group Psychology and the Analysis of the Ego" (1921)[6] Freud analyzed leadership in terms of the leader who had "few libidinal ties." We shall seek to explain precisely what this means psychoanalytically, and grapple with its consequences in detail in Chapter 3. Here we can say in general terms that the leader with "few libidinal ties" points at the character traits in an individual that may permit him to deny the normal bonds of friendship, feeling, and affection, and to eliminate all human consideration in the name of devotion to the revolution. A Robespierre can send his friends, Desmoulins and Danton, to the guillotine without any compunction. A Lenin refuses to listen to Beethoven's *Sonata Appassionata* because it may weaken his revolutionary resolve. As Stendhal reminds us in *The Charterhouse of Parma*, "revolutions are not made with kid gloves"; in the novel, the failure out of squeamishness of some Spanish revolutionaries to eliminate some of their opponents meant the failure of their revolution itself.

For Freud's phrase, "few libidinal ties," I am using the term "displaced libido," meaning that the individual has few libidinal, or loving, ties to individuals, but has displaced them onto an abstraction, in this case the revolution.[7] It is the combination in a true revolutionary of displaced libido with traditional ascetic traits that I have in mind when I speak of the "revolutionary ascetic."

Thus I am seeking to combine inspirations from sociologist Max Weber and psychoanalyst Sigmund Freud in investigating the phenomenon of "revolutionary asceticism." Weber concentrated on asceticism as traditionally defined, and then traced its historical development in the West; he paid no attention to the problem of libidinal ties. Freud gave surprisingly little attention to the analysis of asceticism, but he did inquire in depth into the leader with few libidinal ties, and offered a kind of "scientific myth" as to how such leaders were fundamental to the establishment of human societies.[8] It seems to me profitable to synthesize the insights and theories of these two great seers into one concept of the "ascetic," and then to link it with the phenomena of revolution: hence, "revolutionary ascetics."

I I I

A BRIEF WORD must now be said about the concept of "revolution" itself. On this subject a vast literature has grown up, and it would subvert our purposes if we became too engrossed in the topic by itself. However, for an understanding of our view of *revolutionary* ascetics we need to establish a few guidelines. First, a definition is in order. While few students of the subject agree precisely on the definition of revolution, samples of some standard ones will be useful. For Sigmund Neumann, revolution is "a sweeping fundamental change in political organization, social structure, economic property control and the predominant myth of a social order, thus indicating a major break in the continuity of development."[9] For Chalmers Johnson, we may paraphrase it as:

Violence directed toward one or more of the following goals: a change of government (personnel and leadership), of regime (form of government and distribution of political power), or of society (social structure, system of property control and class domination, dominant values, and the like).[10]

If we accept some such definition of revolution, we are then faced with the task of discriminating among different types of revolution. Historians, political scientists, and sociologists have all tried their hand at establishing typologies of revolution. At the very least one is aware of so-called colonial revolutions, nationalist revolutions, modernizing revolutions, and so forth. More precise efforts at typology are embodied in, for example, James Rosenau's division of revolution into three major types of "internal war:" that is revolution: what he calls "personnel wars," "authority wars," and "structural wars." Chalmers Johnson suggests a sixfold typology: jacquerie, millenarian rebellion, anarchistic rebellion, Jacobin Communist revolution, conspiratorial coup d'état, and militarized mass insurrection.[11]

Such typologies of revolution, and the definitions given earlier, still leave us with numerous problems. Do any of these ideal types help us decide whether the Nazis led a revolution?

What is the difference between a "colonial revolution" in the name of modernization under the presence of Western imperialism and one animated by a root-and-branch opposition to all things Western? Is the Chinese Revolution an example of the latter? Was the Cuban Revolution originally intended by Castro and his followers as a "structural war," or did it become so accidentally? Such questions suggest the complications of understanding revolution and, by extension, the nature of leadership in such differing types of revolution.

There is also the historical dimension to be considered. Is revolution the same thing in the seventeenth century as in the twentieth century? Is it the same in a period or society dominated by religious modes of thought as against one in which modern scientific-technological modes of thought dominate? Does the existence of a prior revolution, such as the French, mold drastically the perceptions about revolution of those who come afterward and try to make their "own" revolution? Such questions, mainly rhetorical, again suggest the diversity of conditions surrounding the emergence of revolutionary personalities, including our revolutionary ascetic.

From this welter of problems surrounding the subject of revolution, for our purposes let us stress a few salient assertions. The first is that revolution is essentially a modern phenomenon, dating in its earliest form from about the seventeenth century. At that time the word "revolution" itself, though used sporadically earlier in Greek and late medieval or Renaissance writings, was taken from the astronomical sphere and applied to the political as well. In both spheres it meant a cyclical movement (as in Copernicus' *On the Revolutions of the Heavenly Bodies*). Such a cyclical movement, or revolution, ended by a return to its original position, i.e., a restoration. Thus political revolution meant an irresistible force, something in the stars mysteriously affecting man's destiny on earth, which caused political affairs to rotate through a cycle. In this usage it echoed the earlier Greek notion, as propounded, for example, in Plato, that states went through a cycle from despotism to democracy and back again.

It was the Glorious Revolution of 1688 which, as Karl Griewank informs us, "permanently introduced the word *revo-*

lution into historical writing and political theory."[12] The earlier events of 1640–1660 had been introduced into historiography by Clarendon, its first historian, as "The Great Rebellion" (it was not until the early nineteenth century that Guizot made it known under the label "The English Revolution," and after the middle of the century that S. R. Gardiner called it "The Puritan Revolution"!). The Glorious Revolution, "revolutionary" as it was, was seen as "restoring" England to its rightful position and liberties before a tyrannical king sought to usurp the situation.

In spite of such a "conservative" usage, however, there *had* been a violent political movement in 1640–1660 which men gradually began to recognize as the first modern, large-scale social transformation of the genus revolution. So, too, 1688–1689 was recognized as a genuine mutation, a transition, as Griewank puts it, "to a new dynasty upon new conditions which, with whatever foundation in law, had been laid down by Parliament."[13] What is more, in the seventeenth century, political change—revolution—was increasingly coupled, even if only half-consciously, with the emergent idea of progress. Such a coupling broke the tie of revolution to cyclical movement, and thus to restoration, and forged a new connection to linear development. As a result, by the end of the seventeenth century a new concept of social transformation, revolution linked to progressive forces, had emerged. The fact that this sort of revolution was no mere accident was confirmed in 1789 and thereafter by the institutionalization of revolution as a means of social change, as evinced both by events (the revolutions of 1830, 1848, and so on) and by men's thinking on politics. It is on the basis of the development sketched above that we have asserted that revolution is a modern, Western development, effectively dating from about the mid-seventeenth century.

The new coupling between "revolution" and linear progress took a while to become obvious. Thus our second point is that modern revolution—and henceforth we mean only this usage—has become an increasingly conscious means of social transformation. Only gropingly present in the English Revolution of 1640–1660 (the so-called Puritan Revolution), in terms of Levellers and Diggers, this fact emerges more convincingly in the French Revolution, and is enshrined in the notion of "ideology" which takes its rise from that momentous event. Henceforth, men consciously plan revolutionary overturns of society.

Such men, and this is our third point, often make revolution their profession. A Blanqui or a Buonarroti, prefiguring a Lenin or a Mao, have no career other than that of professional revolutionary. It is their sole "calling." And at this point we can see how a connection can be made to Max Weber's theory of ascetic traits, hitherto religiously oriented, then utilized for economic activity, and now placed in the service of revolutionary activity.

This notion leads to our fourth point, which concerns the question of "modernization." While we cannot say much about this large topic here, we need to signal its importance in relation to revolutions. Modernization is a complex notion, usually taken to involve such factors as industrialization, increasing rationality, secularization, and urbanization. Whatever the precise nature of modernization and of the earlier modern revolutions (i.e., through the French Revolution) in this regard, the revolutions of the twentieth century have tended to be either "modernizing" revolutions, or else revolutions involved in some way with problems arising from the phenomenon of modernization. In short, as we come to more "modern" revolutions, meaning those of the twentieth century, we must assume that they are centrally concerned with "modernization"—that is, at the very least with coming to terms with the problems involved in existing in a world society characterized by widespread modern technology and science, and with the cultural attitudes that cohere to their use.

Our last point about revolution per se, preliminary to our inquiry into revolutionary ascetics, takes up again the point made earlier about our having to view revolution in an historical dimension. Now we can see that revolution has undergone, and is undergoing, an historical development. This fact has generally been neglected by historians, sociologists, and political scientists, who have tended to offer static typologies in place of dynamic theories. True, they have sought to understand the *internal* dynamics of revolution as well as its nature—one thinks, for example, of Crane Brinton's *Anatomy of Revolu-*

tion, with its phases of revolutionary development—but this is not the same thing as depicting and analyzing the dynamics of revolution in the sense of changes in the phenomenon itself over *historic* time.[14] There is simply no satisfactory "history of revolution" as there is, say, a history of liberalism or a history of science.

The absence of such a study complicates our task, for throughout I am assuming the changing, historical nature of revolution itself. Revolutionary asceticism, therefore, insofar as it exists in a given leader and his followers, exists in differing revolutionary contexts. By means of the broad points sketched above concerning the changing nature and context of revolution, I have tried to indicate the most general outlines of that development. In the light of that development, my thesis, crudely put, is that revolutionary asceticism becomes more and more prominent and more and more functional as we move toward more modern, conscious, and professional revolutions.

I V

IN SEEKING to understand the transition from traditional religious to worldly asceticism, Max Weber wrote his famed work, *The Protestant Ethic and the Spirit of Capitalism*. We are now trying to extend his analysis, and the historical development he studied, to revolution; paraphrasing Weber, we might have called our work "The Ascetic Ethos and the Spirit of Revolution." To avoid such a direct comparison and to allow for the dual inspiration of Freud, we have chosen a more neutral title.

Something of what we are concerned with has been foreshadowed in classic political philosophy in passages on the superhuman founders of states, godlike men who are above normal human passions. Chapter 2, therefore, is a quick glance at the elements of this tradition. From this we move to Chapter 3, which examines in detail our key concepts of displaced libido and asceticism, with the psychoanalytic and political aspects intermingled wherever possible.

At this point we should have our ideal type of the revolutionary ascetic clearly before us. Then we shall use it heuristically to explore certain revolutionary episodes and leaders in history, at the same time as we use history to test and perhaps qualify our ideal type. Our starting point (Chapter 4) is a renewed look at Weber's treatment of traditional religious and worldly asceticism, mainly to establish the context for our own work. The natural follow-up to this effort is a consideration, in our terms, of the Puritan Revolution and Cromwell (Chapter 5). This is, of course, the first major revolution, ushering in the phenomenon of revolution as a preponderant force in modern history; thus it is the first place to look for historical information about and a test of our ideal type. Does the epithet "puritan" mean that the revolution of 1640–1660 was actually "puritanical"? Is this the equivalent of "revolutionary asceticism"? Was Cromwell himself a prototype of the revolutionary ascetic? The answers to these questions are not as obvious as they might at first seem.

The French Revolution (Chapter 6) irrevocably introduced the phenomenon of revolution into historical consciousness, and then became the model and inspiration for all those that followed in the nineteenth and early twentieth centuries. In this light, the American Revolution had mainly a parochial effect; while it inspired and influenced some French and British thinkers, its force was dissipated by distance and smallness (America's population was only about two and one-half million at the time), and its waves merely lapped rather than shook the foundations of the political world. The French Revolution inundated the whole of the European universe, and flowed into the Near and Middle East as well as Latin America. Its armies, as well as its ideas, spilled out into the surrounding countries. Until the advent of Napoleon, whom many view as the counterrevolution, Robespierre stood out as the leader of the French Revolution, symbolizing its power and virtue. While relatively little attention has been paid to the "puritanical tendencies" of the Revolution itself, much has been said of Robespierre as a sort of ascetic. Was his "ascetic" leadership exercised in an ascetic vacuum? What, in fact, was the nature of Robespierre's asceticism, and is he an example *par excellence* of our revolutionary ascetic? These are some of the questions we shall seek to answer.

At the end of the eighteenth century another revolution flourished concurrently with the French Revolution. Indeed, as it waxed in the early nineteenth century it borrowed its name of revolution from the French inspiration, for though not a violent political upheaval it was seen as effecting the same profound transformations in society as the events of 1789. This movement, of course, was the Industrial Revolution. Henceforth revolution was bound to have as significant an economic as a political component. Future revolutions would have to come to terms with what we have loosely called the problem of modernization. In seeking to understand how worldly asceticism, first placed in the service of capitalist economic activity, began to be turned in the direction of revolutionary, modernizing activity, we shall look at materials falling under such headings as utilitarianism, victorianism, and nineteenth-century Russian thought (Chapter 7). As we shall see, ideas and movements have a way of subtly running underground for a while before bursting out into the open. At the end we shall try to confront directly what I call the true "modernization" stage of historical revolutionary development as it manifests itself in the twentieth century in the Russian and Chinese revolutions, and in the persons of Lenin and Mao.

Our consideration of these latter subjects will not be detailed; we are not trying to write a history of the Russian or Chinese revolutions. We shall seek only to sketch the general context in which revolutionary asceticism manifests itself in the twentieth century. With this done, we shall undertake detailed portraits of Lenin (Chapter 8) and Mao (Chapter 9) as revolutionary ascetics. Lenin was chosen originally because I believed that he would reveal himself as our prototypic revolutionary ascetic, the closest figure in actuality to our ideal type. I have not been disappointed. Mao was chosen at first because I thought he would demonstrate the limits of the revolutionary ascetic concept. It also seemed useful to test my concept here in a non-Western context. Initially I viewed Mao as rather removed from any strong revolutionary ascetic elements, i.e., as a very different type from Lenin. On review, and after greater acquaintance with the context of Chinese culture, I have concluded that the revolutionary ascetic elements in Mao are much deeper than I had originally contemplated. However, such a conclusion must be among our most tentative ones.

Finally, in Chapter 10, we take a look into the future of revolutionary asceticism. It becomes at last necessary to compare it to revolutionary aestheticism (with which it is not to be confused), a phenomenon increasingly evident at the present time in advanced, or so-called developed, societies. At this point we should once again be clear that revolutionary asceticism can be properly understood only in the context of the development of revolution itself. In short, while the revolutionary ascetic is an ideal type, we ought not to think of him as a timeless personality. "He"—the ideal type as it manifests itself as part of the personality of an actual revolutionary—is merely one kind of leader in the vast movement of violent social transformation we have come to know as revolutionary, a movement which itself changes over time. Our hope is that in understanding "revolutionary ascetics" in theory, we shall also gain a better understanding of revolutions in general, and especially of revolutionary leadership as it has actually manifested itself in history.

CHAPTER 2

The Godlike Legislator

THE PROBLEM of how man creates, or discovers, his political order has occupied men's minds since the beginning of states. In early times men generally conjured up legendary heroes from the mists of time: a half-god, a messiah, a great warrior. Thus, for example, the founding of Rome was explained by resort to the figure of Romulus. Little critical or analytic thought was expended in seeking to understand the nature of such semimythical founders. With the possible exception of the great Greek thinkers, not till the beginning of modern times, in the period of the Renaissance, was a serious attempt made to explain political leadership and its creation of new states (and political states of being) in essentially secular and rational terms.

Not surprisingly, it is the author of *The Prince* who consciously opens up what he calls a "new route." Machiavelli tells us in Chapter IX of *The Discourses*, the work in which *The Prince* originally appeared:

We must take it as a rule to which there are very few if any exceptions, that no commonwealth or kingdom ever has salutary institutions given it from the first or has its institutions recast *in an entirely new mould, unless by a single person* [italics added]. On the contrary, it must be from one man that it receives its institutions at first, and upon one man that all similar reconstruction must depend.[1]

What sort of man recasts institutions "in an entirely new mould"? Machiavelli expounds the answer in terms of a Prince who pursues his *virtu* as a "legislator" by using methods far different from those we are accustomed to hear described as virtuous. It is, indeed, by force and fraud that the Prince *creates* a polity, which then protects and allows for happiness among the lesser men who comprise its citizenry. There is no personal depth to Machiavelli's Prince; he is described in terms of his external function, his political actions, with nothing said of his personal motivations.

When Rousseau comes to take up anew the subject of the legislator, we expect from the author of the *Confessions* and a progenitor of introspective romanticism a special sort of insight into such a man. Instead, in the *Social Contract* (1762), we are presented with what appears to be a superficial treatment of the founders of societies. In highly impersonal terms, Rousseau informs us:

In order to discover the rules of society best suited to nations, a superior intelligence beholding all the passions of men without experiencing any of them would be needed. This intelligence would have to be wholly unrelated to our nature, while knowing it through and through; its happiness would have to be independent of us, and yet ready to occupy itself with ours; and lastly, it would have, in the march of time, to look forward to a distant glory, and, working in one century, to be able to enjoy in the next. It would take gods to give men laws. . . . He who dares to undertake the making of a people's institutions ought to feel himself capable, so to speak, of changing human nature, or transforming each individual, who is by himself a complete and solitary whole, into part of a greater whole from which he in a manner receives his life and being; of altering man's constitution for the purpose of strengthening it. . . .[2]

A closer look at these passages offers us a startling possibility. The godlike legislator must behold "all the passions of men without experiencing any of them"; he, who is "wholly unrelated to our nature," must nevertheless "feel himself capable, so to speak, of changing human nature." What sort of man can rise to these godlike, i.e., *inhuman*, heights?

Plato, to whom Rousseau appealed so frequently, offered one prototype: the philosopher-king. Plato has Socrates pontificate:

Then if we say that people . . . ought to be subject to the highest type of man, we intend that the subject shall be governed, not, as Thrasymachus thought, to his own detriment, but on the same principle as his superior, who is himself governed by the *divine element* within him. It is better for everyone, we believe, to be subject to a power of *godlike wisdom* residing within himself, or failing that, *imposed from without*, in order that all of us being under one guidance, may be so far as possible equal and united [italics added].³

Do we hear echoes of this passage in Rousseau's conception of the general will? In any case, Rousseau, though perhaps not clearly, perceived the inner mechanism of the godlike wisdom involved. He informs us:

Wise men, if they try to speak their language to the common herd instead of its own, cannot possibly make themselves understood. . . . This is what has, in all ages, compelled the *fathers of nations* [italics added] to have recourse to divine intervention and to credit the gods with their own wisdom, in order that the peoples, submitting to the laws of the state as to those of nature, and recognizing *the same power in the formation of the city as in that of man* [italics added], might obey freely, and bear with docility the yoke of the public happiness.⁴

There is one more quotation we must add here. It deals again with the timeworn analogy of the ruler to the father of a family, but Rousseau gives it a new twist at the end:

The family then may be called the first model of political societies: the ruler corresponds to the father, and the people to the children; and all, being born free and equal, alienate their liberty only for their own advantage. The whole difference is that, in the family, the love of the father for his children repays him for the care he takes of them, while, in the State, the pleasure of commanding takes the place of the love which the chief cannot have for the peoples under him.⁵

We need only add the term "founding" to "father" to connect this passage to the earlier ones on the Prince and the legislator.

As one scholar puts it, "It has seemed as natural for many human societies to attribute their existence to the work of a 'founding father' as it has seemed for many religions to attribute the existence of the world itself to a creative god."[6]

At this point let us pause. I have been trying to establish quickly a tradition of thought in the context of which we might pursue our own work. Political societies, according to the strand of the tradition that we are trying to unravel, are founded by a single, godlike individual who acts for the greater whole like a father to his family. This particular father, however, *does not experience the passions of men,* and, moreover, *cannot love the peoples under him.* His satisfaction, we are told, comes from *the pleasure of commanding them.* He commands by what to lesser men might seem immoral means, and certainly by fraud, in the sense that he attributes his actions to a higher being.

Today we can see that there is much political wisdom, along with much floundering, in these particular formulations. The first thing to note is that Rousseau's writings about the legislator, the "founding father," were a theoretical precursor to the actual problem of *founding* new states, encountered shortly thereafter in the American Constitutional Convention and the French Constituent Assembly. In Rousseau's theory, of course, the godlike legislator had total power to create order out of chaos or, to use other terms contemporary to Rousseau, to operate in a vacuum, or to inscribe the lineaments of his new human nature on a blank tablet.

Needless to say, the reality was different: The Americans in 1787–1789, and the French in 1789–1793, were founding their states in an ongoing historical situation, within the constraints of a given tradition, and with divergent political groups fighting over power and ideology.[7] Moreover, although in America George Washington was a "founding father" of sorts (the mythology actually arose in the nineteenth century), the new Constitution was not the work of one godlike legislator but of a number of very able, and very human, legislators. In fact, America in 1787–1789 gave rise to a "group legislator," a political elite not envisioned by Rousseau.

In France events seemed closer to Rousseau's theory. Robes-

pierre tried to institute the Reign of Virtue and, although he
was only one member of the Committee of Public Safety, to
rise, godlike at least in his putative incorruptibility, above the
rest. Still, even Robespierre was constrained by having to try to
lead a *party*, the Jacobins (though in practice he did it badly
and unwillingly), and thus to violate Rousseau's injunctions
against political divisions or sects. What should have become
clear then, as it is now, is that the godlike legislator, at least in
modern times, can only create a new society or state by *first*
creating, or capturing, a *political party*. The party then molds
the state. In so doing, the party fulfills Rousseau's command
that the legislator embody the general will. However, in this
case it is the party, now made "totally" congruent with society,
that embodies all virtue.

This new situation was partly obscured, I suspect, because
the first truly charismatic leader of modern times, Napoleon
Bonaparte, did not exercise power through a party, but usurped
old forms—monarchy, draped in the new toga of emperorship
—to effect his aims. Thus, to look at the matter in Hegelian
terms, he failed to carry out his historical role to the full, and
rested at a midway point.

Whatever else, however, 1789 and its aftermath introduced
new political concepts to match the emergent political world.
Leadership took on a new dimension. Kingly "fathers" gave
way to charismatic "upstarts," that is, to new "founding fathers" who were self-made men (not descendants of dynas-
ties), "making" other men's natures anew in political states of
their own creation. (Such, at least, was the ideal of the future.)
So, too, in place of the old "ranks" and "estates" of a fossilized
and feudalized society, "classes," primarily economic in nature,
entered upon the stage of history. At first an estate, aristocracy,
gave way to political rule by the "middle class." By the end of
the nineteenth century this class was itself yielding to a new
theoretical entity, the "elite," whose content was still to be
determined. Most important, the political party emerged as the
prime figure of the state.

Political parties, elites, classes, and, even if mainly on the
horizon, charismatic leaders—these were the constituents of the
new political world of the nineteenth century. True, in the hey-

day of parliamentary democracy in the late nineteenth and early twentieth centuries, Machiavelli's Prince and Rousseau's legislator seemed dim and musty shadows of ancient godlike leaders. In the twentieth century, however, they took on new life. Rousseau's legislator now became the "founder" of a new party, rather than of a state; such a party, claiming power to the exclusion of all others, then eliminated all existing classes and created a New Society, populated by a New Man. (Unsympathetic observers saw the party as a new elite, although the party generally saw itself as the mere embodiment of the general will.)

In the realm of theory, the first formally to see the extensions to Rousseau's conceptions made necessary by the developments just summarized was the Italian Marxist, Antonio Gramsci. Perhaps his imprisonment by the "charismatic" leader of the Fascist party, Benito Mussolini, sharpened Gramsci's perceptions. In his "Notes on Machiavelli's Politics," Gramsci declared:

The modern prince, the myth-prince, cannot be a real person, a concrete individual; it can only be an organism; a complex element of society in which the cementing of a collective will, recognised and partially asserted in action, has already begun. This organism is already provided by historical development and it is the political party: the first cell containing the germs of collective will which are striving to become universal and total. . . . *The Modern Prince* must contain a part dedicated to *Jacobinism* [italics added] . . . as an example of how a collective will was formed and operated concretely, which in at least some of its aspects was an *original creation* [italics added], *ex novo*. It is necessary to define collective will and political will in general in the modern sense; *will as working consciousness of historical necessity* [italics added], as protagonist of a real and effective historical drama.[8]

Where does this leave us? With an awareness, if we add to Gramsci's emphasis on the party an emphasis on the party leader as well, that in the modern period, i.e., from the French Revolution on, the godlike legislator, Rousseau's unmoved Mover, must operate through a political party which he must either create or shape in his own image, and which embodies his own will.

More than this awareness is now possible to us. In 1900

Sigmund Freud published his *Interpretation of Dreams,* and psychoanalysis became part of public knowledge. For the first time in history, deep insight into *human* nature was possible in terms of concepts and theories scientifically elaborated and grounded in sustained clinical observation. Thus we may now ask what sort of *man* is it who, as a political leader founding a party that intends to reshape man and society, claims to be godlike, beholding "all the passions of men without experiencing any of them"; and what sort of men follow such a leader? Now, too, we can seek our answer in naturalistic, psychoanalytic terms. That task, in the context of the political tradition so briefly sketched above, is, to put it in the simplest terms and as a complement to our previous formulation, what this present work is about.

CHAPTER 3

Displaced Libido and Asceticism: Theory and Function

I

IT IS OUR THESIS that in the last few hundred years a new version of the godlike legislator, a special kind of modern political type, the revolutionary ascetic, came to the fore, functionally endowed in a unique way to perform certain historical tasks. Through Freud we can gain insight into the element of displaced libido involved. Combining some brilliant intuitions of Max Weber with Freud, we can come to grips with the problem of asceticism per se. Thus equipped with a sure grasp of the relevant theory, we can proceed to analyze the way in which displaced libidinal and ascetic traits *may* function politically and, eventually, how they *have* functioned historically.

Freud's theory is basically libidinal. In *Group Psychology and the Analysis of the Ego* he applied his libidinal, or sexual, theory to the problem of leadership. According to Freud:

From the first there were two kinds of psychologies, that of the individual members of the group and that of the father, chief, or leader. The members of the group were subject to ties just as we see them today, but the father of the primal horde was free. His intellectual acts were strong and independent even in isolation, and his will needed no reinforcement from others. Consistency leads us to assume that his ego had few libidinal ties; he loved no one but himself, or other people only in so far as they served his needs. To objects his ego gave away no more than was barely necessary.

He, at the very beginning of the history of mankind, was the "superman" whom Nietzsche only expected from the future. Even today the members of a group stand in need of the illusion that they are equally and justly loved by their leader; but the leader himself need love no one else, he may be of a masterful nature, absolutely narcissistic, self-confident and independent.[1]

To be absolutely narcissistic is to be totally in love with oneself. Whereas most mature people are capable of object-love, that is, love of another person, the narcissistic personality takes itself as its own love object. Of course, all of us are narcissistic to a certain extent. As Freud remarked, the "narcissistic organization is never wholly abandoned. A human being remains to some extent narcissistic even after he has found external objects for his libido."[2] But the person, or leader, with few libidinal ties goes well beyond the average in his self-love or egotism.[3]

Why this is so is not entirely clear. Basically, the process is unconscious; for whatever reasons, perhaps acute disappointment or injury in earlier efforts at object-love, the narcissistic character is unable to love, or allow himself to love, those around him who would normally become the object of his libidinal drives. There is also a possible conscious element to the process, a deliberate withdrawal of libidinal ties from personal loved objects—because of frustration, danger, dysfunction, and other reasons shortly to be investigated.

Absolute narcissists, however, rarely enter history. They do not become revolutionary leaders unless they are also able to displace their self-love onto an abstraction with which they then totally identify. Thus it is the Revolution, the People, Humanity, or Virtue which the leader glorifies and extols; only "accidentally" does he happen to embody it. As we can readily perceive, in loving the abstraction he is also loving his "better self."[4]

Real people are another matter. Almost always, the revolutionary who loves Humanity cannot abide its visible representatives. It is almost as if he loved Humanity because he hated human beings. Barras tells us of a visit to Robespierre in 1794, and his gaffe in addressing him by the familiar "tu," used among themselves by all the old revolutionaries, instead of the formal "vous." Correcting the error found no favor in Robespierre's eyes, for he "did not betray the slightest sign of satisfaction at this sign of deference." Barras concludes, "I never saw anything so impassive, either in the icy marble of statues or in the faces of the buried dead." As a later commentator, Adolph Thiers, sums it up, "He was without sympathy . . . pity in revolutions destroys its possessor."[5]

Such love for an abstraction, on the other hand, is "safe." The abstraction, by definition, never disappoints, never withdraws love or allows ambivalent feelings to annoy the lover. In the name of love for that ideal, the revolutionary is then free to act in the most determined, positive, and willful fashion. He is "free" from the feelings of ordinary mortals.

In this freedom, as Freud suggests, he could "love" all his followers equally—and abstractly. They, in turn, love him "equally" and just as abstractly as the ideal father-leader. All-powerful, all-knowing, immune (especially if asceticism is added to displaced libido) to the vagaries of the flesh, the leader is perceived by them as godlike—and just as impersonal. As he loves Humanity, so they love Him, and imperfections on both sides do not exist to mar the emotional relationship. In this shared and perfect love the followers are able to love one another as fellow worshipers. These bonds of love are made tighter by the freedom to hate those outside the group; as the truism has it, nothing unites more (besides the leader) than a common enemy.

Freud was not the first to call our attention to the role of love in constituting human groups by both widening and constricting the circle of shared emotion. Kant, in his "Idea for a Universal History from a Cosmopolitan Point of View," spoke of man's social and unsocial nature, and of how the two sides ceaselessly warred against one another in ever-widening circles of social cohabitation. And Adam Smith, before Kant, called our attention to the dialectic of self-love and altruism. What

marks Freud off from his predecessors is his enlarged definition
of love as *libido,* and his analysis of the latter in terms of its
fundamental biological-sexual nature, which is then transformed into object-relations, narcissism, displacement, and so
on. It is this *analysis* of the abstraction, love, that makes it an
operational concept for the first time, and allows us to apply it
in detail to specific cases.

I I

IN EXPLAINING how a leader holds a group together by
libido, or love, Freud also examines the role of "suggestibility."
It is a concept closely related to hypnosis, and to the frequently
noted hypnotic powers of the leader. While not all observers
are struck by the mesmeric qualities of the leader—suggestibility seems to be in the eyes of the beholder—enough (both
opponents and followers) are so as to make the confirmation
overwhelming.[6]

Unfortunately, the precise makeup of such hypnotic power
is still not clear. Freud's idea that the hypnotist returns us to a
childlike sleep, commanded by the all-powerful parents, is no
more than evocative. In the days before Freud the power was
called "animal magnetism," and perhaps some basis in physical
science (or chemistry) actually exists; we are all familiar with
the concept of a "fatal" attraction. Originally made popular by
Anton Mesmer, "mesmeric" power was quickly allied to political
power even in the eighteenth century. At that time, Robert
Darnton informs us, "although it originally had no relevance to
politics, it became, in the hands of radical mesmerists like
Nicolas Bergasse and Jacques-Pierre Brissot a camouflaged political theory very much like Rousseau's."[7]

Our prime interest is not in hypnosis as a political theory,
but as a technique of political power. As technique, it seems to
have had its major use initially in the phenomenon of religious
trance. As the modern world became increasingly secularized,
however, it was only natural that the technique of hypnosis
would be translated from the religious to the political realm.

For example, we seem to see an intermediate stage in the person of the youthful Saint-Simonian leader, Barthélemy Prosper Enfantin. Evidence of his hypnotic powers—presumably used in the service of his political-religious version of Saint-Simonism —manifested itself dramatically at his trial in 1832. As Frank Manuel describes the episode:

In a self-conscious manner, whose motives he [Enfantin] openly explained to the court, he taught the audience a lesson in the superiority of emotions and of tactile values over reason. While the advocate-general ranted about the violation of articles in the penal code, Enfantin with majestic calm extolled the power of beauty. He slowly surveyed the judge, the jury, and the prosecutor with his magnetic eye, forcing them into uncontrollable outbursts of rage as he lingered over every one of them, caressing them, thus demonstrating by example the greater strength of his moral being expressed in the eye over their rationalistic juridical arguments. He was the Father preaching, not defending himself. At a signal, the slightest movement of his brow, members of the cult spoke or were silent. The protracted pauses charged the atmosphere in the courtroom. When the judge tried to break the tension by asking, "Do you want to compose yourself?" Enfantin replied "I need to see all that surrounds me. . . . I want to teach the advocate-general the potent influence of form, of the flesh, of the senses, and for that reason I want him to feel the eye." "You have nothing to teach me, neither about looking nor anything else," was Delapalme's exasperated retort. Enfantin was unperturbed. "I believe that I can reveal the whole of my thoughts on my face alone. . . . I want to make everyone feel and understand how great is the moral force of beauty in order to cleanse it of the stains with which your contempt has caused it to be sullied." Despairing of ever getting this romantic hero, who used the techniques of Mesmer popularized in the *feuilleton* novels everyone was devouring, to return to the well-trodden paths of legal procedure, the president closed the session and the good bourgeois on the jury proceeded to find them guilty.[8]

Closer to our own time, there is Adolf Hitler (whom we will consider as a revolutionary, though of a special sort), whose hypnotic or magnetic powers are attested to by numerous observers. One of the most dramatic accounts is given by Gregor Strasser, an early follower, who later turned against him:

Hitler responds to the vibration of the human heart with the delicacy of a seismograph, or perhaps of a wireless receiving set, enabling him, with a certainty with which no conscious gift could endow him, to act as a loudspeaker proclaiming the most secret desires, the least admissible instincts, the sufferings, and personal revolts of a whole nation. . . . I have been asked many times what is the secret of Hitler's extraordinary power as a speaker. I can only attribute it to his uncanny intuition, which infallibly diagnoses the ills from which his audience is suffering. If he tries to bolster up his argument with theories or quotations from books he has only imperfectly understood, he scarcely rises above a very poor mediocrity. But let him throw away his crutches and step out boldly, speaking as the spirit moves him, and he is promptly transformed into one of the greatest speakers of the century. . . . Adolf Hitler enters a hall. He sniffs the air. For a minute he gropes, feels his way, senses the atmosphere. Suddenly he bursts forth. His words go like an arrow to their target, he touches each private wound on the raw, liberating the mass unconscious, expressing its innermost aspirations, telling it what it most wants to hear.[9]

All such material is absorbing and enormously stimulating. But more important for our purposes of understanding what binds a group together in lasting fashion is not so much the concept of hypnosis per se as the overall, more general phenomenon of suggestibility. And there is one part of this phenomenon that relates specifically to our study of the revolutionary with "few libidinal ties."

Once again it is Freud who gives us our lead. Talking of transference, he declares:

It is a universal phenomenon of the human mind, it decides the success of all medical influence, and in fact dominates the whole of each person's relations to his human environment. We can easily recognize it as the same dynamic factor that the hypnotists have named "suggestibility," which is the agent of hypnotic rapport and whose incalculable behaviour led to such difficulties with the cathartic method. When there is no inclination to a transference of emotion such as this, or when it has become entirely negative, as happens in dementia praecox or paranoia, then there is also no possibility of influencing the patient by psychological means.[10]

Transference, the same factor as "suggestibility"! Here is our clue. Freud had earlier defined transference as "an intense emotional relationship between the patient and the analyst *which is not to be accounted for by the actual situation*" (italics added). Let us substitute for "patient and analyst" the terms "followers and leader." The follower is obviously transferring emotions

onto the leader, and the latter "knows" exactly how to evoke
and guide this transference (almost in an hypnotic way, although this last manifests itself mainly in direct contact). But
what of the leader? If we reverse Freud's formulation, we see
that for him there is "no inclination to a transference of emotion" and thus "there is also no possibility of influencing" him.
In a fundamental sense the leader is a sort of analyst whose
freedom from libidinal ties does for him what sustained training
and analysis does for the psychoanalyst: it liberates him from
the dangers of countertransference. He, the leader-analyst, can
evoke and receive the transferences of his followers (as in the
quotation about Hitler) without himself becoming libidinally
involved. What uses he makes of his power and his own self-
control are another matter. Whether to "heal" or to make
"crazed" is an historical, not a psychological, decision.[11]

Of course, no one—leader or psychoanalyst—is totally free
from transference and countertransference. The leader, for example, is *not* unmoved by the crowd (Rousseau's godlike legislator is not an unmoved Mover). As an orator he is often
caught up in his own hysteria. No one who has seen pictures of
Adolf Hitler smirking in a satisfied way at his own performance
and the reaction of the Nuremberg rally crowd can believe
otherwise. To take another instance, to read Trotsky's descrip-
tions of the effect *on him* of the crowd's response to his
speeches is to realize fully how interrelated the feelings of the
leader and his followers can be.[12]

Yet the general thesis still stands. To an almost "inhuman"
degree, the revolutionary leader of whom we are talking is not
subject to countertransference or "suggestion" from outside. He
is, therefore, "masterful" and "independent" because he has
"mastered" his own libidinal impulses, generally by displacing
them on a "loved" abstraction.

III

THE IDEAL revolutionary ascetic, we are arguing, is one who
has identified his self-love with an abstraction, and is also able

to avoid countertransferences to his followers and to control
them by means of "suggestion." He is also "ascetic" in the
more usual sense of the word; that is, he abstains from "wine,
women, and song." More precisely, as the dictionary definition
would have it, asceticism includes: 1) systematic self-denial for
some ideal; and 2) the religious doctrine that one can reach a
higher spiritual state by rigorous self-discipline and self-
denial.[13]

It was, as we have said, the great German sociologist Max
Weber who took the concept of asceticism and placed it in a
vast historical framework. Weber first contemplated asceticism
as a religious doctrine, and then showed, in *The Protestant
Ethic and the Spirit of Capitalism*, how the ascetic traits developed in a "worldly" manner, supplying the core character type
for the emergence of capitalism. In fact, as we shall see, Weber's
analysis was more sociological than it was psychological.

We can follow Weber's line of thought by means of a few
revealing quotations. Weber informs us:

The great historical significance of Western monasticism, as con-
trasted with that of the Orient, is [for example, that in] the rules of
St. Benedict, still more with the monks of Cluny, again with the
Cistercians, and most strongly the Jesuits, it has become emancipated from planless other-worldliness and irrational self-torture. It
had developed a systematic method of rational conduct with the
purpose of overcoming the *status naturae*, to free man from the
power of irrational impulses and his dependence on the world and
on nature. It attempted to subject man to the supremacy of a
purposeful will, to bring his actions under constant self-control
with a careful consideration of their ethical consequences.[14]

With the Puritans, we are on our way to the "worldly" use of
"constant self-control," i.e., asceticism. Labor, for the Puritans,
is:

An approved ascetic technique, as it has always been in the Western Church in sharp contrast not only to the Orient but to almost all
monastic rules the world over. It is in particular the specific defence
against all those temptations which Puritanism united under the
name of the unclean life, whose role for it was by no means small.
The sexual asceticism of Puritanism differs only in degree, not in
fundamental principle, from that of monasticism; and on account
of the Puritan conception of marriage, its practical influence is

more far-reaching than that of the latter. For sexual intercourse is permitted, even within marriage, only as the means willed by God for the increase of His glory according to the commandment, "Be fruitful and multiply." Along with a moderate vegetable diet and cold baths, the same prescription is given for all sexual temptations as is used against religious doubts and a sense of moral unworthiness: "Work hard in your calling."[15]

The calling, according to Weber, gradually became the rational pursuit of money—through hard work. Benjamin Franklin exemplifies the new, worldly "saint," and Weber tells us that we need only read him to see that "the essential elements of the attitude . . . called the spirit of capitalism are the same as what we have just shown to be the content of the Puritan worldly asceticism."[16]

Let us catalogue the traits of asceticism, religious (Christian) or worldly, revealed by the dictionary definition and the quotations from Weber. Leaving aside for the moment its purpose ("some ideal"), there is self-discipline and self-denial. There is self-torture (made "rational" in Western monasticism); freedom from irrational impulses; freedom from dependency; a power of constant self-control; hard work; defense against the unclean life; fear of sexual enjoyment; a vegetable diet, i.e., no self-indulgence of appetite; and cold baths, i.e., physical "torture" and toughening. The word "self" runs through many of the items, but the meaning of "self-discipline" or "self-control" remains vague. Still, as a provisional classification, one may set up the following subcategories: 1) some sort of turning against the "baser" impulses of the self: the appetites for sex, rich food, the comfortable life, the slovenly life; these "desires" must be "punished" by rigid denial; 2) a need for freedom from any "irrational" dominance of the self by anything outside it, i.e., a rejection of dependency on anything outside one's own will; this is what is meant, I believe, by self-control; and 3) a need for labor, for hard work.

Can we now flesh out the psychological understanding of ascetic phenomena by adding the insights of Freud to Weber? Alas, Freud himself, as we remarked earlier, scanted the topic as such. Fortunately, there are materials at hand in psychoanalytic theory that allow us to construct for ourselves a position on the subject.

The main psychological treatment of asceticism, such as it is, seems to revolve around the concepts of sadism and masochism. In the simplest terms, sadism affords an individual erotic gratification through the infliction of physical pain on another person; masochism offers gratification through the infliction of physical pain on oneself. Looked at this way, sadism and masochism are sexual perversions.

But sadism can also be a conscious or unconscious wish to cause psychological as well as physical pain to others, and masochism the same to oneself. Freud's follower, Otto Fenichel, combines the physical and the psychological when he explains:

In the same way that certain sadists torture others for the purpose of denying the idea that they might themselves be tortured, masochists torture themselves (or arrange for their torture through self-made plans and directions) in order to exclude the possibility of being tortured in an unexpected manner and degree.[17]

Fenichel makes the explicit connection to asceticism in only two places. In the first he states:

In this same category is the psychology of asceticism. In ascetics, who strive to mortify the flesh, the very act of mortifying becomes a distorted expression of the blocked sexuality and gives a masochistic pleasure. This type of masochism is, as a rule, a more anal one, characterized by retention and the capacity for tension. Related to it is the "pride in suffering" exhibited by many children who try to deny their weakness in sustaining tension.[18]

In the second he explains:

The analysis of ascetic pride regularly exhibits the idea of self-sacrifice for the purpose of regaining participation in omnipotence, the pride signifying the triumph over having achieved this participation. "I sacrifice myself for the great cause, and thus the greatness of the cause falls on me." That is what priests do who castrate themselves in order to dedicate themselves to God. Their self-castration is a means of entering into the great protecting union.[19]

Without involving ourselves in a prolonged discussion of the psychological issues as such, let us see how the theory of masochism applies to each item in our previous catalogue of ascetic traits. Subcategory 1 would seem to be most obvious, in which the self is punished for its "baser" impulses, perhaps to avoid a fancied punishment by others; subcategory 2 is relevant through rejection of anything outside one's will, especially when the will is then linked to and identified with some godlike abstraction, thus affording participation in omnipotence; and subcategory 3 pertains if we think of work as God's punishment for man's sexual transgressions. Of course, in each particular "revolutionary ascetic" the constellation of ascetic traits would be different, and be present for different psychological reasons (e.g., hard work may be a sublimation rather than a masochistic punishment of the self). It is enough, for the purposes of constructing our ideal type, to say that masochism may underlie many of the purely ascetic qualities that we encounter in our revolutionary ascetics.

There is in psychoanalytic theory another approach to the phenomenon of asceticism, one that is concerned with the "normal" manifestation of asceticism at the time of adolescence. Here the conception is mainly in terms of ego defense. We can follow Anna Freud as she explores the role of asceticism in the psychosexual development of the individual. She centers on adolescence, when the instinctual wishes threaten to overwhelm the youthful character. It is worth quoting her at length:

Young people who pass through the kind of ascetic phase which I have in mind seem to fear the quantity rather than the quality of their instincts. They mistrust enjoyment in general and so their safest policy appears to be simply to counter more urgent desires with more stringent prohibitions. Every time the instinct says, "I will," the ego retorts, "Thou shalt not," much after the manner of strict parents in the early training of little children. This adolescent mistrust of instinct has a dangerous tendency to spread; it may begin with instinctual wishes proper and extend to the most ordinary physical needs.

We have all met young people who severely renounced any impulses which savoured of sexuality and who avoided the society of those of their own age, declined to join in any entertainment and, in true puritanical fashion, refused to have anything to do with the theatre, music or dancing. We can understand that there is a connection between the forgoing of pretty and attractive clothes and the prohibition of sexuality. But we begin to be disquieted when the renunciation is extended to things which are harmless and necessary, as, for instance, when a young person denies himself the most ordinary protection against cold, mortifies the flesh in every possible way and exposes his health to unnecessary risks, when he not only gives up particular kinds of oral enjoyment but "on principle" reduces his daily food to a minimum, when, from having enjoyed long nights of sound sleep, he forces himself to get up early, when he is reluctant to laugh or smile or when, in extreme cases, he defers defecation and urination as long as possible, on the grounds that one ought not immediately to give way to all one's physical needs.[20]

Such repudiation of instinct differs from ordinary neurotic repression. In the latter a substitute is generally found for the rejected gratification (for example, the hysteric finds sexual excitation in other bodily zones or processes; that is, he sexualizes them). Instead, the "normal" adolescent repudiates gratification completely, and then almost invariably swings over "from asceticism to instinctual excess . . . suddenly indulging in everything which he had previously held to be prohibited and disregarding any sort of external restrictions." Therefore, the ego *defends* itself against the sudden accession of libido in the adolescent by wild swings from asceticism to indulgence, as befitting his ambivalent feelings toward his wishes.

Another defense, according to Anna Freud, is intellectualization. Here "the *thinking-over* of the instinctual conflict" can be safely undertaken, without necessarily involving irreversible actions and the dangers thereof. Thus the instinctual problem is reified. As Anna Freud puts it, "the point at issue is how to relate the instinctual side of human nature to the rest of life, how to decide between putting sexual impulses into practice and renouncing them, between liberty and restraint, between revolt against and submission to authority." Or, in another phrasing pertinent to our problem:

The philosophy of life which they construct—it may be their demand for *revolution* [italics added] in the outside world—is really their response to the perception of the new instinctual demands of their own id, which threaten to revolutionize their whole lives.

The formulations just given involve a real danger of reductionism. The demand for "revolution" is not simply a libidinal resolution; it occurs only in certain political, social, and cultural settings—in fact, revolution itself as we have maintained, is, properly speaking, only to be found in modern history—and for all sorts of conscious reasons.[21] With this qualification we can profit from Anna Freud's theory. In general, our revolutionaries do deal with libidinal impulses in terms of both asceticism and intellectualization. What distinguishes them from most young people is that they make these "defenses" central to their lives even after adolescence. More importantly, for our purposes, asceticism (and intellectualization) becomes "adaptive," providing great political strength for our revolutionaries.

It is this problem—political as well as psychological—that is at the heart of this book. Displaced libido and asceticism have functional significance on the political as well as the psychological level; the two levels joining in what we may call the psychohistorical realm. We are postulating, in fact, that there is an enormously explosive power in "revolutionary asceticism," that the traits of displaced libido and asceticism are highly functional in the real world of revolution. Control over other people is a key political issue, often approached in terms of the question of authority. We claim that the subject must also be approached psychologically; that we must inquire how "control" over one's instinctual desires fosters and facilitates "control" over one's followers in the political arena.

I V

LET US NOW LOOK at the way revolutionary asceticism (which has, incidentally, an overlap with Weber's theory of charisma) arms the leader for his historical task of revolution.[22] We contend that the revolutionary ascetic, our new version of Rousseau's legislator, does not experience "the passions of men," or, rather, experiences them in a *controlled* fashion, and thus enjoys real political advantage from his character. The first functional advantage emerges from the denial of libidinal ties. On the most prosaic ground, a revolutionary leader is vulnerable if he has loved ones. For example, under

Tsarist Russia, suspected social democrats were constantly exiled and torn apart from their wives; children were hostages to fortune. The dedicated revolutionary learned quickly that he must not allow himself to be caught up in emotional ties of a family nature. (How this affects the sort of woman involved in revolutionary relations we shall consider later.)

On another level, a professional revolutionary simply has no time for ordinary family concerns. He is devoted to the revolution at all hours, and when other men go home to their wives and children, he is still making speeches and organizing supporters. How, then, can he "love" in the ordinary way? (In many ways he is like the typical achieving businessman of the free enterprise system, whose whole life is his business activity, with little time *or emotion* left over for his family; once again one thinks of Weber's ascetic entrepreneur, to whom we have added the notion of libidinal withdrawal.)

In sum, the revolutionary leader must reject existing family and social relations, and break the ties binding him to them. It was Christ, after all, as Hegel emphasized, who told his disciples: "Follow me, and forsake thy Father and Mother"—and set the example for them! Today it is Mao Tse-tung who takes up the refrain, exhorting his followers to abjure their family ties and relate only to him and the party, providing the model for this action in his own life. Psychologically and historically, the construction of a "new" society, either on the familial or national level, requires destruction of the old; this means destruction of the emotional ties to the people who comprise that outmoded group.

An integral part of this process is a denial and rejection of the past. For the revolutionary leader this usually means a rejection of both his personal past and that of his "nation." To symbolize the personal break he frequently takes a new name or mode of address (as with Lenin, or Stalin, or Citizen Robespierre). Coming almost always from the upper or middle class, the revolutionary leader looks with horror upon the softness and exploitation of his childhood existence or, as with Mao, upon his parents' worldly ambitions. He becomes a "new man," a professional revolutionary sharply cut off from his adolescent, amateurish past.

He also spurns the national past. As Weinstein and Platt, discussing the French Revolution, remind us:

To remember the past was to have feelings about it, and if one judged it fairly, then there was the good as well as the bad. But if one could remember the good, it became difficult to act, and both past and feelings were therefore denied, at least in their positive aspects; because the past was not available to him, Robespierre could act.[23]

Hence the king was seen only as a tyrant, and the past as a time of superstition and despotism deserving only to be obliterated —in memory as well as in fact.

Such breaking of emotional ties—to the past and the present, personal and national—can only be done by a leader who has become a "new man." I shall take as my prototype the Russian populist Chernyshevsky, who in turn served as the model for Lenin. While we shall deal with Chernyshevsky at greater length, here for the moment is the description of him offered by Isaiah Berlin:

Chernyshevsky's harsh, flat, dull, humourless, grating sentences, his preoccupation with concrete economic detail, his self-discipline, his passionate dedication to the material and moral good of his fellow man, the grey, self-effacing personality, the tireless, devoted, minute industry, the hatred of style or of any concessions to the graces, the unquestionable sincerity, the combination of brutal directness, utter self-forgetfulness, indifference to the claims of private life, innocence, personal kindness, pedantry, moral charm, capacity for self-sacrifice, created the image that later became the prototype of the Russian revolutionary hero and martyr.[24]

The "new man," as advocated by Chernyshevsky in his novel, *What Is to Be Done?*, as well as exemplified by his own character, was to be "hard," to be without feelings, to distrust sentiment, to reject spontaneity, and to deny his passive wishes. The self-indulgent character Oblomov, pictured by the contemporary Russian novelist Goncharov, was the reverse image, the negative identity, the abomination to be despised. As Nathan Leites has tried to show in his *Study of Bolshevism*, Chernyshevsky's values became internalized as the "operational code" of the Bolshevik leaders from Lenin onward.[25]

V

WE HAVE STRESSED that the leader's rejection of the past and any annoying ties to it not only strengthens his self-confidence but also permits his followers to break from their thralldom to existing institutions. What the revolutionary ascetic does, in fact, is provide an ego-ideal which can serve as an alternative to the dominant values of the society. Unlike the superego, which is derived from the punitive aspect of parents and generalized authority, the ego-ideal is taken from some aspect of the original loved object, e.g., the parent, and made into an all-encompassing inner vision of what a right and just world would look like. Thus, and we cannot emphasize the point too strongly, in this aspect of his existence the revolutionary ascetic is a creator. He is exercising ego as well as id functions and providing his disciples with new ways of perceiving and judging the world around them.

In this situation, the libido formerly attached to real persons is now displaced onto the ego-ideal by the revolutionary ascetic; as we have seen, it is extended to the followers by a chain of libidinal relations to which they are enslaved, but from which the revolutionary ascetic is himself left free. In return for their "enslavement" to the leader and the new ego-ideal, the followers now have a sense of "entitlement," that is, they are allowed (nay, made) to feel justified in the release of aggression, previously forbidden by internalized values, against their former rulers and values.

It is of such psychological dynamics that revolutionary social change is made. The revolutionary ascetic conjures up a new ego-ideal and, literally, fantasies, or dreams, of a new reality. However, unlike an Oblomov (see Chapter 8, on Lenin), he has the character traits and energy needed to organize reality in a way that will make his dream come true.

The danger is that, like Don Quixote, the revolutionary may wander in the land of windmills forever. Lenin, well aware of this issue, remarked that he would hide himself behind the back of Pisarev (a nineteenth-century Russian populist):

"There are differences and differences," wrote Pisarev concerning the question of the difference between dreams and reality. "My dream may run ahead of the natural progress of events or may fly off at a tangent in a direction to which no natural progress of events will ever succeed. . . . Divergence between dreams and reality causes no harm if only the person dreaming believes seriously in his dream . . . and if, generally speaking, he works conscientiously for the achievement of his fantasies. If there is some connection between dreams and life then all is well."[26]

Later Lenin added that "it would be stupid to deny the role of fantasy even in the strictest science: cf. Pisarev on useful dreaming, as an impulse to work, and on empty day-dreaming." In short, we may add that if a dream could reveal the mathematical nature of the world to Descartes, and serve as the basis of Freud's mental science and therapy, it can also serve as the means by which the revolutionary ascetic places before himself and his followers a new ideal toward which they may work—and fight.

By his creative fantasy, his new ego-ideal, the revolutionary ascetic supplies the beliefs and values on which a new community of believers, bound to him by ties of love, can come together. Organizational abilities can then make the ties cohesive. A new society can be created in which shared "interests" arise to supplement the new beliefs and values already held in common. This effort usually requires tremendous sacrifices of the followers, and it is the leader's revolutionary asceticism, as we have seen, that justifies the demands he places upon them. His creative fantasy and his ego-ideal keep them moving toward the promised land when all other incentives are lacking. In turn, the hosannahs of his followers provide enormous libidinal satisfaction to the leader's narcissism.

VI

MEN SUCH AS our revolutionary ascetics are obviously not only rejecting libidinal ties but also practicing the classic ascetic virtues per se (e.g., self-discipline, self-denial). Because of their godlike nature (though they would not put it in these terms), they believe in their right to rule over their followers. Their own repression of instinctual gratification seems a fitting price for the purchase of leadership. As with earlier religious martyrs, the revolutionary ascetics seem to gain a victory over the rest of us through their "suffering." They, and we, conceive their right to rule as a "duty" imposed on them, rather than as an indulgence of desire; after all, are they not repressing their desires in their personal lives? As Philip Mason puts it in another context:

Often the privilege of rank carries with it much from which the commoner would shrink, sometimes a harsh austerity of bodily discipline and a lifelong training for death, as with Spartans, Aztecs, Zulus, and Prussians.[27]

With our type of revolutionary leaders, moreover, such rule is almost always exercised in the name of the general will, and therefore, by definition, selflessly and as a duty. Thus revolutionary asceticism justifies the revolutionary leader *to himself* (as well as to his followers, as we shall see), and allows him to rule—and, if necessary, to kill—with a clear conscience.

Finally, the conquest of oneself through classic asceticism serves two further purposes. It permits the leader to conquer his own fears. Such fears, as we have noted earlier, whether coming from internal, threatening impulses, or from external threats of torture or deprivation, hold less terror for the man who has already "tested" himself by self-imposed penalties. In addition, conquest of oneself, enhancing one's sense of autonomy, also gives confidence in one's ability to conquer the outside social and physical world. It also enhances the leader's feeling (on the unconscious level, of course) of rightness to rule: If he can rule and control himself "correctly," then he is rightfully entitled to rule and control others.

VII

SO FAR we have concentrated on the functional advantages of revolutionary asceticism for the leader, and have alluded only indirectly to the effect on his followers. Let us now analyze more explicitly its importance for the followers. Our thesis is that the leader's revolutionary ascetic qualities make him seem superhuman, a viewpoint enhanced by his own supreme self-confidence and total belief in the rightness of his mission. The result for the followers is that they can follow the leader "blindly," "slavishly," and without fear. They can give way safely to their desires for complete dependency.

However, the term "followers" is too all-inclusive. Weber's theory of leadership can help us by suggesting that we ought really to differentiate between immediate followers—disciples —and general supporters. It is the former whom Weber usually has in mind. Thus, one commentator, Robert C. Tucker, re-marks about the followers:

Oftentimes, the relationship of the followers to the charismatic leader is that of disciples to a master, and in any event he is revered by them. They do not follow him out of fear or monetary induce-ment, but out of love, passionate devotion, enthusiasm.[28]

As a case in point, Tucker quotes from the memoir of a thirty-year-old Russian Marxist commenting on Lenin:

No one could so fire others with their plans, no one could so impose his will and conquer *by force of his personality* [italics added] as this seemingly so ordinary and somewhat coarse man who lacked any obvious sources of charm . . . only Lenin represented that rare phenomenon, especially rare in Russia, of a man of iron will and indomitable energy who combines fanatical faith in the movement, the cause, with no less faith in himself . . . [he] had the feeling that in him the will of the movement was concentrated in one man. And he acted accordingly.[29]

It is not only the immediate followers, the disciples, who can submit themselves more or less completely to the leader be-cause of his fanatical faith in both himself and the movement. The general supporters can also follow without fear or ques-tion, though perhaps with less intense manifestations of im-mediate love and devotion.[30] Moreover, according to an addi-tional interpretation which builds on the Weberian theory of charisma and is perhaps exemplified best in the thinking of Robert Lifton and Philip Rieff, the leader with fanatical faith offers his followers not only certain victory, but salvation. The idea is that the leader has conquered for himself the fear of death (usually through some episode in which he has confronted it directly; he has passed through the "shadow of the valley of death"), and therefore, symbolically, done the same for his followers. In part, too, the victory of the proposed revolution is "millennial," and thus offers a form of immortality. Death is overcome in a twofold way, and the charismatic leader *cum* revolutionary ascetic brings a multiple form of salvation.

Whatever the precise mechanism, it is clear that my revolutionary ascetic leader, especially through his displaced libidinal qualities, provides his followers with the security of total commitment. In this he is like God, the perfect Father, and partly for this reason is often revered as a "superhuman" figure.

As for revolutionary ascetic leader's specifically classic ascetic qualities, these appeal to followers in many ways. Often, for example, the revolutionary leader appears in the midst of what is perceived as a "corrupt" society. Pure himself, he is therefore qualified to purify and "clean up" the rotten mess. Even in basically noncharismatic, bureaucratic political systems, such as in the United States, we are aware of the electoral attraction of the slogan, "Clean out the rascals," and how, for example, this worked to the advantage of General Eisenhower. How much more critical it is that the leader in a revolutionary situation seem pure and incorruptible: Mirabeau's venality, and the alleged venality of Danton, worked seriously against them both in the power struggle.

Further historical comparison may be useful here. In the Middle Ages the Cathari, a movement within the Christian church, insisted that sacraments were only valid if the priest administering them was personally pure. So, too, in charismatic politics. The purity of the leaders vouches for the rightness and purity of the movement. There is also a nice God-Devil split afforded to the followers, for all the "pure" and "good" feelings can be isolated and concentrated on the all-good God, and all the "bad" feelings fixed upon some noxious enemy.

On a slightly different note, we can guess that the ascetic leader, uncorrupted by the lures of money, flesh, or sensuality in general, is perceived by his followers—incorrectly, as I have suggested—as without self-love or self-interest. Sans self-interest, it is then assumed that he can judge the competing claims of the interests of others impartially and fairly; above the fray, he is therefore just. He can, so to speak, act disinterestedly in affairs of state because he has no "interest" in his own private affairs.

All of these diverse sources of influence over followers—the evocation of feelings of total, secure dependency, the luxury of isolating all the good and bad feelings, the belief in incorruptibility and disinterestedness—are brought forth or enhanced by the leader's presumed possession of ascetic qualities and a displaced libidinal nature. Together, these revolutionary ascetic qualities hold out to the followers the pleasurability of complete, slavish love of and dependency on a superhuman being. To the revolutionary ascetic, in turn, his special qualities secure enormously powerful political and social support. Small wonder that so many revolutionary leaders have been revolutionary ascetics!

VIII

LET US NOW draw a number of strands together. In seeking to understand the psychological dimensions involved in displaced libido and asceticism, we have called upon such Freudian concepts as narcissism, displacement, suggestibility, and masochism. Next, we have tried to see how such character traits are functional, psychologically *and* politically, for both the leader and his followers: for example, justifying the "selfless" exercise of power, giving the appearance, if not the reality, of "purity" to such exercise, "testing" the leader for the possibility of torture and deprivation and "toughening" him for the commission of "unsentimental" acts, turning the leader into a professional revolutionary totally dedicated to his "calling," and allowing him to give the disciples the security of following a leader who holds out certain salvation.

At the end, such a leader is a new version of the godlike legislator, only we have tried to delineate his superhuman qualities in terms of our ideal type, the revolutionary ascetic. What is more, we have been able to *analyze* the elements that make up both his personality and the psychological source of his leadership. In addition, we have sought to estimate his ability to break emotional ties to the past, for both himself and his followers, and to offer a new ego-ideal. Having done all this (and, admittedly, we have not attempted to examine the limitations inherent in his "driven" nature, especially for postrevolutionary society), we now wish to bring the leader out of the heavens and to place him firmly on the ground of actual historical life. Using Max Weber's sociological and historical insights, we have postulated ascetic and displaced libidinal traits as moving from the service of religion, to capitalist economics, to modernizing revolution.

All these assertions are still in the realm of theory and ideal type. The task ahead is to examine actual leaders and revolutions, and to see what in fact is the fit between the psychological type and the historical revolutionary. Our claim, to repeat, is that modern revolutions are modernizing ones, and that there is a special fit between the revolutionary ascetic character and the needs of such revolutions. To put it another way, revolution is itself a changing historical phenomenon; as it changes more and more in the direction of becoming a modernizing revolution, it turns increasingly to a particular character type: the revolutionary ascetic. This character, at least until the present, corresponds with the historical demands of modern revolution, and vice versa. Theoretical assertion must now be tested and illustrated by appeal to the historical record.

PART TWO

THE HISTORICAL
STAGES

CHAPTER 4

The
Religious Stages

I

WE SUGGESTED EARLIER a possible "ascetic ethos and the spirit of revolution" as a complement to Max Weber's work on the spirit of capitalism. To carry out such a task, we need first to have a clear idea as to what is and has been involved in the religious use of asceticism. In fact, we need to reexamine Weber's original work.

As Weber recognized, asceticism in itself, i.e., nonrevolutionary, is hardly a new or modern phenomenon. Its connection for many centuries with religion of many kinds is abundantly evident. For our purposes, we need merely single out a few general points.

The first point is that, psychologically, asceticism in its Western religious guise appears frequently to be practiced not only so as to reach a higher ideal, but so as to assuage feelings of guilt. Thus one rids oneself of sin, scourges the flesh, fasts, or refrains from sex as a form of self-punishment. Basically, it is asceticism out of fear of the superego. In this form asceticism is not practiced primarily in order to obtain self-control.

Of course, religious asceticism is not solely of this form. For example, in so-called primitive religions, such as some American Indian religions, fasting and flagellation are perceived as giving power over the self, and thus a claim to power over the tribe. The prevalence of religious asceticism out of a sense of guilt will depend, therefore, to a large extent on the nature of the superego in various cultures. Generally, however, where there is a strong sense of sin in the culture and the religion, there we can expect guilty asceticism. Such asceticism differs significantly from what I have been trying to analyze as a component part of revolutionary asceticism, and poses the problem of identifying the historical stages by which we move from one to the other.

The second point emerges from what has just been said. Different religions will make use of asceticism in varying degrees and in varying ways. It is imperative, in seeking to understand a particular revolutionary ascetic, to be aware of the religious tradition of asceticism in which he is operating. Christianity (even where overtly rejected) offers one set of resonances to the revolutionary asceticism per se of a Robespierre or a Lenin; Hinduism offers a very different tonality to that of a Gandhi. To take only one example: In Christianity sexual intercourse is often linked with a sin against God, the Father, wherein the lusts of the flesh are seen as evil, and giving way to them as a diversion from the requisite devotion to God (who alone, presumably, should have the powers of procreation). In the Hindu religion, the classic writings suggest that the loss of semen is the loss of an irreplaceable life force, and weakens the powers of the brain (there are overtones of this in Christianity, but in a much less consciously expressed degree). Thus sexual abstinence, or control, in a Lenin or a Gandhi "mean" different things both to them and to their followers. For an understanding in depth of revolutionary asceticism, it is therefore necessary to place each case in its particular religious and cultural context.

I I

FOR OUR PRESENT PURPOSES we shall move from all possible religions with ascetic elements to a consideration only of Christianity and its asceticism. We shall take Max Weber as our guide, and move with him in ever-narrowing circles from Christianity to Catholicism, to Protestantism, to Lutheranism, and to Calvinism and its related developments. Specifically, in *The Protestant Ethic and the Spirit of Capitalism* Weber is interested in explaining how capitalism is uniquely characteristic of the West, and ascetic Protestantism characteristic of capitalism, and why this is so.

Weber's famous thesis, in brief, is that modern European civilization is uniquely characterized by rationality, which manifests itself especially in economic and scientific life. Weber's main concern is with economic life, which he equates with capitalism (though once capitalism exists, the possibility of rational socialism is also present). Capitalism is the rational, calculated, and constant pursuit of profit, and forever renewed profit. It involves such developments as the rational capitalistic organization of free labor, a regular market, and rational business bookkeeping.

How did this system come about? Weber's answer is subtle and sensitive. While keeping an eye on multiple causation—actually coexisting processes—he rejects the simple, or vulgar, Marxist notion of capitalism as an historically necessary result of certain material changes, and emphasizes instead the crucial shaping role of the "spirit" of capitalism.

That spirit is ascetic Protestantism. How did this spirit arise, historically, and in unintended and accidental fashion? As Weber points out, greed for profit has existed in most societies. Indeed, we can say that *capitalism* of a sort has existed in many societies:

For the purposes of this conception, all that matters is that an actual adaptation of economic action to a comparison of money income with money expenses takes place, no matter how primitive the form. Now in this sense capitalism and capitalistic enterprises, even with a considerable rationalization of capitalistic calculation, have existed in all civilized countries of the earth, so far as economic documents permit us to judge. In China, India, Babylon, Egypt, Mediterranean antiquity, and the Middle Ages, as well as in modern times.[1]

The crucial point about modern Western capitalism is that it is the *restrained* and *rational* tempering of the irrational greed for gain. Moreover, this restraint is achieved by internal and not external controls, and this is an essential difference between ascetic Protestantism and Catholicism. Once we have such internalized restraint, we can have deferred gratification of all desire, and the way is open, among other things, to the rational accumulation and use of capital. Further, once in existence, capitalism no longer needs its religious underpinnings, according to Weber, and under the thrust of competition proceeds inexorably along as a self-generating mechanism (in this way it resembles its companion, Western science, which is also now self-perpetuating).

The starting point for this development is Western monasticism; its turning point is Martin Luther. Western monasticism had taken the existing individual asceticism of early Christianity and, in contrast to the religions of the Orient, institutionalized and regulated it. In the monastery the monk was placed under a *rule*, and a systematic method of rational ascetic conduct imposed (presumably self-imposed) upon him. Yet, as a monk, he had removed himself from the world and its activities. As Weber puts it:

Thus asceticism, the more strongly it gripped an individual, simply served to drive him further away from everyday life, because the holiest task was definitely to surpass all worldly morality.[2]

It was Luther's life work to take asceticism out of the monastery and to involve it with worldly activity. Luther did this as a personal experience. There is a nicety in his making the move from the monastery to the world in his own life, testing it existentially, so to speak, at the same time as he worked out the consequence of this shift in his theology. There is a further nicety in that not only Weber, but Erik Erikson as well has taken "Young Man Luther" as the central revolutionary figure for modern times.[3] For Weber, Luther leads (unintentionally, of course) to capitalism; for Erikson he leads (unconsciously, though also sometimes consciously) to a revolutionary challenge to authority. At first, in an effort to rid himself of a feeling of sin, Luther immured himself in a monastery, scourging his flesh, fasting, and subjecting himself to minute controls upon all his impulses. It was the failure of this effort—a most creative failure!—to achieve a sense of salvation by monastic asceticism that led Luther back into the world with a new version of the uses of asceticism.

According to Weber, the central doctrine in this transvaluation of value was the conception of the *calling*. The calling, as expounded by Luther, meant a "life-task, a definite field in which to work" (p. 79). Therefore, "the only way of living acceptable to God was not to surpass worldly morality in monastic asceticism, but solely through the fulfillment of the obligations imposed upon the individual by his position in the world. That was his calling" (p. 80). Thus at one stroke Luther and the Reformation justified worldly activity as acceptable and praiseworthy in the sight of God, and not, as previously conceived, as diverting and seducing man from Him.

Though Luther was the revolutionary turning point in the secularization of asceticism, he was only a midpoint in the whole development. With him the concept of the calling remained traditionalistic. Having justified worldly activity and work, Luther nevertheless preached the old doctrine that each individual was to remain "in the station and in the worldly occupation in which the call of the Lord had found him" (p. 84). Explicitly, he opposed both social mobility and rational capitalism. Implicitly, the reason he opposed monastic asceticism was that he had finally decided that it was a form of "good works," and as such could not lead to salvation. Only an inner change, a feeling of faith, could bring the security he sought so avidly for his spiritual future.

It was Calvin who took the giant step, again unintentionally, to ascetic Protestantism as the inspiring spirit of capitalism. If the concept of the calling was central to Luther, the concept of *predestination* was the rock upon which Calvin founded his church. Predestination meant the final and rigorous rejection of all good works and sacraments as aids to salvation: God had made his election of individuals for salvation or damnation at the beginning of time, and his eternal decree was hardly to be affected by childish attempts at persuasion. How, in the face of such a razorlike dogma, could the uses of asceticism be of any consequence? Surely asceticism would bring one no closer to God and salvation?

There are three consequences, or developments, of Calvin's concept of predestination that need to be commented upon. First is the psychological consequence. In what Weber calls its "magnificent consistency," it left a man with "a feeling of unprecedented inner loneliness" (p. 104). No one and nothing could help him: neither priest, nor sacrament, nor his own efforts. One could only trust in God, and this meant that one ought not to trust in the aid or friendship of men, or even of one's own family. We shall see later how this enforced feeling of total independence from other men (purchased at the price of total dependency feelings toward God) had consequences for revolutionary behavior, but here we wish only to stress its usefulness for the development of laissez-faire capitalism. To stand on one's own feet, psychologically, allowed one to enter new entrepreneurial fields with courage and heroism.

But the "magnificent consistency" of Calvin's predestination was too harsh for most of his followers to accept undiluted. They needed additional security, and they found it in the modified doctrine of the elect. This is the second consequence of Calvin's dogma. The theory of the elect simply states that some individuals *have* been elected for salvation by God. While the practice of good works, the definition of which in its Calvinist dress we shall need to explore further in a moment, cannot influence one's election, it *can* provide a sign that one *has* been elected. Thus, psychologically, the fear of damnation is assuaged by outward evidences. When we realize that good works for the Calvinist means the practice of an ascetic worldly existence, carried out in one's calling (now open, however, to self-determination), and that this asceticism is not the Catholic practice of isolated and disjointed single good works, but the unified, constant, total system of ascetic *character* in the individual, we perceive the new and true features of ascetic

Protestantism. I would suggest for it the label of "elitist asceticism," for it is basically a life style only of the elect.

Weber suggests a third consequence to Calvin's predestination. He sees it as an important step "in the development of religions, the elimination of magic from the world" (p. 105). This, of course, plays a major role in Weber's thesis that the distinctive quality of modern European civilization is its progress to rationality. Where God cannot be influenced in any way, there is no point in resorting to "magical" sacraments, prayers, and confessions. The world is a determined, lawlike place, and one can see how this attitude ramifies not only into rational capitalism, but into rational science as well.[4]

The Calvinists, according to Weber, were the main carriers of the pure spirit of ascetic Protestantism. The core of their doctrine was predestination, with all of its bracing psychological ramifications. Other Protestant sects can, in a sense, be placed on a continuum in terms of their deviation from that central doctrine. Weber deals briefly in this manner with Pietism, Methodism, and the Baptist sects as the other forms of ascetic Protestantism. Each is interesting in the variations it introduces to the basic worldly asceticism.

Pietism placed a greater emphasis on the emotional side of life than was acceptable to orthodox Calvinists. The positive result was greater fervor in leading the strict life. The negative result was that "religion took on a positively hysterical character, resulting in the alteration which is familiar from examples without number and neuro-pathologically understandable, of half-conscious states of religious ecstasy with periods of nervous exhaustion, which were felt as abandonment by God" (p. 130). Moreover, in some branches of Pietism apostolic poverty was glorified, and this led directly away from rational asceticism as defined by Weber. It is of interest, too, to note that Pietism seemed to appeal to a strata of society different from that attracted to Calvinism: to "on one hand . . . the faithful official, clerk, labourer, or domestic worker, and on the other . . . the predominantly patriarchal employer with a pious condescension" (p. 139).

Methodism, which in many ways was the Anglo-American counterpart to Continental Pietism, added to the latter's emphasis on feeling a methodical means of inducing the emotional act of conversion. Attainment of repentance was accompanied, as Weber points out, by "an emotional struggle of such intensity as to lead to the most terrible ecstasies, which in America often took place in a public meeting" (p. 140). We shall deal later with the psychological aspects of this methodized conversion; here we wish only to call attention to an aspect of the phenomenon unmentioned by Weber. As anyone familiar with American revival meetings knows, the people who come to them are for the most part sober, ascetic folk in their daily lives—the characters of Grant Wood's famous portrait of the mid-American farm couple. In the revival meeting they experience a total release of emotions. After the conversion episode, of course, they return to their ascetic ways, but with a new confidence in their destiny. Can one see in these meetings a form of "orgy" as met with in other religions? One thinks of primitive religions, with their fertility rites, or of Catholicism, with its Mardi Gras and Holy Week. (The latter is especially strong in the "puritanical" areas of Catholic Spain, around Salamanca in the North and Malaga and Seville in the South.) Thus even the ascetic life seems to need its institutionalized moments of release, in order not to run into the Savonarola-type reaction.

The last group of ascetic Protestants dealt with by Weber is composed of the Baptist sects (that is, Baptists, Mennonites, Quakers, and so on). As against a Church, Weber defines a sect as "a community of personal believers of the reborn, and only these" (p. 145). Whereas Calvinism included elect and nonelect in its Church—for who could tell which was which until the Day of Judgment—the sect is comprised only of those who have truly been born again. While waiting for this rebirth, the Baptists (to use the term generically) rejected all sacramental assistance as a form of magic, and avoided unnecessary intercourse with the world and worldly people. In the latter action they went so far as to reject the state, and any service to it (for example, the Quakers and Mennonites refused to bear arms or to take oaths).

Yet what truly distinguished the Baptists from the Calvinists was their rejection of predestination; they are at the end of the continuum mentioned earlier. In their view, anyone, given the proper spiritual preparation—that is, worldly ascetic life—could be reborn. Once touched by the Spirit, he could then voluntarily join the sect. As Weber describes the experience, "the peculiarly rational character of Baptist morality rested psychologically above all on the idea of expectant waiting for the Spirit to descend . . . the purpose of this silent waiting is to overcome everything impulsive and irrational, the passions and subjective interests of the natural man" (p. 148). Thus, even on a very different doctrinal basis which eschewed predestination, Baptism, like Calvinism, ended as a form of ascetic Protestantism.

It may be well to describe the Baptist sects as a form of "democratic asceticism" open to all (in fact, it tended to appeal to the lower and lower middle classes), and compare it to the "elite asceticism" of Calvinism. The usefulness of this classification is that, as we turn to a consideration of the development of revolutionary asceticism, we have available to us the categories of an asceticism of the leader, of an elite, and of a mass democracy. While we would hardly profit from mechanical application of these categories, it may be useful to bear them in mind as rough "ideal types," to which aspects of revolutionary experience sometimes correspond.

III

WE OUGHT TO SAY A WORD in passing about the connection of Methodism and revolution. According to the well-known thesis of Elie Halévy, the presence of Methodism among English workers in the eighteenth century strongly mitigated against the possibility of revolution (such as occurred in 1789 in France). In this theory, the Methodist workers were "quietists" politically because: 1) they were concerned solely with salvation in the next world and not in this; 2) they were sober, ascetic workers, because of their religion, and accepted the necessity of laboring hard and obediently in the station and task to which God had called them, without aspiring higher;

and 3) they derived emotional comfort from the revival meetings and church gatherings offered by Methodism. In short, religious asceticism was diametrically opposed to revolutionary asceticism, in that no bridge lay between them; rather, the converse was true. Whatever asceticism was available was preempted for religious uses.

We can hardly solve this historical problem here. It is, for example, the contention of E. J. Hobsbawm that there is no problem.[5] Methodists were no *less* revolutionary than any other group. If this is so, then nothing needs to be explained (at least in Halévyian terms). If, on the other hand, Halévy's facts are correct, our concern would not be with rebutting him, but with studying the process by which asceticism as a social force left its religious moorings and became attached, or at least available for attachment, to revolution. We shall approach this task more directly, by a consideration of the so-called Puritan Revolution, in Chapter 5.

I V

BEFORE TURNING to that task, we might say a preliminary word in comparison of Weber with Freud. Weber and Freud share two overriding convictions. The first is that mankind has been progressing from superstition and magic belief to rational thought and action (and that this progression is desirable). Modern civilization, especially in its European form, is defined by Weber as characteristically *rational*. Rationality, as we have seen, is soon equated with control and, specifically in capitalism, ascetic control. Freud, too, as in his *Civilization and Its Discontents*,[6] seems to subscribe to the idea that modern civilization is built on the increasing renunciation of instinctual gratification. (In addition, both Weber and Freud are deeply troubled by the overrepressive features of their own civilization, although they applaud earlier developments that led to this stage. However, this is to open up another problem, not requisite here.)[7] While Freud would give a modified interpretation to what is meant by "rational," he is at one with Weber in thinking it the basis of Western civilization and, properly defined, a desirable direction of man's historical evolution.

The second conviction held in common is a belief in "spirit," that is, man's mental attributes, as absolutely central in man's historical development. While neither Weber nor even Freud neglects the material, or environmental, factors completely, they are as one in rejecting Marx's primacy of the economic conditions. To use Freudian terms, "psychic reality" is even more fundamental than "actual reality."

The question narrows down to what each man, Weber and Freud, understood by "spirit." Weber, like Freud, was concerned with man's psychology. Thus he comments that:

We are interested rather [than in "what was theoretically and officially taught"] in something entirely different: the influence of those *psychological* sanctions which, originating in religious belief and the practice of religion, gave a direction to practical conduct and held the individual to it (p. 97).

So, too, Weber understood the difference between the merely logical and the psychological:

The Calvinistic faith is one of the many examples in the history of religions of the relation between the logical and the psychological consequences for the practical religious attitude to be derived from certain religious ideas. Fatalism is, of course, the only logical consequence of predestination. But on account of the idea of proof (that is, the problem of "election") the psychological result was precisely the opposite (p. 232).

Nevertheless, with all of his compliments to the psychological, Weber was primarily interested in the influence of *rational* ideas on behavior. When he does deal with the psychological, it is in terms simply of intuitive or surface psychology. There is nothing of Freud's dynamics of the unconscious in Weber's psychology.

With no derogation to Weber, it will be useful to add Freudian psychology to his analysis. We may see what is possible here with a few examples. At one point Weber remarks that "the truth is that both Luther and Calvin believed fundamentally in a double God ... the gracious and kindly Father of the New Testament, who dominates the first books of the *Institutio Christiana*, and behind him the *Deus absconditus* as an arbitrary despot" (p. 221). I submit that we obtain a deeper understanding of the *meaning* of this belief for Luther and Calvin if we add to Weber's insight the explanation by Freud concerning our ambivalence toward father figures. As Freud tells us, we split our love-hate feelings toward our own parent into the "good" and the "bad" father.[8] The Christian religion usually accomplishes this in terms of a "good" God and a "bad" Devil; Luther and Calvin have also achieved the comforting isolation of each set of feelings by envisioning a "double God." What Freud tells us is that ambivalent feelings *always* exist toward father figures, and *must* be expressed in some way. Such a view sets before the scholar a task of inquiry that he might otherwise shirk.

Another, probably more familiar, example concerns the notion of accumulation of money. Weber, who gives it an important role in ascetic Protestantism, puts it thus: "When the limitation of consumption is combined with this release of acquisitive activity [i.e., Luther's notion of the calling, as developed by Calvin], the inevitable practical result is obvious: accumulation of capital through ascetic *compulsion* [italics added] to save" (p. 172). Weber makes the subject even more tantalizing when he quotes Benjamin Franklin to the effect that "money is of the prolific, generating nature," and then adds, "If we thus ask, *why* should 'money be made out of men,' Benjamin Franklin himself, although he was a colorless deist, answers in his autobiography with a quotation from the Bible, which his strict Calvinistic father drummed into him again and again in his youth: 'Seest thou a man diligent in his business? He shall stand before Kings'" (p. 53).

Such an answer might satisfy Franklin and Weber. After Freud, it no longer satisfies us. One need only refer to the huge literature on the connection of accumulation, and especially of money, with anality to make our specific point.[9]

My general point, however, has not been that Freud contradicts or replaces Weber but that he supplements him. And the way in which he can do this is unconsciously hinted at by Weber himself when, talking of the puritan outlook as the most important and consistent influence in the development of a rational bourgeois economic life, he adds, "It stood at the *cradle* [italics added] of the modern economic man" (p. 174). And so it did. Only when we study the ways in which conscious puritan belief specifically affected, in unconscious ways, the family and social upbringing of the child—its "socialization"— do we understand more fully the dynamics that the process involved.[10] In Freudian terms, the "internalization" of the "superego" is crucial here, and one small part of that process can be discussed under the heading of the "anal stage" and of toilet training.[11]

On the other hand, in any such discussion today a fuller, if not stricter, infusion of Weberian sociology into Freudian psychology is also desirable. Such a development has been taking place at the hands of the eminent sociologist Talcott Parsons and his disciples, such as Weinstein and Platt.[12] Less obviously Weberian, though still enjoying his inspiration, are the general developments now occurring under the heading of "psycho-history," and here, as is well known, the psychonalyst Erik H. Erikson is the influential pioneer, as in his *Young Man Luther*.

CHAPTER 5

The Puritan
Revolution and
Cromwell

I

WITH OUR INSPIRATIONS clear now, we can turn back to
the task of tracing the divergence of religious asceticism into
revolutionary asceticism. At first, of course, the two were apparently identical, symbolized as such in the Puritan Revolution. Weber, however, gives little direct attention to the Revolution. In *The Protestant Ethic*, and then only in a footnote, he
remarks that Cromwell's army, though partly conscripted, felt
that it was an army of citizens fighting solely for the glory of
God, and not at the behest of an earthly sovereign. In another
essay Weber generalizes:

Under certain conditions, however, revolutionary consequences
may follow from a genuine virtuoso religiosity. . . . One form
springs from inner-worldly asceticism, wherever this asceticism is
capable of opposing an absolute and divine "natural law" to the
creatively wicked and empirical orders of the world. It then becomes a religious duty to realize this divine natural law, according
to the sentence that one must obey God rather than man, which in
some sense holds for all rational religions. The genuine Puritan

revolutions, whose counterparts can be found elsewhere, are typical. This attitude absolutely corresponds to the obligation to crusade.[1]

Inner-worldly asceticism, of course, is not worldly asceticism, as studied by Weber in its Calvinist transmutation into the "spirit" of capitalism. We are not informed as to how worldly asceticism worked its way into the actual Puritan Revolution of 1640; perhaps Weber thought it so implicit as not to need extended comment. In any case, we know that the Puritan Revolution was not a simple matter of worldly asceticism at work, but a complicated interplay of religious, political, and constitutional issues (with an important but, in my view, subordinate addition of social and economic considerations).[2] Gradually, it seems, those who embraced worldly asceticism appear to have taken a stronger and stronger role in the prosecution of the Civil War and, especially on the military side, their ascetic way of life gave them a real advantage over their opponents. Ultimately, if I had to sum up the role of worldly asceticism in the Puritan Revolution, I would be tempted to describe it as an unusual case of "democratic revolutionary asceticism," with some elements of "elite revolutionary asceticism."

We cannot, however, let the matter stand at this level. If we wish really to understand the way in which asceticism and displaced libido were gradually placed in the service, not of religion or economic activity, but of revolution, we must press on. Such a discussion can start with the suggestive work of Michael Walzer. It is he who has most recently taken up the thought of Max Weber in this area, developed it in a critical spirit, and carried it into the political realm.[3]

Walzer's thesis is that the puritan saints are "the first of those self-disciplined agents of social and political reconstruction who have appeared so frequently in modern history."[4] The Calvinists, he claims, first introduced "revolutionary organization and radical ideology," the latter as "a kind of mental and moral discipline" (p. 1). The saints presented "a novel view of politics as a kind of conscientious and continuous labor" (p. 2). Moreover, if we turn to the libidinal area, Walzer informs us that "they joined forces with any man who might help them without regard to the older bonds of family and neighborhood. They sought 'brethren' and turned away if necessary from their relatives; they sought zeal and not affection. Thus there arose the leagues and covenants, the conferences and congregations which are the prototypes of revolutionary discipline. . . . The results of that labor can best be seen in the English Revolution of 1640" (p. 3).

Now clearly, for our purposes, this is an exciting view. According to Walzer, asceticism is already directly and fully placed in the service of revolution in 1640. The revolution is, indeed, a "puritan" revolution (though he calls it an English Revolution), made by disciplined, ascetic men, free of older ties of sentiment, and now bound only to one another by a new revolutionary organization and ideology. Surely this can be seen as an exemplification and confirmation of our thesis on revolutionary asceticism; and, in part, it is.

There are, however, qualifications necessary to the notion that the "Puritan" Revolution is a full-blown instance of what we have been calling "revolutionary asceticism." Let me list a few such qualifications. The first is that, as Walzer himself recognizes by use of the term "English Revolution," the revolution can really be called "puritan" only in its later stages, from somewhere around 1648. The saints played a role, perhaps a major one, in the events of 1640–1642, but only as part of a much larger *dramatis personae*. In this, perhaps, they were similar to the Bolsheviks in early 1917 Russia. But beyond this the analogy breaks down. In spite of any possible implications in Walzer's rather broad language, the saints were *not* an organized and ideologized political *party* as we understand that term. They lacked, as William N. Chambers puts it, "the degree of order, visible continuity and relative clarity of political formations or positions, and stable rationalization of political methods, which may be countered among the characteristics of modern party politics."[5] Similarly, as Robert Walcott points out, Macaulay was wrong when he traced his Whig ancestry back to the Roundheads of the time of Charles I, and, selecting a certain day in October of 1641, wrote in his *History of England* that "from that day dates the corporate existence of the two parties which have ever since alternatively governed the country."[6]

The saints, then, were not a political party such as the later Whigs and Tories (of the nineteenth century). While events did conspire to bring some of them into a position of power in revolutionary England, it was on the basis of military power, as we shall see, and not political party organization or even ideology. In short, the continued and steady discipline, the renunciation of libidinal attachment to persons outside a revolutionary political party, can hardly be attributed to puritanism as such. The saints were a sect, a faction, a caucus, or a "connection," but not a true professional, revolutionary political party.

Nor can we talk about the puritan as a *professional*, political revolutionary whose life is steadily devoted to the overthrow of existing authority and its replacement by a consciously devised and created "new state." During the Commonwealth and Protectorate, it is true, we seem to catch glimpses of possible forerunners of the sort of revolutionaries with which we are familiar today, such as Levellers and Fifth Monarchy Men. But we must not mistake their minds for the minds of twentieth-century men.

Just as some people pursued economic profit before Weber's rational capitalist entered the scene in force, so some people pursued political power without thereby turning their asceticism and displaced libido to the service of rational, disciplined revolutionary activity. It is this last that is intended by the use of the term "revolutionary asceticism." With these qualifications, however, it is evident that Walzer's formulations concerning the saints offer an important insight into the ways in which religious inspiration began to merge into secular revolutionary activity. As Eric Hobsbawm has argued, in fact, it was "primitive rebels," with millennial and anarchistic aspirations, who marked a nineteenth-century transitional stage to full-scale revolutionary movements.[7] The puritans were hardly "primitive," and most were not millennial, but they too are usefully seen as a transitional stage in the development of revolutionary asceticism.

Walzer himself tries to get deeper into the psychological

processes of puritanism. Once again his insights are suggestive and valuable, with "discipline" and "disciplinarians" the key words. "The association of the brethren," Walzer tells us, "was voluntary indeed, but it gave rise to a collectivist discipline marked above all by a tense mutual 'watchfulness'. . . . The crucial feature of the Puritan discipline was its tendency to transform aggression into self-control. . . ."[8] But how shall we explain this clearly evident fact of intense puritan discipline and self-control, what Walzer calls "fanatical self-control" (p. 68)?

His explanation is that the puritans turned to extreme self-control as a method of defense against overwhelming anxiety. First he offers a generalization: "Anxiety seems to appear in acute form only among men who have experienced some great disorder or who are caught up in a process of rapid, incomprehensible change: the breakdown of some habitual system of conventions and routines, a departure to an unaccustomed world, the aftermath of epidemic or war" (p. 77). Specifically, "Puritan fearfulness is best explained in terms of the actual experiences of exile, alienation, and social mobility about which the saints so often and insistently wrote. Discipline and repression are responses to these experiences, responses which do not aim at a return to some former security, but rather at a vigorous control and a narrowing of energies—a bold effort to shape a personality amidst 'chaos' " (p. 81).

While he acknowledges aggressive impulses, Walzer's stress is on external forces: "confusion, change, alienation and exile" (p. 83).[9] To these, I believe, can usefully be added a deeper analysis of the internal forces at work. The puritans, as Walzer himself recognizes, had a special anxiety and fear of sudden and violent death. The world they saw around them seemed insistently to be threatening their destruction. We must ask, however, how many of these destructive anxieties came *from* the puritans themselves, projecting outward on the world their own violent and aggressive fantasies? While objective reality undoubtedly confirmed the Puritan fears in some cases, I suggest that much of the impetus for the Puritan "ideology" came from internal sources.[10]

Thus Calvin sees external aggression everywhere, where we would not expect it: "Now, whithersoever you turn, all the objects around you are not only unworthy of your confidence, but almost openly menace you, and seem to threaten immediate death. . . . All the ferocious animals you see are armed for your destruction."[11] Even more supportive of my analysis—for one might argue that Calvin is talking either in realistic or metaphysical terms—is the puritan view of children. In a famous treatise on *A Godly Form of Household Government*, we are told that "The young child which lieth in the cradle . . . is altogether inclined to evil. . . . If this sparkle be suffered to increase, it will rage over and burn down the whole house. . . ."[12] Moreover, a glance at Cromwell's life, to which we shall turn in a moment, indicates the wrathful aggression and temper which he characteristically exhibited in his general behavior.

Erik Erikson, too, has seen more sharply what Walzer has glimpsed in this matter. Erikson remarks about the role of puritanism: "This much-maligned puritanism, we should remember, was once a system of values designed to check men and women of eruptive vitality, of strong appetites, as well as of strong individuality."[13] In *Gandhi's Truth* Erikson sees Gandhi making a comparison of *Ahimsa*, or passive, but not therefore weak, nonviolence, with puritanism: "*Ahimsa*, he realized, had not been invented by meek or defenseless people, even as in Western civilization puritanism was the way of life not of 'repressed' people, but of essentially lusty ones."[14]

My task here is not to sustain this insight in any detail. It is merely to add the assistance afforded by Walzer's stress on external sources of puritan anxiety—rapid change, exile, and so on—to our effort to understand the ascetic and displaced libidinal character in its puritan guise, and to extend Walzer's analysis by pointing to the internal forces of aggressive and destructive impulses that underlie it. In short, in this particular historical instance, I believe that there is a good deal of evidence to show that revolutionary asceticism, insofar as it exists at the time of the puritans, arises not only out of narcissistic and sadomasochistic libidinal elements, but out of peculiarly intense aggressive impulses as well.

I I

HOW GREAT IS THE presence of revolutionary asceticism in the outstanding leader of the Puritan Revolution, Oliver Cromwell? Was he a revolutionary ascetic leader and were his followers inspired by this aspect of his character? Perhaps in seeking to answer these questions we can also secure an oblique glance at the role of aggressive impulses in Cromwell, a puritan.

Oliver Cromwell was born into the most important family in Huntingdon, a royal borough, in 1599. His immediate family, though only a collateral branch, took their importance from the time of the Reformation, and the rise to power and wealth through service to Henry VIII of Thomas Cromwell. The Cromwells were originally beer makers: hardly an ascetic beginning! In addition, one side of the family was descended from Morgan Williams, of Welsh origin, another brewer.

Oliver's father, Robert, was relatively well-to-do, though not wealthy. It was Oliver's uncle, Sir Oliver, who had inherited the bulk of the estate and was now proceeding to dissipate it lavishly. One form of that dissipation was in providing magnificent entertainment for James I when he came to visit; one author has noted that "the beer, once brewed at Putney to sustain the Cromwell income, flowed freely and copiously upon the lawns of the Palace of Hinchingbrooke, while the King shot his pheasants or hunted foxes."[15]

Oliver grew up as a fairly typical member of the English gentry. There seems some evidence that he was spoiled by his mother, the stronger member of the family, married to a somewhat dreamy husband who was apparently not in the best of health. Oliver seems to have taken after the mother in his robust, active character, and his youthful interests lay in sports rather than in intellectual or cultural pursuits.

If he was spoiled by his mother, it may be because Oliver was the sole surviving son—an older brother, Henry, died shortly after Cromwell's birth, and another brother, Robert, born eight years later, died shortly after birth. There were also seven sisters. Death in general seems to have surrounded Oliver;

while death fears may have been commonplace in the early seventeenth century, they seem to have taken on a special intensity for Cromwell. When Oliver was two years old his father's cousin, Captain Henry Cromwell, died in their house. When he was four Queen Elizabeth died, and his biographer reminds us that "The mourning for her was the earliest national event of which he could well have been conscious."[16] At eight, as we have said, his brother Robert died, and at eighteen his father Robert, leaving Oliver as head of the household to take care of his mother and sisters.

At this remove, and with the sparse data at our disposal, it is difficult to be sure of the effect of such events on the young Oliver. If the story of Sir Philip Warwick can be believed, however, Cromwell was preoccupied with the subject. Warwick, having conversed with Cromwell's physician, Dr. Simcott, reports that the latter "assured me that for many years his patient was a most splenetic man, and had fancies about the cross in that town, and that he had been called up to him at midnight, and such unreasonable hours, very many times, upon a strong fancy, which made him believe he was then *dying* [italics added]." Warwick adds, and this may be mere partisan animus, that "there was a story of him, that in the day-time, lying melancholy in his bed, he believed that a spirit appeared to him and told him that he should be the greatest man (not mentioning the word king) in this kingdom."[17] For us, the fear of dying and the fancy of a kind of resurrection tie in directly with the problem of death and destruction fantasies that we talked about earlier.

Cromwell's family, as we remarked, was a Reformation family with extensive kinship ties to other such families. Puritanism was a serious matter for them, and Oliver's education was entrusted to a puritan divine, Thomas Beard, master of the Free School at Huntingdon. He made an enormous impression on Cromwell, and it was Beard's name that Cromwell invoked in his maiden speech in the House of Commons. We can sense the nature of that influence from Abbott's comments that Beard's lectures were against the dissolute and sinful habits of his age. His *Theatre of God's Judgments* stresses, we are told, "God's immediate concern with all the petty details of men's lives and

His presence among them ... [it] concerns itself chiefly with the darker side of life. Its God is less the loving Father than a stern avenging Deity."[18] Yet Oliver emerged with great love, or at least respect, for Beard and his views.

Two themes running through Cromwell's life culminate in the "conversion crisis" that he experienced sometime around his twenty-eighth year. They undoubtedly make up a large part of the sense of "sin" he felt at that time. The first theme concerns his angry and destructive impulses. Warwick referred to him as a "splenetic" man; all other observers agree. Clarendon, for example, spoke of his "indecency and rudeness," his "great fury."[19] Ashley speaks of him as a "natural leader of men whose strong temper sometimes took complete control of his being even to the extent of affecting his health."[20] Abbott sums up his early life as rude and unmannerly, if not worse ... "a strong man, vigorous, turbulent, uncontrolled, passionate, tending to that melancholy which is often associated with the 'Celtic temperament. ...' "[21] Later, in Parliament, he was noted for the personal animosity with which he verbally attacked an opponent, and especially for the lack of restraint in his language.[22]

The second theme involves Cromwell's "bad habits," or rather his excessive conscience about lapses into the dissoluteness of his age that Beard had warned against. Thus, Carrington, in the *Perfect Politician*, tells us that Oliver returned home from one year in college (Cambridge) after his father's death, and "There for some time he spent his life not altogether free from the wildnesses and follies incident to youthful age, to the wasting of some part of that small estate his father had left him."[23] If this report is true, then Oliver was "living up" to the dissipating nature of his uncle, Sir Oliver. We have stories, too, indicating "his love of horse-play and of practical jokes in something less than the best of taste."[24] Another story, from after his conversion, confirms our theme. According to Heath, Cromwell grew so "scrupulous a Conscience, that having some years before won thirty pounds of one Mr. *Carlton* at play, meeting him accidentally, he desired him to come home with him and to receive his money, telling him that he had got it by indirect and unlawful means, and that it would be a sin in him to detain it any longer."[25]

Up to this point, we have a Cromwell who loved vigorous bodily expression, took great "delight in horse and field exercise," had severe death and destruction fears, had strong outbursts of uncontrollable anger and temper, indulged in some small measure of "dissolute" behavior—and had a strong, and eventually overwhelming, sense of sin about himself. The conflict appears to have come to a head around 1628.

Abbott tells us about the conversion crisis in Cromwell's life:

It would appear that it had been caused, or accompanied by, or had resulted in, profound disturbances, emotional and perhaps physical. For this, apart from the words of Cromwell's earliest biographers, there are two pieces of apparently indubitable evidence. The first is the case-book of a certain Dr. Theodore Mayerne, sometime physician to James I, who, in the course of his practice, which seems to have been in part at least what is now called "psychiatry," set down under date of September 15, 1628, that, consulted, by "Mons. Cromwell," he had found him "valde melancholicus," that is to say, extremely melancholy.[26]

A friend who knew Cromwell at the time wrote, many years later, the following account of the crisis:

This great man is risen from a very low and afflicted condition; one that hath suffered very great troubles of soul, lying a long time under sore terrors and temptations, and at the same time in a very low condition for outward things: in this school of afflictions he was kept, till he had learned the lesson of the Cross, till his will was broken into submission to the will of God. Religion was thus "laid into his soul with the hammer and fire"; it did not "come in only by light into his understanding."[27]

Most important of all is Cromwell's account. In 1638, responding to a request of his cousin, Mrs. St. John, he replied:

I live . . . in Mesheck, which they say signifies Prolonging; in Kedar, which signifieth *Blackness*: yet the Lord forsaketh me not. Though He do prolong, yet He will (I trust) bring me to His tabernacle, to His resting-place. My soul is with the congregation of the firstborn, my body rests in hope. . . . You know what my manner of life hath been. Oh, I lived in and loved darkness, and hated the light; I was a chief, the chief of sinners. This is true, I hated godliness, yet God had mercy on me.[28]

Then he added, "if here I may honour my God either by doing or by *suffering* [italics added], I shall be most glad. . . . He it is that enlighteneth our blackness, our darkness. I dare not say, He hideth his face from me. He giveth me to see light in his light. . . ."[29]

After his "conversion," Cromwell gave up whatever dissolute habits had preyed on his mind. We can now see him as seeking self-control through asceticism of sorts. His denial of aggressive impulses was partly successful for, as Ashley tells us, "Later as a figure upon the national stage he learned to keep his temper in check, except when under provocation it burst out beyond denial."[30] Rather than denial, perhaps we ought to speak of sublimation of his aggressive drives in terms of "spiritual warfare," since it was primarily over religious issues that Cromwell first became a "revolutionary." It would be a mistake, however, to exaggerate the ascetic qualities in Cromwell: throughout his life he liked his ale and wine, he hunted and hawked (excellent training for a cavalry leader), and he cultivated his taste for music. While living a fairly simple life, he kept most of the tastes—including the taste for sports—of the country gentry from which he came.

On one level there is little to indicate that Cromwell tried to cut himself off from libidinal ties to other persons; quite the opposite. The evidence is overwhelming that he maintained a deep and abiding love for his mother, who lived with him almost all his life. When he was twenty-one he married, fathered nine children of whom eight survived to be reared, and seems to have been a warm and devoted father. On the death of his eldest son, Robert, in 1639, and even more so, it seems, on the death of his daughter Elizabeth in 1658, Cromwell was distraught. As we are told by a contemporary, for fourteen days after his daughter's death Cromwell was "unable to attend to any public business whatever . . . [he] was a most indulgent and tender father."

As for his wife, who wrote him in 1650 that "My life is but half a life in your absence," Cromwell replied, "Truly, if I love you not too well, I think I err not on the other hand much. Thou art dearer to me than any creature; let that suffice"; and we have no reason not to believe him.[31]

On another level, it is true, Cromwell could suppress any libidinal feeling about people by investing all his impulses in the abstraction God, or Providence. At these times he could permit himself military acts of cruelty and rage, under the guise of what he called "cruel necessity." Thus we see Cromwell justifying actions, such as his brutal policy in Ireland, with the claim that "It is easy to object to the glorious actings of God, if we look too much upon instruments. Be not offended at the manner; perhaps there was no other way left." Cromwell did not, in fact, see himself as a leader, but as one led—through the wilderness, in order to serve God, perhaps by seemingly cruel means. In his defense he declared, "I have not sought these things, truly I have been called unto them by the Lord, and therefore am not without some assurance that He will enable His poor worn and weak servant to do His will."[32]

Cromwell, then, was only in small part an example of our ideal type, the revolutionary ascetic. His semiascetic "conversion" did give him a growing control over his destructive impulses, which he could then turn to use in "spiritual warfare," where his anger could serve an angry God. In this sense he became "disciplined" and partly free of ordinary libidinal ties. But his nonascetic inclinations lingered on strongly, and his libidinal ties to wife and children, kinsmen and friends (even when they became political enemies), persisted throughout his life. He was indeed a puritan, but not "puritanical."[33]

What sort of leadership did he offer his followers in this respect? Were the Independents and the soldiers of the New Model army more like "revolutionary ascetics" than Cromwell? Clarendon seems to hint at a devious and Machiavellian use of the outward signs of asceticism by Cromwell, though without questioning the fact of the army's "disciplined" nature:

Cromwell had been most strict and severe in the forming the manners of his army, and in chastising all irregularities; insomuch that sure there was never any such body of men so without rapine, swearing, drinking, or any other debauchery, but the wickedness of their hearts: and all persons cherished by him, were of the same leaven, and to common appearance without the practice of any of those vices which were most infamous to the people, and which drew the public hatred upon those who were notoriously guilty of them. But then he was well pleased with the most scandalous lives of those who pretended to be for the king, and wished that all his were such, and took all the pains he could that they might be generally thought to be such; whereas in truth the greatest part of those who were guilty of those disorders were young men, who had never seen the king, and had been born and bred in those corrupt times, "when there was no king in Israel." He was equally delighted with the luxury and voluptuousness of the presbyterians, who, in contempt of the thrift, sordidness, and affected ill-breeding of the independents, thought it became them to live more generously, and were not strict in restraining or mortifying the unruly and inordinate appetite of flesh and blood, but indulged it with too much and too open scandal, from which he reaped no small advantage; and wished all those, who were not his friends should not only be infected, but given over to the practice of the most odious vices and wickedness.[34]

Other sources suggest that we must qualify our view of the ascetic nature of the army. For one thing, even by May 1645 over one-half of the infantry in the New Model Army were impressed. In the next few years many of the recruits to the army came from the King's soldiers, as his defeated armies disbanded. Not until 1651 was impressment forbidden, and only volunteers taken.[35] We cannot expect impressed and royalist soldiers to be models of ascetic behavior, and of course they were not.

In fact, at the start of the Civil War, the Parliamentary armies were notorious for their lack of discipline. Swearing, drunkenness, and plundering were frequent crimes, as well as illicit amours and breaches of manners by the soldiers when quartered in homes. However, in 1642 Hampden finally prevailed on Parliament to institute martial law. This was followed by a "Laws and Ordinances of War Established for the Better Conduct of the Army." The same rules applied to the royalist armies, and it was only the vigorous administration and enforcement of the laws in the Parliamentary army that began to give it a reputation for discipline. This, and more regular pay, made the difference.[36]

The real difference, however, manifested itself primarily in the Independents. A minority in the army, their effective takeover of power in 1647, led by Cromwell, made for the character of a "puritan" army. Their strength was in the cavalry (the best-paid and highest-educated segment of the army; pay for the troopers, for example, was three times that of the infantry).[37] This elite may be looked upon as ascetic.

As an ascetic military elite, their controlled and disciplined nature was highly functional, offering great military advantages. Well-behaved, they were welcomed rather than rejected by the local inhabitants of areas in which they were quartered or fighting. As one newspaper account described Cromwell's early regiment of picked men: "No man swears but he pays his twelvepence; if he be drunk he is set in the stocks, or worse ... insomuch that the counties where they come leap for joy of them, and come in and join with them. How happy were it if all the forces were thus disciplined."[38] So, too, in battle their ascetic spirit was at least a psychological match for the cavaliers of the King. As Cromwell told John Hampden in around 1642, after the failure of Parliament to win the battle of Edgehill, "Your troopers are most of them old decayed serving men and tapsters and such kind of fellows: and ... their [the royalists'] troopers are gentlemen's sons, younger sons, persons of quality. Do you think that the spirit of such base and mean fellows will be ever able to encounter gentlemen that have honour, courage and resolution in them? ... You must get men of a spirit ... that is likely to go on as far as a gentleman will go, or else I am sure you will be beaten still."[39] Cromwell's ascetic elite was not to be "beaten still."

If, however, we look at the basic inspiration for the asceticism of Cromwell's Independents, we shall see that it was religious, not revolutionary conviction. They were saints, not bolsheviks. Officers, including Cromwell, preached to their men, but mainly about things of the spirit. Though there were "frequent meetings of the [army] Council and long prayer-meetings in which, as the phrase ran, the officers 'waited upon God' and 'confessed their sins,'"[40] these sins were religious, not political. When challenged by more politically minded men, Cromwell retorted that the kingdom of God was spiritual and not of this earth. The reign of Christ was to be taken in a spiritual, not a literal, sense.

True, some Independents went further. These are the Levellers and the Fifth Monarchy Men. In the Army Debate of 1647 the Levellers argued for an "Agreement of the People" which would bring real revolution to England in the form of universal manhood suffrage, equal electoral divisions, abolition of king and House of Lords, and introduction of a democratic republic. Their effort to put their ideas into effect by seizing control of the army was crushed by Cromwell, who had their ringleader tried and shot on the field. Moreover, their shift from religion to politics was a late and rapid development, for it was only in 1645 that the Leveller's leader, John Lilburne, had finally come to see that true justice and equality could only come through political upheaval and awakening. Before the publication of his pamphlet, "Englands Birth-Right Justified" (1645), "The earliest statement of radical policy to appear in the revolution," Lilburne was "a pious and enthusiastic separatist who held no considered political theory."[41]

Whether the Levellers were a true political party—and I have already indicated my serious doubts in this matter—they never captured the "Puritan Revolution." *That* revolution was primarily a religious matter (though the "English Revolution" as a whole, from 1640 to 1660, was definitely political, i.e., mainly constitutional in nature). Cromwell and *his* Independents were most concerned with establishing and maintaining their right to pursue their religious beliefs as they saw fit. It was in the service of this ideal that they placed their asceticism, insofar as it existed. For this reason I hesitate to recognize them as true representatives of the concept of revolutionary ascetics. For me, Cromwell and his followers are transient figures in the movement that displaced asceticism and shifts libido from the service of religion to the service of revolution.

I I I

WE HAVE NOW COMPLETED our brief treatment of Cromwell and the Puritan Revolution. As an aside to our discussion of religious and revolutionary asceticism in its puritan stage, however, we may momentarily look at the phenomenon of conversion and compare it to modern-day "brainwashing" and "thought reform." The "conversion" phenomenon, as mentioned by Weber in his discussion of the Methodists and Baptist sects, has been amply studied, especially in its "revivalist" form.[42] The similarity of the latter to hypnotic experiences has been emphasized, and, in general, its psychological and psychoanalytic nature closely examined. The peculiar fact that *Protestant* conversion of this sort has led in general to worldly asceticism has fallen to Max Weber to explain.

How does this sort of conversion experience manifest itself in non-religious terms? Robert Lifton, among a number of others, has devoted an interesting work to this subject. He informs us that:

Whatever its setting, thought reform consists of two basic elements: confession, the exposure and renunciation of past and present "evil"; and reeducation, the remaking of a man in the Communist image. These elements are closely related and overlapping, since they both bring into play a series of pressures and appeals—intellectual, emotional, and physical—aimed at social control and individual change.[43]

The similarity of this process to religious conversion is obvious. To nonbelievers, of course, it is perceived pejoratively, as "brainwashing" (yet note the positive, though reluctant, unconscious admission of a "cleansing" experience). "What we see," Lifton reminds us, "as a set of coercive maneuvers, the Chinese Communists view as a morally uplifting, harmonizing, and scientifically therapeutic experience."[44]

What is the connection of this "morally uplifting" experience to worldly asceticism? Our clue can come from one of the case studies appended by Lifton to his book. It is the "Confession Document" of Professor Chin Yüeh-lin, made during the thought reform campaign of 1951–1952. In the first paragraph he tells us what we need to know:

Born of a bureaucratic landlord family, I have always led a life of ease and comfort. I went abroad at nineteen and stayed there for eleven years to absorb the way of life and predilection for pleasure of the European and American bourgeoisie. The principal source of my various pleasures lay in the decadent philosophy of the bourgeoisie, and for thirty years I played a game of concepts. I was engrossed in this game of concepts because it was the only way for me to feel happy and free, and to escape from the restrictive realities of society. I thus cultivated the habit of running away from realities, despising realities, and leading a life isolated from realities. However, since I still had to live in a society of realities, the only way for me to maintain this life isolated from the realities was to gain certain privileges. I needed those privileges, and I thus fell a victim to the ideology of special privileges.[45]

Chin Yüeh-lin is a bourgeois, not an aristocrat, and his "special privileges" are the "life of ease and comfort" of the bourgeoisie, not the aristocracy, but the fundamental dynamics are the same as in many earlier puritan conversions. In the name of the revolution and its ascetic requirements, instead of in the name of religion (and all of this, of course, in a Chinese setting), Chin must go through a conversion experience in which he learns, *willingly and from internal commands* (though these have been inculcated with the help of external coercion), to repress and control his soft, fleshly desires. He must harden himself to the demands of being a new man in a new China. One requires the other.

In this brief episode we can see how, in conjunction with our basic theme, one aspect of religious asceticism can be converted into revolutionary asceticism. The Chinese Revolution echoes the earlier experience of the Puritan Revolution.[46] Both together illustrate how a general transition from worldly asceticism in the services of religion, as in the puritan conversion, to the service of revolution, as in Chinese thought reform, can occur.

CHAPTER 6

The French Revolution and Robespierre

REVOLUTION came to France in 1789. It was not, however, inspired by a group of religious ascetics or, indeed, of worldly ascetics. Mirabeau is typical of the nonascetic leader of the early years, to be followed in a position of power by Danton. Only as the Revolution progressed and became involved in war and counterrevolution did revolutionary ascetic leadership emerge in the shape of Robespierre, Saint-Just, and their immediate followers. If they had been Huguenots, perhaps we would have a case for the transition of ascetic Protestantism into revolution; but they were not. Rather, it would appear that Robespierre was in the tradition of a Savonarola. For a moment, events and moods conspired so that asceticism held a powerful appeal for the mass of people; then the moment of restraint was over, and the *jeunesse dorée* and the Directory entered the scene. Robespierre's revolutionary ascetic leadership was neither religiously inspired in any specific sense nor able to appeal forcefully to any tradition of religious asceticism. It *was* revolutionary, but it was never able to institutionalize itself. Thus, like the *sans-culotte*, whom it temporarily led, its fate was simply to vanish from the stage of history, and linger on merely as a legend.

Yet legends, which have some basis in fact, often unduly color our picture of an event. It behooves us, therefore, to look more closely at the role of revolutionary asceticism in the French Revolution. This is tantamount to saying that we must study Robespierre. Although there is no evidence that his followers were revolutionary ascetics, as with the Independents in the New Model Army, it seems clear that part of Robespierre's leadership appeal was based on his reputation as a revolutionary ascetic.

What was the reality behind the reputation? The basis for an answer, at least as far as Robespierre's early life, is distressingly thin and unreliable.[1] Nevertheless, certain facts and salient features do emerge from even a brief consideration of his character and development. The overwhelming event in Robespierre's early life was the death of his mother in childbirth when Robespierre was six, leaving him with his father, two sisters, and a younger brother. Within four months of the mother's death the father deserted his young children, leaving them in the care of aunts and grandparents. Intermittently returning after a year's absence, the father finally disappeared completely when Robespierre was fourteen, leaving behind him not only his children, but various debts—one of the reasons frequently given for his original desertion—and a vague cloud of disgrace.[2]

We can only guess at the psychological legacy of these events for Robespierre. A profound feeling of desertion would be natural. So would an attitude of distrust, coupled with a fear of ever again loving an object that might suddenly be removed. At a very deep level, the seeds of distrust of sexuality may also have been sown: the conceiving of children implied death. Moreover, Robespierre's father, besides being improvident, seems to have been strongly sensual, for his marriage was hastily contracted—Robespierre was born four months after the wedding—and the other siblings followed about as fast as possible, including the fifth which did not itself survive the mother's death.[3] The father, in deserting his family, had "rejected"

Robespierre; did Robespierre in turn reject his father's sexuality?

We cannot know for sure. Robespierre seems never to have mentioned his father. The mother, however, according to Robespierre's sister Charlotte, was another matter. In Charlotte's memoirs she tells us that "My brother Maximilien could not recall her [the mother] without emotion. Every time we spoke of her in our intimate conversations, I heard his voice change and saw his eyes glisten."[4] As for Robespierre, according to Charlotte, the death of his mother and the desertion of his father had turned him "from a normally cheerful boy (*étourdi, turbulent, léger*) into a sedate and conscientious young head of his family (*posé, raisonnable, laborieux*)."[5]

Laborieux, hard-working, was one of the key traits Robespierre seemed also to have exhibited at school, first at the Collège d'Arras, and then at the Collège Louis-le-Grand in Paris where he was sent on scholarship at the age of eleven. Here he stayed for twelve years, establishing an excellent record as a classical scholar and later pursuing legal studies. As a result, in 1781, aged twenty-three, he was able to return to his birthplace, Arras, as a promising young lawyer. At first he prospered to an unusual degree. Helped by older lawyers, he secured a goodly number of cases for a beginner. He was taken into the Academy of Arras within two years of his return, as well as being elected to the select Rosati Club (rose-lovers) where he tried his hand at carefree verses. In short, he appeared to be a fine young man, prospectively a good marital catch, making his way into the higher echelons of Arras society.

Some scholars detect a cloud gathering in his choice of an essay contest in which first to try his literary skill. In 1784 the Academy of Metz proposed the question: "What is the origin of the public attitude that assigns to all the individuals in a family a share of the shame arising from the condemnation of its one guilty member?" Robespierre submitted an entry, showing much passion on the subject, which he had originally delivered as his inaugural speech at the Academy of Arras; it won a medal and 400 livres. In 1786 he delivered another oration on the laws of bastardy. But only hindsight suggests that these topics may have been overdetermined by his youthful origins. At the time, no one would have paid undue attention to a passage of what appears to be typical enlightenment political sentiment:

The mainspring of energy in a republic, as has been proved by the author of *L'Esprit des Lois*, is *vertu*, that is to say, political virtue, which is simply the love of one's laws and of one's country; and it follows from the very nature of these that all private interests and all *personal relationships* [italics added] must give way to the general good. Every citizen has a share in the sovereign power ... and therefore cannot acquit his *dearest friend* [italics added], if the safety of the state requires his punishment.[6]

Only a crotchety scholar pursuing the theme of revolutionary asceticism might feel that a special sort of personal passion might later come to lend additional meaning and importance to these youthful words which, in themselves, expressed unreproachable, high-minded, and, indeed, abstractly correct views.

One thing above all was evident about Robespierre. He was ambitious, and ready at every turn to promote his own cause. It sits in odd combination with his idealism, and one comes later to feel that he wished to repress any memory of this less-than-virtuous self, submerging it in constant professions of virtue and in murderous attacks on other "self-interested" men. In any case, the early record is clear. At the very beginning of his career he wrote to Dupaty, a leader of the Paris bar and author of a book on criminal law, asking for advice: "I want to be a lawyer," Robespierre declared. "I know how many qualities are needed for fame in that profession. One at least I can claim to possess—keen ambition and an unqualified desire for success."[7] Similarly, Robespierre was extremely forward in publishing his initial legal pleas and academy essays, sending them to the "right" people and often not making full acknowledgment of his debt to others, e.g., using all the ideas of the scientist Buissart on lightning-rods, worked up in a *mémoire* for a case that Robespierre was asked to plead, the plea of which Robespierre published without a word of acknowledgment to Buissart![8]

What happened to this ambitious, hard-working young lawyer, whose many virtues seemed to outshine his minor vices?

Gérard Walter, Robespierre's most trustworthy and painstaking biographer, suggests that 1788 was the decisive point ("Au tournant d'une route," is his phrase) in Robespierre's life. I shall follow Walter in his account. Hints of what were to come manifested themselves in the two or three preceding years. In the so-called "Affaire Deteuf," Robespierre had seemed unnecessarily to have attacked his erstwhile friends and patrons, and to have exhibited an unusual concern to make of the case a platform whereby he could call into question the moral integrity of those involved.[9] This and other such incidents should have prepared Robespierre for a certain coolness toward him on the part of his former friends. Thus in 1788 his legal cases exhibited a steady drop. In the same year, when the new president of the Council of Artois summoned a group of outstanding lawyers to an important juridical conference, Robespierre was not invited. He felt the slight keenly, and published a sharp pamphlet to show his displeasure. In this "Lettre" he admitted his resentment and confessed himself "to be very chagrined and disgusted." Then, in what was to become a compulsive trait, he explained away the incident in terms of a conspiracy theory, giving full reign to his basic distrust of others. "Among impossible things is certainly that of obtaining universal approval; there is always someone who will destroy your happiness and secretly plot your downfall."[10] As another biographer perceptively observes, "A gospel which emphasizes the doctrine that to feel justified is to be justified must produce in its followers a large amount of self-pity."[11]

The way into the "Establishment" was now closed to Robespierre. Henceforth his writings took on a new and sharper quality. As we all know, the change in him mirrored changes in mood going on in all of France in 1788. When he talked in his first openly political pamphlet, "A La Nation Artésienne," written to advance his own political ambitions, of a "conspiracy of the enemies of the common people," the passion may have come largely from his personal "triste expérience" (or so, at least, he perceived it). No matter; it corresponded perfectly with the gathering fears of a significant part of the French population. It is well to remember, however, that at this time Robespierre, again echoing the rest of the country, was still appealing in his pamphlet to the King to "save the country." It would take another three years or so for Robespierre to realize that the providential man "whom the Lord in his infinite goodness had designated for us," as he put it, would not be Louis XVI—but himself!

We need not linger over the details of Robespierre's coming to power. Making his appeal mainly to the artisans and peasants of Arras, rather than to the middle class, Robespierre waged a clever electoral campaign for the Estates-General, in the course of which he broke harshly with another former friend, Dubois de Fosseux (a fellow member of the Academy of Arras, who has the additional distinction of having corresponded at length with Babeuf). A few days before his thirty-first birthday, Robespierre was elected deputy from Arras to the Estates-General. His refusal to accept "compromise," which had lost him so many friends, had gained him admiring supporters who saw in him a model of political rectitude.

At this point let us pause. Our intent is not to offer a full psychohistory of Robespierre, but simply to indicate the elements of revolutionary asceticism insofar as they manifest themselves in his life.[12] The asceticism, though so frequently remarked upon, appears mainly to have been a matter of simple tastes, with some interesting exceptions. Robespierre's ambition did not seem to run to material things. He worked hard, but not to a point of excess. As a deputy in Paris, at the height of his power, he still lived in a few rooms in the "obscure house" of a carpenter. As a visitor typically observed, "His household is one of extreme simplicity." Food seemed not particularly to interest him. Only in dress did he have rather more elegant tastes. As the same visitor observed, "Robespierre dresses with scrupulous care and with a complete absence of caprice." His famous green coat was always neat, his shirts clean, his hair carefully dressed, and he refused to wear the red Phrygian cap: in short, the complete bourgeois.[13]

For Robespierre's followers, all this bespoke the simple "man of the people" who happened to come from a class above them. Clearly he was not "self-interested," in the sense of acquiring material rewards for himself. In contrast to Mirabeau, and perhaps Danton, he was obviously not "corruptible." His one care was not himself, but the People; his one aim, not aggrandizement, but the exercise of any power that he possessed in bringing about and preserving the reign of virtue. There is much that is attractive in this picture of Robespierre; and it undoubtedly attracted to him numerous followers among the poor and downtrodden, as well as, at least initially, among the lovers of liberty.

What of his libidinal life? He had deeply loved his mother, as we have seen. He remained close to his sisters, especially Charlotte, who kept house for him for five years in Arras, and to his brother Augustin, who supported and served him in Paris during the Revolution. While in Arras, we are told by Charlotte, Robespierre fell in love with Anais Deshorties, stepdaughter of one of his aunts, spoke to her of marriage before leaving for Paris, and was "painfully affected" when he returned to Arras in 1791 and found her married to the son of a friend. If true, this story would suggest that once again Robespierre learned the painful lesson that he could not "trust" others. I find myself skeptical as to the story's authenticity, for it simply doesn't seem to fit Robespierre's character. More in character is his relation to Eléonare Duplay, the plain but earnest daughter of his landlord in Paris. We are told by the family doctor, Souberbielle, that the couple "were fond of each other, and they were engaged to be married, but nothing immodest passed between them. Without affectation or prudery, Robespierre kept out of and even put a stop to, any kind of improper talk; and his morals were pure." We can well believe this last, especially if we recall Robespierre's horrified reaction to Danton's definition of virtue as what he did with his wife in bed at night (and if we also remember the probable meaning of sexuality for Robespierre in his childhood experiences). Undoubtedly more revealing of his relation to the good Eléonare is Robespierre's reported comment: "She had the soul of a man, and would have known how to die as well as she knew how to love." Needless to say, Robespierre's enemies, seeking to shatter his image of "incorruptibility," spread rumors to the effect that he was having improper relations with Eléonare, living as he did in the room opposite hers. There is also the rumor that he kept a mistress, again a very dubious matter.[14]

As for men, perhaps aware that their "soul" knew how to
die, Robespierre demonstrated a constant pattern of putting
aside "personal relationships" and not only not "acquitting,"
but rather accusing his "dearest friend" when he thought the
safety of the state required it. We have mentioned his behavior
in Arras, where one after another he broke with patrons and
friends in the name of principle. In Paris, and in power, he
accentuated this trait, putting to death his "dearest friend"
Danton and his former schoolmate Desmoulins, among numerous others who perished during Robespierre's reign of virtue. If
these men were really threatening the safety of the state, then
Robespierre's behavior could not be faulted. But the evidence
suggests that they, like so many other good revolutionaries, had
simply run afoul of Robespierre's unacknowledged ambition for
power, masked for himself in terms of a noble service to Virtue
(which, by happy chance, turned out to be embodied in Robespierre).

We can be in no doubt that Robespierre was prepared to cut
his libidinal ties to friends, if such existed at all, easily and
frequently. Did he turn his libidinal energies inward? Was he, in
short, an example of the narcissistic revolutionary ascetic? In a
rare admission of fault on the part of her brother, Charlotte
suggests how ungiving and self-centered he could be. "My aunts
and I," Charlotte recalls, "were irritated by his frequent moments of distraction, by the wandering of his mind during our
gatherings. In fact, when we played cards or talked of petty
family concerns, he would remove himself to the farthest corner
of the room and was soon lost in thought, quite *as if he had
been alone*" [italics added].[15] Even more revealing is Robespierre's own account of his reaction to a trivial slight (not being
greeted by some "of the town's customs collectors," "employés
de l'octroi" when returning to Artois): "That sign of dis-
respect," Robespierre admitted, "hurt me deeply, and for the
rest of the day my ill-humor made me unbearable." Then he
confessed in an unusual moment of self-awareness, "My pride
and conceit [*amour-propre*] know no limits."[16] We must take
him at his word.

The words above are in a letter of 12 June 1783 to Buissart,
Robespierre's scientific guide in the matter of the lightning-rod

case. There is one other, most revealing note in this letter, written from the town of Carvin, where Robespierre, after the successful conclusion of the case, had been invited by his cousins. Robespierre tells Buissart that his visit to Carvin was a veritable triumph: "Townspeople of all walks of life gave ample evidence of their desire to see us; the cobbler downed his tools to contemplate us at his leisure; the barber, abandoning a beard half-trimmed, ran to look at us, razor in hand; the housewife, in order to satisfy her curiosity, even risked burning her cakes. I even saw three gossips interrupt their frantic conversation to rush to the window."[17] Now, it is true, as Walter remarks, this is said with a tone of irony. Is Robespierre mocking his own wishes? Did it really happen as described, or is Robespierre fantasying? Whatever the precise answer, we can be sure that it represents a desire on Robespierre's part for applause and recognition, and we can note that his desired audience is the common people—shoemakers, barbers, bakers, and commercial travelers. Their adulation can satisfy his "amour-propre." Do we have here, then, a forecast of Robespierre's desires in 1789?

Robespierre, we must remember, was a disciple of Jean-Jacques Rousseau, and Rousseau, too, had glorified the people. Though both Robespierre and Rousseau abandoned intellectually the religion in which they had been raised, they transmuted many of its ideas into a secular ideology. Thus it is not strange to hear Rousseau announce that "The voice of the people is, in fact, the voice of God." Such a formulation allows for an interpretation in which a given individual, perhaps one of our revolutionary ascetics, may speak for both parties. Robespierre, in becoming that person, could rely heavily on Rousseau's formulations, such as those in the "Discourse on Political Economy." There, Rousseau asked the question: "In order to determine the general will, must the whole nation be assembled together at every unforeseen event?" "Certainly not," was his answer. "It ought the less to be assembled, because it is by no means certain that its decision would be the expression of the general will. . . . The rulers well know that the general will is always on the side which is most favorable to the public interest, that is to say, most equitable; so that it is needful only to act justly, to be certain of following the general will." This was no accidental statement. Rousseau repeated the notion a few paragraphs farther on. He commanded, "as virtue is nothing more than this conformity of the particular wills with the general will, establish the reign of virtue." What more could Robespierre want in order to believe that he was following Rousseau in setting up his Republic of Virtue? To confirm his view, Robespierre needed only to read further: "We ought not to confound negligence with moderation, or clemency with weakness. To be just, it is necessary to be severe; to permit vice, when one has the right and the power to suppress it, is to be oneself vicious."[18]

Robespierre's identification with Rousseau is powerfully put in a dedication to him which he wrote either in 1789 or 1791:

It is to you that I dedicate this writing, Spirit of the Citizen of Geneva, so that if it is called to see the light of day, it may do so under the protection of the most eloquent and virtuous of men. Today, more than ever before, we need eloquence and virtue. Divine Man, you taught me to know myself. Whilst I was still very young you made me appreciate the dignity of my nature and reflect on the grand principles of the social order. The old edifice has crumbled and the outline of a new building rises on its ruins. It is thanks to you that I also have brought to it my store. Receive then my homage. Feeble as it is it should please thee, for I have never flattered the living. I saw thee in thy last days and this memory is for me a proud joy. I have looked on thine august features; I have seen there the mark of the heavy grief to which the injustices of men condemned thee. Since that moment I have understood all the pangs of a noble life devoted to the cult of Truth. They have not frightened me. The consciousness of having willed the welfare of his fellow men is the reward of the virtuous man. The gratitude of the multitude, who surround his memory with honours, bestows on him the due which his contemporaries denied him. Like you, I would purchase such a prize at the cost of a laborious life and even of a premature death.[19]

Had Robespierre actually met Rousseau? Robespierre's sister, basing her contention on the passage above—"I saw thee in thy last days"—claims he had, but Walter explains the phrase more plausibly as meaning that Robespierre had probably seen his hero by chance, at a distance, in a crowd in Paris. As Robespierre has reminded us in his dedication, he had read Rousseau's books while in the Collège Louis-le-Grand—their being forbidden books must have made them all the more attractive—and fallen under his spell immediately. By 1789 he obviously thought of himself as Rousseau's spiritual son; indeed, as his reincarnation.

A glance at Rousseau's life suggests how overdetermined this identification actually was; it was not simply a matter of intellectual affinity (though that was one part of it). Rousseau, as is well known, also lost his mother during childbirth—made worse in his case by the fact that it was *his* birth—and grew up without the presence of maternal love. So, too, Rousseau's father deserted him, probably around the age of seven to nine, fleeing Geneva after wounding a man in a quarrel, and committing Rousseau to the care of an uncle.[20] Similar childhood experience—taken in the gross sense—of parental loss and desertion appear to have led to similar feelings in Rousseau and Robespierre of insecurity and distrust. The need of both men to "justify" themselves and to demonstrate their own virtuous nature seems to have been severe. Both appear to have turned inward, and to have sought solitude.

Later in life Rousseau experienced acute moments of what we must call paranoic attacks, culminating in the affair with David Hume.[21] Here his generalized distrust of others, a sort of spiritual attitude, took on concrete form as Rousseau "acted out" his suspicions. Do we find the same interference with reality, and by 1793 on a massive scale, of paranoic suspicions in Robespierre? A contemporary observer—a young Englishman —offers us the following description of his encounter with the "Incorruptible":

He was reading at the time, and wore a pair of green preservers [spectacles]; he raised his head, and turning up his spectacles on his forehead, received me most graciously. My introducer having stated that I was *un petit ami de Dorival Albitte—un petit Anglais, Que veux-tu? que demandes-tu?* was his brief and abrupt question. I referred him to the contents of my memorial, on which he cast a mere glance, and then said, "If it were in my power to liberate an Englishman, until England sues for peace, I would not do it—but why come to me? Why not apply to the Comité? Every one applies to me, as if I had an omnipotent power." Here a strange twitching convulsed the muscles of his face. At this present moment I recollect the agitation of his countenance. He then added, "Your brother is much safer where he is. I could not answer for the life of any Englishman were he free. All our miseries are the work of Pitt and his associates; and if blood is shed, at his door will it lie. Do you know, *enfant*, that the English here set a price on my head, and on the heads of every one of my colleagues. That assassins have been bribed with English gold—and by the Duke of York—to destroy me? The innocent ought not to suffer for the guilty, otherwise every Englishman in France should be sacrificed to public vengeance."

I was astonished. After a short pause he added, "Do you know that the English expected that this Duke of York would have succeeded the Capets? Do you know Thomas Paine and David Williams?" he continued, looking at me with an eagle eye; "they are both traitors and hypocrites."

He now rose, and paced up and down his room, absorbed in thought; he then suddenly stopped, and, taking me by the hand, said "*Adieu, mon petit, ne crains rien pour ton frère.*" He then turned off abruptly, and my guide led me out.[22]

Overdramatized, perhaps, unfriendly to Robespierre, yet this account accords with numerous others. As two modern scholars sum it up:

The absolute moral sense, the need to maintain total control, and the determination to eliminate dissonant elements were exaggerated reflections of qualities that had existed in Robespierre before his advent to power. These qualities stemmed from anxieties that grew worse as the situation grew worse. Robespierre had always been excessively distrustful of those around him, a trait which predisposed him to exercise total control, and which was quite evident to his contemporaries. Pétion said of Robespierre that he saw everywhere conspiracies, treason, and plots; he never forgave an insult to his self-esteem ... and always believed that he was being watched and persecuted.[23]

In sum, the emotional origins of Rousseau and Robespierre display a striking general similarity, and so does an important aspect of their psychological later life that we can only look upon with deep misgivings. We must not forget, however, that both men functioned throughout much of their lives in highly creative fashion. Rousseau's creativity, surely the greater of the two, is abundantly known and need not occupy us further here.[24] But what of Robespierre? What happened to him, considered for our purposes as a revolutionary ascetic?

On the purely ascetic side, we encounter mainly simplicity of life in Robespierre, though this had a definite political function of the kind discussed earlier in regard to our ideal type. While by no means of the deep inner significance and compulsiveness that we find, for example, in Gandhi, Robespierre's asceticism probably gave him a sense of greater control over himself, and of lesser dependence on others. It seemed also to allow simple and common people to identify with him, though only to a certain extent, and, more importantly, to trust him as a completely disinterested and pure representative of their needs and desires.

Robespierre's ascetic and virtuous nature initially helped him to lead his fellow French citizens, at least for a while, in the direction of greater liberty, fraternity, and equality. The tragedy is that his excess of virtue turned into a vice. As Weinstein and Platt suggest, starting as a spokesman for increased autonomy, Robespierre ended as an apostle of intense authoritarianism. In their view it was Robespierre's own emotional ambivalence concerning these polarities that brought about his downfall: "The psychological qualities that characterized Robespierre won him popularity and support while he was the critic of authority; these same qualities, compounded by the enormous pressure, made him intolerable as a leader."[25]

In the process, however, the other element in Robespierre, his lack of strong libidinal ties to other persons, gave him the power to lead others to disrupt *their* ties to the past. To follow Weinstein and Platt again, discussing this aspect of the French Revolution, they assert that "it was necessary to repress affective attachments in order to act, and the greater the demands the more perfect the repression. The attempt to blot out the past was felt eventually in every area of culture connected to the old order." In introducing, for example, the new calendar, the revolutionaries showed their basic intent: "to escape the past, to deny that anything of significance had occurred before the year I of the Revolution, and through Republican fetes and holidays, to fix the public in the struggles of the present and point them toward the future."[26] Robespierre, wishing to escape his own family past and having attenuated his libidinal ties to others, was in a particularly good position to lead in this matter.

In some senses, then, Robespierre is an example of our revolutionary ascetic. While actually somewhat removed from our ideal type—a surprising conclusion considering the stereotype —those aspects of his character that correspond to it were functional; they helped him obtain power.[27] For a brief period they also helped lead France in the direction of greater freedom. Then the expansive nature of his narcissism (his "amour-propre"), his rejection of libidinal ties, and the malignant growth of his distrust and suspicion, resulting in a form of paranoia and allowing no possibility of stabilizing the Revolution, proved his undoing. His immediate colleagues, or at least the majority of them, as well as the common people, finally turned upon him. That is one of the meanings of Thermidor, the moment in July 1794 when Robespierre fell from power.

If Robespierre had been able to use his revolutionary ascetic qualities in the formation or control of a true political party, as did Lenin and Stalin, he might have been able permanently to control those around him and to institutionalize his paranoiac system. (Certainly this was a lesson Lenin learned from him; no Bolshevik Thermidor was ever permitted.) But Robespierre never wished to be a leader of a party, or even of the Jacobins. Perhaps out of ideological conviction—following Rousseau's admonitions against sects—and certainly out of psychological wishes, he refused to identify with a party, choosing only the "People." Thus, as Marat correctly noted, "Robespierre . . . is so little suited to be the leader of a party that he avoids any group in which there is a tumult and pales at the sight of a saber." Marat's observation was matched by Robespierre's own self-knowledge and self-admission: "I only listen to my duty. I wish for no one's support or friendship. I am not trying to make a party for myself."[28]

True, he did manage to acquire a small core of followers— St. Just was the outstanding example—who followed him lovingly to the end. For a time he held sway in the Jacobin Club, which fulfilled for a while some of the functions of a political party, but it eventually fell away from him. At no time did he acquire any sort of a mass following dedicated to the main propositions of revolutionary asceticism. Thus Robespierre must be thought of as a pioneer, though not a prototype, of revolutionary asceticism. Thermidor showed that neither the French people themselves, nor even the bulk of the revolutionaries, had become fundamentally enamored or under the sway of revolutionary asceticism. At best it was only a brief flirtation, soon forgotten in the excesses of the Directory.

CHAPTER 7

From Legislator
to Bolshevik:
Robespierre to Lenin

I

WITH Rousseau's legislator we are still in another world from
that of the revolutionary as we know him in the twentieth century. The French Revolution is basically preindustrial, not consciously aiming at modernization. A substantial gap separates a
Robespierre from a Lenin.

In this chapter we shall focus on the process that allowed for
the change of one into the other, realizing, of course, that one
cannot encapsulate a century's development in any simple
formula. What we are doing, therefore, is indicating a line of
march, abstracted from the complex surrounding reality.

The line we postulate is, on the face of it, unlikely. It starts
from the initial modernization, the industrialization of Europe
in the late eighteenth-early nineteenth century. In its first manifestation, in Great Britain, this movement took a capitalist
form. Weber's thesis on the Protestant ethic applies, except that
in the British case, religious asceticism, i.e., Protestant Calvinism, was no longer directly connected to the spirit of capitalism

but was itself transmuted into utilitarianism. Utilitarianism was the secular form of the Protestant ethic, which supplied both the value system and the ideal personality type of the Industrial Revolution in Britain.

The utilitarian is almost a caricature of the ascetic and displaced libidinal man, only now his character is placed in the service of economic and governmental rather than religious activity. But what was caricature for the early nineteenth-century contemporaries of the actual utilitarians becomes for us an ideal type. Of course, although they were intimately connected to the Industrial Revolution, the utilitarians were not connected to political revolution. Instead, they were at the forefront of reform: one thinks of Bentham, James Mill, Place, Grote, Chadwick, and so on.

Only as utilitarianism passes into the mainstream of European life and culture, and especially into Russian thought, does it become connected with revolutionary activity. Nineteenth-century Russian revolutionary thinkers drew upon many sources: utopian socialists such as Robert Owen, Saint-Simonians, Fourierists, Hegelians, Marxists, anarchists, and so on. As we shall try to show, however, the ideal *character* of the future Russian revolutionary increasingly took on the lineaments of our revolutionary ascetic, mediated through the inspiration, in large part, of utilitarianism. The key figure in this transmission was Chernyshevsky, who provided a direct inspiration to Lenin.

Chernyshevsky himself, like most of his radical colleagues in the mid-nineteenth century, was not enamored of a modern industrial state in Russia. He and his colleagues were more communitarian and utopian in their dreams. Yet, paradoxically, it was Chernyshevsky who pictured and praised the hard, unloving, and ascetic type of character, a kind of utilitarian, as the ideal person to bring about a revolution that would realize communitarian aims. It seems Chernyshevsky was unaware how sadly out of joint his unyielding revolutionary was with his pliant, cooperative society-to-be.

Lenin was more realistic in joining character type and revolution. He, and others like him in the generation following Chernyshevsky, had an aim different from the communitarian, utopian one: a powerful, centralized, modernized Russian state. In Lenin's famous definition, communism was "Soviets plus electrification." Fusing the capitalist-utilitarian personality and the Russian revolutionary tradition, with Chernyshevsky as his mentor, Lenin emerged with the hard, unyielding, "loveless" figure of our revolutionary ascetic in Bolshevik dress.

II

AT FIRST SIGHT, utilitarianism seems an unlikely companion to asceticism of any kind. While definitely an ideology of social change, utilitarianism itself was nonrevolutionary in its aims. During the time that the Revolution of 1789 raged in France, utilitarianism began to gather strength in England as an alternative theory of social transformation. Instead of appealing to social contracts and natural rights, it turned to the concept of utility. Instead of Rousseau it had Jeremy Bentham as its mentor. Publication of his book, *Introduction to the Principles of Morals and Legislation*, in 1789 can be taken as a fitting symbol of the new developments, though the real political fruits of his work came later in the nineteenth century.

What is striking is that in his theory Bentham attacked the notion of asceticism. The principle of utility was that "the greatest happiness of the greatest number is the foundation of morals and legislation." To measure happiness, Bentham sought to discover a "felicific calculus" wherein the amount of pleasure in any act could be measured against the amount of pain. The aim, of course, was to maximize pleasure. Asceticism, as Bentham explained it, was one of the two principles adverse to utility, for it opposed itself to pleasure. Thus it was the inverse of utilitarianism: "approving of actions in as far as they tend to diminish his [man's] happiness; disapproving of them in as far as they tend to augment it."[1]

Considering Bentham's opposition to one major component of our concept of revolutionary asceticism, it might seem absurd to suggest that utilitarianism became a nineteenth-century "carrier" of revolutionary asceticism—though without the revolution. Yet that is exactly our thesis: Utilitarianism served as an important way station in the transformation of asceticism and displaced libido from the service of religion to the service of revolution.

There is a hint of what happened in Bentham himself. The other principle that he set in opposition to utility was the principle of sympathy and antipathy. By this, Bentham meant:

That principle which approves or disapproves of certain actions, not on account of their tending to augment the happiness, nor yet on account of their tending to diminish the happiness of the party whose interest is in question, but merely because a man finds himself disposed to approve or disapprove of them: holding up that approbation or disapprobation as a sufficient reason for itself and disclaiming the necessity of looking for any extrinsic grounds.[2]

From this principle one could proceed (though it is not a necessary procession) to the view that libidinal attachments must be overcome in the name of "the greatest good of the greatest number"; this was certainly the view held by Chernyshevsky, who became a devoted proponent of utilitarianism in nineteenth-century Russia.

Behind Bentham's utilitarianism stood Max Weber's asceticism in Calvinist dress. Weber himself has pioneered in tracing this evolution from Calvinism to a *nonreligious* world asceticism. Describing the development from the sixteenth to the eighteenth century, he points out that:

The full economic effect of those religious movements, whose significance for economic development lay above all in their ascetic educative influence, generally came only after the peak of the purely religious enthusiasm was past. Then the intensity of the search for the Kingdom of God commenced gradually to pass over into sober economic virtue; the religious roots died out slowly, giving way to utilitarian worldliness.[3]

In a more limited vein, Weber quotes Baxter's *Christian Directory*: "It is for action that God maintaineth us and our activities; work is the moral as well as the natural end of power. . . . It is action that God is most served and honored by. . . . The public welfare or the good of the many is to be valued above our own," and remarks, "Here is the connecting-point from the will of God to the purely utilitarian view-point of the later liberal theory."[4]

Specifically, Weber suggests the connection between Calvinism and utilitarianism in relation to sexual intercourse. He summarizes the opinion, in this case of pietistic groups, that:

The highest form of Christian marriage is that with the preservation of virginity, the next highest that in which sexual intercourse is only indulged in for the procreation of children, and so on down to those which are contracted for purely erotic or external reasons and which are, from an ethical standpoint, concubinage. On these lower levels a marriage entered into for purely economic reasons is preferred (because after all it is inspired by rational motives) to one with erotic foundations. . . . The transition to a pure, hygenically oriented utilitarianism had already taken place in Franklin, who took approximately the ethical standpoint of modern physicians, who understand by chastity the restriction of sexual intercourse to the amount desirable for health, and who have, as is well known, even given theoretical advice as to how that should be accomplished.[5]

In the area of both work and love—Freud's famous *Liebe und Arbeit*—Bentham exhibited traits of the revolutionary ascetic in his own life. He led a pure and seemingly disinterested existence, devoting himself to legal, educational, and political reform. He had neither wife nor child, and proudly bore the title of "Hermit of Queen's Square Place." His life seemed wrapped up completely in hard work.

We ought not, however, to make too much either of Bentham's character or his doctrines as a precursor of revolutionary asceticism. Others, such as James Mill, established the image of ascetic and displaced libidinal utilitarian man, both as caricature and ideal type, in far more compelling fashion. Starting as a Calvinist, Mill "converted" to utilitarianism and ended up serving as a fitting link between the two. For example, Mill both extolled and illustrated the ethic of hard work. "He who works more than all others," Mill admonished his son John Stuart Mill, "will in the end excel all others."[6] And Mill suited his actions to his words, putting in prodigious hours at his writing and editing. As for libidinal ties, much of his reputation and political power derived from his seeming absence of feeling. Even Mill's friendly biographer, Bain, admitted as much:

It is a consequence of the determined pursuit of one or two all-comprehending ends, that a man has to put aside many claims of egoism. More than that, I hated friendship and I could not avoid the feeling of satisfaction for being unable to see you and others."[13]

Thus for Belinsky ideas, and his love and devotion to *them*, became his entire life. He described his nature admirably to a friend:

You do know my nature: it always takes an extreme position and never hits the center of an idea. I depart from the old idea with difficulty and pain and go over to the new one with all the fanatacism of a proselyte. I have now reached a new extreme—it is the idea of socialism, the idea of ideas, the way of ways of living, the problem of problems, the alpha and omega of belief and knowledge. Everything derives from it, exists for it, and goes to it. It has absorbed for me history, religion, and philosophy, and that is why I explain in its terms my life, your life, and the life of all those whom I meet on the road of life.[14]

In the name of "the idea of ideas [socialism]," he was prepared to sacrifice all concrete human beings. As Belinsky boasted:

God is my witness—I do not have any personal enemies. This is because of my nature (and I can say it without boasting) which stands above personal wrongs. But the enemies of public good—oh, let their intestines be thrown out so that they can hang themselves on them! I am ready to offer them the last service—to prepare knots and to put them on their necks.[15]

So, too, speaking of his "wild, frenzied . . . love for the freedom and independence of the human person," he exclaimed, "I am beginning to love mankind à la Marat: to make the least part of it happy I believe I could destroy the rest of it with fire and sword." Then he added, "People are so stupid that you have to drag them to happiness . . . in any case, what is the blood of thousands in comparison with the humiliation and sufferings of millions?" It was with great self-awareness that Belinsky wrote of himself: "What can I do? I love in my own fashion."[16]

Yet Belinsky remained a member of the intelligentsia, with somewhat revolutionary ideas; he did not become a revolutionary. It was Nicolay Chernyshevsky who both exemplified the "new man" in his own life, and, in his book *What Is to Be Done?*, offered the model for the revolutionary ascetic of element of rapprochement, it can only provide a fellow believer, but friendship requires an acknowledgement of a person and not his ideas." And, relating directly to our thesis, Herzen added, "Feasting goes with fullness of life, ascetic people are usually dry, egoistic people. . . ."

Belinsky took a different view of the matter. He loved only ideas, not persons; indeed, he had no life other than ideas. As Martin Malia puts it:

If worse came to worse, a Bakunin or a Herzen could make it up with father and find refuge on the family estate; a Belinsky, a Chernyshevsky, or a Dobrolyubov, if they wished to exist as "human beings," indeed if they wished to exist at all, had no choice but to labor at the tasks of intelligentsia. This faculty alone conferred on them at the same time dignity, personality, and the freedom of a livelihood which permitted them to escape from the oppression of their origins yet which did not make them dependent on the state.[12]

This explanation tells us only about the sociological, or perhaps economic, basis of Belinsky's devotion to ideas; it does not tell us anything about the psychological basis. In fact, it was the very "friendship group" which, by allowing gentry and *raznochintsy* to meet on terms of intellectual equality, probably served to awaken severe feelings of resentment and humiliation in the breasts of the socially inferior intelligentsia. It was all very well for Herzen to praise "feasting"; it must have had a mocking ring to Belinsky, the sick and overworked son of a poor provincial doctor. So, too, dependency feelings were threatening, not only if they related to the state, but even if they were extended to those members of the upper orders whose friendship and patronage might seemingly be removed at any moment.

In any case, Belinsky found it safer to relate to people solely in terms of ideas, which in fact became his only social ties. According to Nahirny, "As early as 1836 Belinsky was convinced that it was not an individual's personality, the 'immediate attributes of a human being' that 'form the bonds of friendship,' but similar beliefs and convictions." Writing to his friend Botkin, Belinsky declared, "I conceive of friendship as a cold feeling, an exchange of vanity, a result of habit, idleness, and

1840s, with their leanings toward idealism and sentimentality.

V. G. Belinsky was the first to make the break. As a literary critic, he symbolized the new type of the intelligentsia: a man of the *raznochintsy*, "persons of various classes," rather than of the gentry (as were, for example, Herzen and Turgenev), and dependent for a living on his professional work, i.e., his writing. In short, he is the professional intellectual, preceding the professional revolutionary.

Until his death in 1848, Belinsky hammered away in favor of the notion that literature has a social function, which is the amelioration of conditions in society. It is, however, not this side of his career that concerns us here, but rather his life in which we are interested: his character and style of living. We shall follow Vladimir C. Nahirny in his discussion of the latter.[11]

According to Nahirny, one significant part of the break within the generation of intelligentsia was over the issue of whether it was love and friendship rather than ideas that bound the group together. For "gentry" intelligentsia such as Herzen, Turgenev, and Ogarev, revolt against kinship ties was still unacceptable. For example, Ogarev wrote to Herzen: "I have not emancipated myself from the control of my father.... But come over here and look yourself at that old man. Even if I intended to get rid of his guardianship and love—do not forget love—then you would retort: unconscionable." As Nahirny sums up their situation, "Far from being uprooted and socially isolated, they were still entrenched economically, socially, and culturally in their social milieu, bound by kinship ties to their families, had friends and a relatively wide acquaintance, and led, for that time, a well-rounded and diversified life."

It was at the universities that members of the gentry mingled with *raznochintsy*, such as Belinsky. In the new friendship circles, men concerned with ideas could mingle freely, irrespective of social background. But "gentry" intelligentsia, such as Herzen or Ogarev, could not give up love for their families and kin; rather they extended love beyond these narrow bonds, but to real people, and not merely to abstractions. Thus Herzen wrote that "Friendship ought to be indulgent and passionate, it ought to love a person and not an idea; an idea is solely an underlying mere affection, feeling, or sentiment. Not that he is necessarily devoid of the warm, social emotions: he may have them, in fair measure; not, however, in an overpowering degree. It is that they stand in his way to other things; and so are, on certain occasions, sacrificed; leading thereby to the reproach of being of a nature hard and unfeeling. Such was Pitt, and such was Mill.[7]

Feeling and passion were exactly what Mill repressed in himself. Indeed, this is what his son John so bitterly deplored: "For passionate emotions of all sorts, and for everything which has been said or written in exaltation of them, he professed the greatest contempt. He regarded them as a form of madness."[8]

The power and the control over feelings necessarily expressed itself in relation to sex. For example, Mill warmly congratulated a friend on being "past the hey-day of the blood when the solid qualities are apt to be overlooked for the superficial"; he opposed dances "such as slide into lasciviousness";[9] and he, who had nine children of his own, extended his personal and psychological needs to public ones and became one of the first exponents of birth control.

Hopefully, we have said enough about Bentham and James Mill—and we could have mentioned a number of others—to establish the lines of the ascetic and displaced libidinal traits in utilitarianism.[10] But the utilitarians were not revolutionaries; by doctrine and action they were reformers in a social setting— early nineteenth-century England—that, partly as a result of a revolution almost two centuries before, had made reform preferable to revolution.

III

THE INTERVENING LINK between utilitarianism and the emergence of a Lenin as a revolutionary ascetic must be sought elsewhere—in mid-nineteenth-century Russia, in its "utilitarian" and "Victorian" phases. The key figure in this development is N. G. Chernyshevsky, surrounded by his contemporaries Belinsky, Dobrolyubov, and Pisarev. Together they mark the break with the generation of intelligentsia of the

Specifically, Weber suggests the connection between Calvinism and utilitarianism in relation to sexual intercourse. He summarizes the opinion, in this case of pietistic groups, that:

The highest form of Christian marriage is that with the preservation of virginity, the next highest that in which sexual intercourse is only indulged in for the procreation of children, and so on down to those which are contracted for purely erotic or external reasons and which are, from an ethical standpoint, concubinage. On these lower levels a marriage entered into for purely economic reasons is preferred (because after all it is inspired by rational motives) to one with erotic foundations. . . . The transition to a pure, hygenically oriented utilitarianism had already taken place in Franklin, who took approximately the ethical standpoint of modern physicians, who understand by chastity the restriction of sexual intercourse to the amount desirable for health, and who have, as is well known, even given theoretical advice as to how that should be accomplished.[5]

In the area of both work and love—Freud's famous *Liebe und Arbeit*—Bentham exhibited traits of the revolutionary ascetic in his own life. He led a pure and seemingly disinterested existence, devoting himself to legal, educational, and political reform. He had neither wife nor child, and proudly bore the title of "Hermit of Queen's Square Place." His life seemed wrapped up completely in hard work.

We ought not, however, to make too much either of Bentham's character or his doctrines as a precursor of revolutionary asceticism. Others, such as James Mill, established the image of ascetic and displaced libidinal utilitarian man, both as caricature and ideal type, in far more compelling fashion. Starting as a Calvinist, Mill "converted" to utilitarianism and ended up serving as a fitting link between the two. For example, Mill both extolled and illustrated the ethic of hard work. "He who works more than all others," Mill admonished his son John Stuart Mill, "will in the end excel all others."[6] And Mill suited his actions to his words, putting in prodigious hours at his writing and editing. As for libidinal ties, much of his reputation and political power derived from his seeming absence of feeling. Even Mill's friendly biographer, Bain, admitted as much:

It is a consequence of the determined pursuit of one or two all-comprehending ends, that a man has to put aside many claims of an important way station in the transformation of asceticism and displaced libido from the service of religion to the service of revolution.

There is a hint of what happened in Bentham himself. The other principle that he set in opposition to utility was the principle of sympathy and antipathy. By this, Bentham meant:

That principle which approves or disapproves of certain actions, not on account of their tending to augment the happiness, nor yet on account of their tending to diminish the happiness of the party whose interest is in question, but merely because a man finds himself disposed to approve or disapprove of them: holding up that approbation or disapprobation as a sufficient reason for itself and disclaiming the necessity of looking for any extrinsic grounds.[2]

From this principle one could proceed (though it is not a necessary procession) to the view that libidinal attachments must be overcome in the name of "the greatest good of the greatest number"; this was certainly the view held by Chernyshevsky, who became a devoted proponent of utilitarianism in nineteenth-century Russia.

Behind Bentham's utilitarianism stood Max Weber's asceticism in Calvinist dress. Weber himself has pioneered in tracing this evolution from Calvinism to a *nonreligious* world asceticism. Describing the development from the sixteenth to the eighteenth century, he points out that:

The full economic effect of those religious movements, whose significance for economic development lay above all in their ascetic educative influence, generally came only after the peak of the purely religious enthusiasm was past. Then the intensity of the search for the Kingdom of God commenced gradually to pass over into sober economic virtue; the religious roots died out slowly, giving way to utilitarian worldliness.[3]

In a more limited vein, Weber quotes Baxter's *Christian Directory*: "It is for action that God maintaineth us and our activities; work is the moral as well as the natural end of power. . . . It is action that God is most served and honored by. . . . The public welfare or the good of the many is to be valued above our own," and remarks, "Here is the connecting-point from the will of God to the purely utilitarian view-point of the later liberal theory."[4]

the future. Born in 1828 into a family of priests, Chernyshevsky at first followed the family tradition by taking up theological studies. When he lost his faith, partly under the impact of the ideas of Hegel and Feuerbach, Chernyshevsky gave up his plans for a clerical career and enrolled instead at the University of St. Petersburg. He retained, however, the ascetic way of life, derived from his religious background. As we shall see, he turned it to other than religious purposes.

At St. Petersburg he became a typical *intelligent*, studying intently the works of the philosophers and social critics and expounding his views in terms of aesthetics and literary criticism, for more direct political or philosophical comments would have been forbidden by the censor. As with Belinsky, Chernyshevsky was impatient with art or literature that served no direct social purpose. Turgenev appears to have hit the mark when he remarked of Chernyshevsky (and Dobrolyubov) that these two men were "literary Robespierres; they wouldn't for a moment hesitate to cut off the poet Chénier's head."[17] Chernyshevsky, however, aspired to be something more than merely a "literary Robespierre"; he also became an active revolutionary (though not a very successful one). Immersing himself in the agitation concerning agrarian problems and peasant communes, he joined in the organizing of underground activities. For this he was arrested in 1862 and placed for more than eighteen months in the Peter-Paul fortress, where he wrote *What Is to Be Done?*, published in 1864. In that same year he was sent to forced labor in Siberia—really to prison—and not freed until 1883. He was then exiled to Astrakhan, where he remained for six years before being permitted to return to his native Saratov. Four months later he was dead.

Chernyshevsky was really a revolutionary ascetic *manqué*. In his own life he pursued an ascetic existence (even before prison) and, like Belinsky, did not allow himself to love people. Approaching his future wife with due deliberation, he satisfied himself that "she is a democrat" and not too religious. He could then declare that "My assumption is correct and now I adore you unconditionally . . . my love is not unconditional. . . . I have heard many things about you, but this prompts me to look at you in a special manner . . . for such a kind of ideas I cannot but love you." Aware of the danger of libidinal object ties for a "professional" revolutionary, Chernyshevsky sought to attenuate them from the beginning, warning his wife that "The nature of my ideas is such that sooner or later I will be caught." (Chernyshevsky's next phrase unwittingly reveals the link between his religious background and his revolutionary commitments: "And thus I await every minute the appearance of the police, and, like a pious Christian, await the Last Day of Judgment.") Momentarily, it seems, Chernyshevsky sought to evade his fate by embracing human ties as a check to his revolutionary activities. In an odd passage, he mused: "I should possess an idea that I do not belong to myself; that I have no right to risk my life. There should be some protection against democratic, revolutionary conviction, and this protection cannot be anything else but the idea of a wife."[18] But the "protection" failed in the face of Chernyshevsky's greater ardor for revolution. Warned of his impending arrest and given a chance to escape, he chose not to take it. There were, as Franco Venturi observes, many reasons for his decision: "his almost religious spirit of resignation; the conviction that he was destined for prison, the desire to give himself one more proof of his resolution about which his conscience had been so tormented ever since boyhood. . . ."[19] For us, additional psychological hints implicit in the ideal type of the revolutionary ascetic also spring to mind. In any case, Chernyshevsky remained for the trial that resulted in his imprisonment. When he was exiled to Siberia, he left behind his wife and a son, Alexander.

Chernyshevsky's revolutionary activity had been nipped in the bud. In his prison novel, *What Is to Be Done?*, however, he left a legacy to future revolutionary activists such as Lenin. The novel really spoke less about "what is to be done" than "who was to do it," for the main thing that emerges from its pages is the prototype of the "new man," the "revolutionary ascetic" who will bring about the Day of Judgment.[20] Its heroes are men like Lopukhóv or Rakhmétov, examples of the "unusual man," and their female counterpart is the heroine, Véra Pávlovna. Rakhmétov, for example, transformed himself into an "uncommon man" by imposing "rules upon himself." "He was poorly clad, though fond of elegance, and in all other things lived a Spartan's life; for instance, he allowed himself no mattress and slept on felt without so much as doubling it up." (His only weakness was for cigars.) Rakhmétov's asceticism, we are told, was not from personal desire but from a temporary, functional necessity of being "hard" in order to carry out the needed tasks.

Meanwhile, although it was also necessary to refrain from "useless expenditures of time," physical exercise was essential. Starting with gymnastics, Rakhmétov proceeded to search for work requiring strength (chopping firewood, forging iron). Adopting the diet of pugilists, "he ate food known exclusively as strengthening, especially almost raw beefsteak. . . ." There is a strong masochistic element to his behavior, though placed in the service of revolutionary "toughening." One night his friend discovers him covered with blood:

The back and sides of Rakhmétov's shirt (he was in his shirt) were covered with blood; there was blood under the bed; the felt on which he slept was covered with blood; in the felt were hundreds of little nails, sticking up almost an inch; Rakhmétov had lain all night on this bed of his invention.

"What does this mean, Rakhmétov?" cried Kirsanov, thoroughly frightened.

"A trial. It was necessary to make it. Improbable, certainly, but at all events it was necessary to make it. I know now what I can do."[21]

Rakhmétov also knew he could break all libidinal ties to persons when necessary. We are told that in his second year as a student at the university, aged seventeen, he broke with his family, "won the curses of his brother, and behaved in such a way that the husbands of his sisters had forbidden them to pronounce his name. . . ." As for erotic relations, these are to be ignored. Elsewhere, discussing a tale by Turgenev, Chernyshevsky had already counseled: "Forget about them, those erotic questions! They are not for a reader of our time, occupied with problems of administration and judiciary improvements, of financial reforms, of the emancipation of the serfs."[22] And this counsel is kept, though in rather teasing fashion, in What Is to Be Done?

Marital relations, too, are not for the "uncommon man."

Chernyshevsky has Rakhmétov live up to the advice he, the author, had given himself, but not been able to take. When a lovely nineteen-year-old widow falls in love with him, Rakhmétov declares that:

"You can see that men like me have not the right to bind their destiny to that of any one whomsoever."

"Yes, you are right," said she, "you cannot marry. But until you have to leave me, love me."

"No, I cannot accept that offer either; I am no longer free, and must not love."

Chernyshevsky then reassures us, rather smugly, "What has become of this lady since? This adventure must have changed her life. In all probability she herself became an unusual person."[23]

The heroine, Véra Pávlovna, does marry, not once but twice (after her husband's idealistic "suicide"). But the relationship, as befits two "unusual persons," has nothing erotic about it. The husband and wife live in separate rooms so as not to disturb one another, and though there is a son, Mitya, he plays no role in the story. As one friend says to Véra Pávlovna, "Your nature has so little of the feminine element that you are undoubtedly about to put forth utterly masculine ideas."[24]

One more trait of Chernyshevsky's "new generation" to which we need to pay attention is its basic moral philosophy and psychology. For Chernyshevsky, all human relations are, and ought to be, ultimately reducible to self-interest. As Lopukhóv, Véra's first husband, informs her early in their courtship, "What are called elevated sentiments, ideal aspirations—all that, in the general course of affairs, is absolutely null, and is eclipsed by individual interest; these very sentiments are nothing but self-interest clearly understood." Véra paraphrases him: "Practical and cold men are therefore right in saying that man is governed exclusively by self-interest." But she adds, "This theory seems to me very cold." To which Lopukhóv replies, "No, Véra Pávlovna: this theory is cold, but it teaches man to procure warmth.... This theory is pitiless, but by following it men cease to be wretched objects of the compassion of the idle."[25]

Do we recognize this "pitiless" theory? It is, of course, utilitarianism. As Isaiah Berlin summarizes the position, "Cherny-shevsky preached a naive utilitarianism. Like James Mill, and perhaps Bentham, he held that basic human nature was a fixed, physiologically analyzable, pattern of natural processes and faculties, and that the maximization of human happiness could therefore be scientifically planned and realized."[26] Happiness, strange as it may seem, was the aim of Rakhmétov's ascetic and libidinal restraints. Chernyshevsky admonishes his reader, "Desire to be happy: this desire, this desire alone, is indispensable. With this end in view you will work with pleasure for your development, for there lies happiness."[27]

Chernyshevsky was an enormously eclectic thinker. Hegel and Feuerbach, as well as the utilitarian thinkers, colored his ideas, and to them he added notions of Saint-Simon and Fourier. Yet central to his convictions was utilitarianism. Indeed, John Stuart Mill, with his own effort at adding Saint-Simonian ideas, especially about the philosophy of history, to his father's utilitarianism, may have prepared the way for Chernyshevsky's less systematic fusion of these schools of thought. In fact, Chernyshevsky translated into Russian Mill's *Principles of Political Economy* (and once added that men such as Cobden and Bright, outstanding proponents of laissez faire, were his ideal). Beyond specific utilitarian ideas, however, Chernyshevsky seems to have taken the caricature of the utilitarian man—ascetic and unfeeling—as his model of the "new man."

What we see in nineteenth-century Russia, therefore, is Chernyshevsky placing utilitarianism and the utilitarian man in the service of revolutionary ideas.[28] But his own effort to carry his revolutionary ideas into actuality was aborted by his imprisonment, and his character as a revolutionary ascetic played itself out solely as an inspiration to others, and even more as a fiction. It remained for Lenin, exiled to his family farm at Kokushkino, to read *What Is to Be Done?* and to translate seriously into life the figure of Rakhmétov. In England the utilitarian man became either an entrepreneur or a reformer. In Russia, and with Lenin, he became a professional revolutionary: hard, tough, without sentiment. Chernyshevsky's revolutionary, as we noted earlier, was to work for a kind of communal or cooperative society, on a simple scale of economic activity. Lenin disliked and distrusted communes, and as a good Marxist (and unconscious Russian nationalist?) wished for a high level of economic productivity. Thus he directed *his* new men, the Bolsheviks, toward a modernizing revolution. In the end, then, Lenin wished to achieve by professional revolutionary activity much of what the earlier utilitarians had been able to attain by reforming efforts. Utilitarian man, in the broadest sense, had become the revolutionary ascetic as I have described him.

I V

ONE LAST STATEMENT must be made, before dealing directly with Lenin, concerning the emergence of the professional revolutionary, the man who spends his entire life "making" revolutions the way a businessman "makes" steel or textiles. This tradition of the professional revolutionary, a fitting component of the general professionalization forced upon men by the Industrial Revolution, probably starts with Blanqui and Buonarroti, though it may be traced back in embryo to Babeuf and the sputtering out of the French Revolution. It reaches fruition in Marx and Engels as theorists, and Bakunin, Nechaef, and perhaps Tkachev in practice. Out of the collaboration of Bakunin and Nechaev emerged the *Revolutionary Catechism*. It is the Bible or, to use more modern terms, the textbook of the professional revolutionary. To quote a few of its paragraphs is to catch the "spirit" of revolution:

The revolutionary is a lost man; he has no interests of his own, no cause of his own, no feelings, no habits, no belongings; he does not even have a name. Everything in him is absorbed by a single, exclusive interest, a single thought, a single passion—the revolution.

Hard with himself, he must be hard towards others. All the tender feelings of family life, of friendship, love, gratitude and even honour must be stifled in him by a single cold passion for the revolutionary cause. For him there is only one pleasure, one consolation, one reward, and one satisfaction—the success of the revolution.

The character of the true revolutionary has no place for any romanticism, sentimentality, enthusiasm or seduction. Nor has it any place for private hatred or revenge. This revolutionary passion which in him becomes a daily, hourly passion, must be combined with cold calculation.[29]

A professional revolutionary in this catechism is, by necessity, a revolutionary ascetic. His "calling" requires him to practice worldly asceticism and to displace libidinal ties from persons to ideas and the "cause." At this point, Weber's ascetic enterpreneur and Freud's leader with few libidinal ties truly have fused into one figure: the modern, and generally modernizing, revolutionary.

PART THREE

TWO
CASE STUDIES

CHAPTER 8

Lenin

I

IN THE SAME WAY that the Russian Revolution replaced
the French Revolution as the model and myth for modern revolutions, Lenin replaced Robespierre as the prototypic revolutionary personality. Unlike the Frenchman, however, Lenin's
whole life involved revolution: It was his profession, as he
became a revolutionary before the Revolution itself, immersing
himself in an existing revolutionary tradition; he was the essential figure in bringing about the October Revolution of 1917;
and he guided that Revolution until shortly before his death in
1924. If ever there was identity between a man and his revolution, it existed between Lenin and the Bolshevik Revolution.

Having said this, we are faced with an extreme paradox.
Lenin, who created the Bolshevik Revolution and stamped his
personality on it, was, or appeared to be, to an extraordinary
degree "without personality." Observer after observer records
his initial disappointment on first seeing the ordinary, uninspir-
ing, and plebeian or middle-class figure of Lenin. Typical was
Maxim Gorky's account of his first meeting with Lenin: "For
me there was something lacking. . . . In a way he was too ordinary, he did not give the impression of a leader."[1] Lenin was
no Napoleon, certainly at first glance; if we may coin a phrase,
he was a "revolutionary in a business suit." Here, at the begin-

ning of the twentieth century, we have the new type of leader, who personifies in himself the amorphous masses of the emerging industrial society. He is the revolutionary ascetic *par excellence*.

Befitting his apparent lack of personality is the absence of any trustworthy accounts of his early, formative years or of the intimate side of his life. He himself was singularly unintrospective. He wrote no autobiography—his one response to a request in 1917 for an account of his life consisted of eight lines!—and left no diary. His letters are dry and businesslike, revealing nothing personal, talking only of money, books, and his philosophical and political interests. Even the memoirs of his wife, Krupskaya, from whom one might have expected more, are of the same nature: dry, pedantic, and, in her case, hagiological in tone and concern. What little we have on Lenin *as a person* is mainly from the memories of adult friends, usually fellow party workers. The most revealing of these is Nikolay Valentinov's *Encounter with Lenin*,[2] supplemented by such other reminiscences as those of Gorky, Balabanoff, and various members of Lenin's family.

Lenin was a pseudonym for Vladimir Ilyich Ulyanov. One may say that the Russian Revolution was made by pseudonymous individuals. Partly this was because of the necessity for secrecy imposed on the revolutionary movement by the pressure of the Tsarist police service—it was a revolution from "underground." Partly the name changes also symbolized the revolutionary's break with his real family, and his taking on a new name in the brotherhood of the ideological group. In any case, Lenin's "underground man" was not Dostoevsky's; of all the great Russian writers, it was Dostoevsky for whom Lenin had the least sympathy, and the former's *Notes from Underground*, with its introspective, guilt-ridden, "possessed" individuality must have set his teeth on edge. Whereas the world of Lenin's slightly older contemporary, Freud, following on Dostoevsky, was peopled with anonymous characters—an Anna O, a Dora, even a Rat Man—whose identity had to be covered because their real personalities were too revealing, the world of Lenin's Bolshevism was filled with pseudonymous figures—a Stalin ("Steel"), a Trotsky (his jailer's name), a

Martov ("Man of March")—who, ideally, had no personality except that of the professional revolutionary.

Lenin himself best personified the new Bolshevik man. As Adam Ulam puts it categorically, "Bolshevism without him was unimaginable."[3] Thus, to know Bolshevik man, one ought intimately to know Lenin. Our available sources make it almost impossible to pursue a true developmental, psychohistorical life study of Lenin. Nevertheless, while the etiology is uncertain, the "patterns" of his behavior, his "life style," are abundantly available for inspection. The traits, if not the origin, of the Bolshevik "new man" as epitomized in Lenin can be easily delineated and even analyzed. Our aim here, then, is to use available Lenin materials as a case study for our general treatment of the ascetic ethos and the spirit of revolution, and our contention will be that Lenin exemplifies asceticism made secular and revolutionary: He is Victorian asceticism turned mainly to political revolutionary ends.

I I

THERE IS, of course, more to Lenin's personality than revolutionary ascetic qualities. In a fuller analysis, one would give equal attention to his ego-ideals, his cognitive powers, and so on. It is only in terms of our particular aims that we can justify our concentration on his personality as a revolutionary ascetic.

In any event, Lenin's personality is at one and the same time consistent and ambivalent. It is consistent because the various parts interrelate and support one another: personal hardness fits with a hard-core political party, personal industriousness coincides with the desire for an industrialized Russia, and so on. Indeed, the overt consistency of Lenin's personality gave him much of his strength, and impressed followers and enemies alike with his apparent singleness of aim, relentlessly pursued. On the other hand, his repressed ambivalence becomes more and more striking as one studies him, until the covert part of his personality becomes the necessary pendant for the over-consistency. For example, Lenin's hardness is necessary because of the sirenlike attraction for him, as for all Russia, of softness; tremendous efforts at self-control were required by the ever-threatening rages within him.

We shall try to deal with both the overt consistency and covert ambivalence, but first our attention will go to the consistency. Lenin thought poorly of Freud; as he remarked to Clara Zetkin, "The extension on Freudian hypotheses seems 'educated,' even scientific, but it is ignorant, bungling. Freudian theory is the modern fashion. I mistrust the sexual theories ... it seems to me that these flourishing sexual theories which are mainly hypothetical, and often quite arbitrary hypotheses, arise from the personal need to justify personal abnormality or hypertrophy in sexual life before bourgeois morality, and to entreat its patience."[4] One of those "quite arbitrary hypotheses," as we have already seen, is Freud's theory of the leader as lacking "in libidinal ties." It is a pleasant irony to suggest that Lenin is the perfect and consistent exemplar, almost to the point of caricature, of this character.

Lenin did not come easily to his breaking of libidinal ties. It was a titanic struggle (and in fact he kept some of the ties to his immediate family). One suspects, however, that the need to deny love was already there early in his childhood, for even at sixteen Lenin is described as taciturn and withdrawn, without friends. There is the story of desertion by so-called liberal friends of the family at the time of his brother's execution (1887); if it occurred as told, it would have encouraged this development. It is around 1900, however, that the complete snapping of the ties seems to have taken place, when Lenin's professed "love" for his older mentor Plekhanov is abruptly made use of in a struggle for power over the journal *Iskra*, and, as Lenin perceives it, betrayed. Before detailing the break itself, uncharacteristically revealed in detail by Lenin himself, let us note the complicated nature of Lenin's "love" relation to Plekhanov.

To Lenin the relation seemed like one between father and son, with Plekhanov as the revered and trusted teacher (as numerous commentators have observed, Lenin's father was a professional teacher). Was the relation perceived in different form by Plekhanov? At one point, discussing the incipient quarrel, Plekhanov said jokingly: "Napoleon had a passion for getting his marshalls divorced from their wives; some marshalls gave way, although they loved their wives. Comrade Akimov in this respect is like Napoleon—he wants to divorce me from Lenin at all costs. But I am showing a stronger character than the Napoleonic marshalls; I am not out to divorce Lenin, and I hope he does not intend divorcing me." According to Krupskaya, who reports this exchange, "Vladimir Ilyich smiled, and shook his head in the negative."[5] Here, then, the imagery is directly sexual—husband and wife—rather than parental. We must, therefore, understand Lenin's severe reaction in terms of this hypercharged "love" atmosphere.

In a fifteen-page outpouring called "How the 'Spark' [*Iskra*] Was Nearly Extinguished," written later in life, Lenin recalled his earlier feelings:

As soon as we found ourselves alone ... we broke into a flood of angry expressions. ... My "infatuation" with Plekhanov disappeared as if by magic, and I felt offended and embittered to an unbelievable degree. Never, never in my life, had I regarded any man with such sincere respect and veneration, never had I stood before any man so "humbly" and never before had I been so brutally "kicked." That's what it was, we had actually been kicked. We had been scared like little children, scared by the grown-ups threatening to leave us to ourselves, and when we funked (the shame of it!) we were brushed aside with incredible unceremoniousness. We now realized very clearly that Plekhanov had simply laid a trap for us that morning when he declined to act as co-editor; it had been a deliberate chess move, a snare for guileless "pigeons." ... And since a man with whom we desired to co-operate closely and establish most intimate relations, resorted to chess moves in dealing with comrades, there would be no doubt that this man was bad, yes, bad, inspired by petty motives of personal vanity and conceit—an insincere man. ... Our indignation knew no bounds. Our ideal had been destroyed; gloatingly we trampled it underfoot like a dethroned god. ... We had received the most bitter lesson of our lives, a painfully bitter, painfully brutal lesson. Young comrades "court" an elder comrade out of the great love they bear for him—and suddenly he injects into this love an atmosphere of intrigue, compelling them to feel, not as younger brothers, but as fools to be led by the nose, as pawns to be moved about at will, and, still worse, as clumsy *Streber* [careerists] who must be thoroughly frightened and quashed! An enamoured youth receives from the object of his love a bitter lesson to regard all persons "without sentiment," to keep a stone in one's sling.[6]

Surely we are in the presence of one of Freud's "traumatic" accounts, overdetermined, of course! As a defense against his thwarted "great love," Lenin turns to great repression: henceforth he will be "without sentiment." It is noteworthy that shortly after this episode he begins to sign his articles in *Iskra* with the pseudonym Lenin.[7] The Ulyanov given to sentiment has been replaced by the hard, unloving, unyielding Lenin. We are now in the presence of the prototypic leader "with few libidinal ties."

The ramifications of this continuous development in Lenin, with numerous corresponding traits of traditional asceticism, are of overwhelming significance. As we see in the above quotation, Lenin perceived (in psychoanalytic terms we would talk of transferences) Plekhanov as both a "grown-up"—indeed, a "god"—with himself in the position of a child, and a brother, with himself as the younger brother. Henceforth Lenin had no "master" and no "brothers" whom he loved. By 1903 he had stopped addressing Martov, the closest friend of his youth, by the familiar "thou" form (one can compare this with Robespierre's behavior), and announced, "Don't look at Martov in the old way. The friendship has ended. Down with any softness."[8]

There were lapses, of course. Lenin was always vulnerable to his pattern of having a "crush" on a new collaborator, and then having to create a "distance" between them. As Krupskaya commented, Lenin "was always having these periods of enthusiasm for people,"[9] and then becoming disillusioned. Such, of course, was his relationship to Valentinov, described in detail by the latter. More startling was the recurrence of this pattern as late as 1911 in relation to Malinovsky, a police spy planted in the Bolshevik ranks, whom Lenin persisted in trusting and favoring until the inevitable denouement (in this case, as late as 1918).

The breaking of libidinal ties with "brother" figures is, I believe, significantly connected with Lenin's coming to terms, in an ideological as well as personal sense, with his own brother Alexander, and with the latter's terroristic beliefs. The evidence is conclusive that what made certain Lenin's evolution into a professional revolutionary was Alexander's unsuccessful assassination attempt on Alexander III, with the brother's resultant execution. We can only guess at the compound of survival guilt, mourning feelings, love, and hate stirred up in Lenin. There can be no question that Lenin loved his brother (as well as unconsciously desiring to supplant, to "replace" him), and in becoming a revolutionary partly identified with him. Yet to be a successful revolutionary Lenin had to disengage himself from his brother's "path," and thus, in the realm of the unconscious, to repudiate him, to "break" with him.

In "What Is to Be Done?" (1902) Lenin unsuspectingly reveals this aspect of himself. Referring to young social democrats (like himself?), Lenin remarks that "Many of them began their revolutionary thinking as adherents of Narodovolists. Nearly all of them in their early youth enthusiastically worshipped the terrorist heroes. It required a struggle to abandon the captivating impressions of these heroic traditions, and *it was accompanied by the break of personal relationships* [italics added] with people who were determined to remain loyal to Narodnaya Volya and for whom the young Social-Democrats had profound respect."[10] Our interpretation of this passage is given support by Krupskaya's personal comment: "This paragraph is a piece of the biography of Vladimir Ilyich."[11]

Lenin's "great wrench" freed him from his "heroic" brother, whose heroism was impulsive and passionate.[12] Impulse and spontaneity, as we shall see, were always threatening to Lenin. The "great wrench" also helped free Lenin from almost all ties of personal friendship and love, leaving room in general only for political "friendships." As one early associate remarked, "I began to be separated from the movement and thus completely ceased to exist for Vladimir Ilyich."[13] Lenin's rejection of libidinal ties allowed him to use dissidents, even if he "disliked" them, as long as they served the cause, and to spurn those whom he might otherwise have "liked" if "objectively" they hampered the movement. "Friendship is friendship, and duty is duty," he characteristically remarked.

Perhaps most important of all, the "great wrench" allowed Lenin to proceed coldly to the formation of a tight, hard-core party organization, totally "controlled" and calculating, tied to Lenin as the leader who correctly interpreted the steely, unyielding, and deterministic dogma of Marxism. But more of this later.

III

LENIN quite clearly freed himself from libidinal ties in the political arena. What about familial and marital ties? Here the picture is more complicated. Lenin's attachment to his mother was strong throughout his life. His letters, especially the early ones, are filled with loving sentiments. Indeed, some critics have postulated a significant oedipal relation to his mother. Lenin also remained in close touch with his various sisters, being especially warm toward his favorite younger sister, Olga, until her death at age twenty. In short, Lenin did not break with his immediate family.

In fact, it seems as if Lenin used his family to shield him from the importunities of the outside world. A few items of special interest, however, must be noted. The death of his father when Lenin was sixteen, and the death of his brother the next year, left Lenin as titular male head of the family; we can only speculate whether an actual "break" or "wrench" from his father and brother would otherwise have been necessary. Next, although head of the family, Lenin seemed to remain continuously dependent on the women of his family. It was his mother who interceded for him with the Tsarist authorities, and to whom he constantly wrote for money. His sisters were continuously asked to procure books for him, and to carry out similar errands. Without seeking to depreciate Lenin, we can say that he used his family in his work (they were also willing to serve), and that he never earned an independent living or helped to support them. Perhaps he took their mutual love for granted. It must surely have given him great emotional security.

What about other women in his life? Wife and marriage? It is not clear what sort of model his own parents provided him. His father, a bureaucrat charged with administration of a school district, was away frequently. Immensely hard-working, he was a loyal supporter of the Tsar, believing that the path to a better Russia was through education and slow change. Toward the end of his life he was disillusioned in this belief. In 1884 he was informed by the Ministry of Education that he would have to resign, for even his loyal and reforming ideas were considered too liberal in the growing reaction of the time. Without adequate financial resources or pension, Ulyanov *père* faced a dismal future. Fortunately, the ministry changed its mind and renewed his service for another five years. But he lived only two years longer, and died in 1886 of a hemorrhage of the brain. The Simbirsk paper described Lenin's father at the time of his death as "extremely successful . . . due . . . to his ability to deal with people of the most different walks of life, different degree of education, and to his warm-hearted and attractive personality."[14] Though described as "accessible to his children, friendly, humorous, full of stories, and eager for games," most accounts also portray him as the typical patriarchial, Victorian master of the house.

The mother, Maria Alexandrovna Blank, was also a hard-working, educated, and dedicated person. She was of superior social status to her husband: whereas his father was a tailor, hers, originally of German origin, was a graduate of Petersburg Medical Academy. He is described as "Somewhat of a Rousseauist, he believed in nature healing, in Spartan living, in simple diet and water cures. . . . He denied his children 'the poison' of tea and coffee, and made them drink cold clean water. He denied them also ample and comfortable clothing: they had to expose their bodies to wind, snow, and frost, and to harden them even more, he treated them to frequent cold compresses." His daughter Maria seems to have followed her father in his child-rearing attitudes, for we are told that she "brought up her children in a Spartan manner too, without however subjecting them to any of the trials she and her sisters and brother had to go through."[15] Thus if the example of hard work came from both parents, the Spartan inclination in Lenin appears to have been implanted by his mother. Unlike the father, who was a believer in religious orthodoxy, she had emancipated herself from any religious belief. Perhaps for this reason, again unlike the father, she was free to support her children's revolutionary aspirations. Lastly, in another sphere, it was the mother, a gifted pianist, who brought music and culture to the household.

Most accounts picture the marriage of Ilya Nikolayevich Ulyanov and Maria Alexandrovna Blank as a contented, happy one. At least one scholar, however, following the account mainly of Marietta Schaginjan, tells a different story, of a moody Maria, dissatisfied with her unromantic husband, sleeping apart and making the best of a disappointing relationship.[16] Alas, the evidence is so fragmentary and untrustworthy that prudence suggests we abstain completely from any judgment in the matter, except to say that the family was an unusually hard-working, dedicated group of individuals (for example, all the children did well at school) who *seemed* tightly-knit and concerned with one another. One statement by Lenin gives us pause. Talking to Clara Zetkin, after the Revolution, of sexual relations, marriage, and the family, Lenin said: "The decay, the corruption, the filth of bourgeois marriage, with its difficult divorce, its freedom for the man, its enslavement for the woman, the resultant hypocrisy of sexual morality and relations fill the most active-minded and best people with disgust."[17] Lenin's own family was "bourgeois" (though his father had actually earned entrance to the lower nobility). Had he been thinking of them when he made this statement? Almost nothing else said by Lenin gives support to this view.

In any case, Lenin did not take the Victorian marriage of his parents as his overt model.[18] In marrying Nadezhda Constantinova Krupskaya he was marrying a "new woman"—the emancipated female—and offering us an exemplar of what we shall call a "new-model marriage." Krupskaya was first and foremost a revolutionary companion rather than an object of romantic love. A schoolteacher, she had early become involved in revolutionary circles in St. Petersburg. Before meeting Lenin she had become impressed with him through one of his writings —on markets. Once married, she shared his exiles and served him faithfully in the cause to which they were both dedicated.

Valentinov describes her as an "unfeminine woman."[19] Affection between her and Lenin was certainly not demonstrative; as Krupskaya remarks revealingly about one of their efforts to elude the police, "we emerged arm-in-arm, which was a thing we never usually did."[20] Moreover, she and Lenin shared as their ideal Chernyshevsky and his vision of the new man and woman, and Chernyshevsky, though a materialist, dismisses summarily the physical aspect of the marital relation. As we remarked earlier, in reviewing a short story by Turgenev, Chernyshevsky declared characteristically: "Away with erotic problems. [This, ironically, is the main concern of his own book, *What Is to Be Done?*] The modern reader has no interest in them. He is concerned with the question of perfecting the administration and the judicial systems, with financial questions, with the problem of liberating the peasants."[21]

All our evidence suggests that Lenin, as an adolescent, showed little interest in girls, although apparently he told one friend that "I used to flirt when I was at school."[22] There is the story that he proposed to another schoolteacher-revolutionary before Krupskaya, but was rejected.[23] Some have suggested that Lenin was impotent; more have postulated that he was infertile. In any case, we are left with the question: Why did Lenin, who seems either to have been constitutionally low-keyed sexually, or else enormously repressed and sublimated in his sexual drives, need to be married? For companionship? Children? Or some deeper psychological need?

Lenin and Krupskaya's marriage, whether or not it was so intended to, served as a model for Bolshevik society. Unlike bourgeois marriage, divorce was open to either partner, without emotion or strings attached. Certainly the woman was not to be "enslaved" (at least in the old sense), nor was she to be a mere sex object; in this important sense revolutionary asceticism became unconsciously tied to the whole movement for "emancipation of women." The object of the marriage was revolutionary service to society, not individual self-fulfillment and concern. Marriage was not based on "sentimentality."[24]

One episode suggests to us that there was another side to Lenin. It is his relationship to Inessa Armand (long hidden by the Soviet idolatry for Lenin). She, too, was a revolutionary "companion," but with what a difference! Married to a member of one of Moscow's rich capitalist families, the beautiful Inessa, aged twenty-eight, left her husband by agreement in 1903, taking their five children (the last one born in that very year), and went to live with his younger brother! This situation, too, did not hold her, and she became an active revolutionary propagandist. In 1910 she met Lenin in France. The attraction was mutual, and gradually Inessa began to share the life of the Lenins. Krupskaya, "new woman" that she was, seems to have accepted the triangular relationship with good grace.

Inessa awakened the passionate, emotional side of Lenin, long submerged and repressed, although their affair was probably not sexually consummated. Krupskaya herself tells us that Inessa "seemed to radiate warmth and ardor ... [she] loved music and made us attend Beethoven concerts. She herself was a good musician and played many of Beethoven's compositions very well indeed. Ilyich was particularly fond of the *Sonata Pathétique* and he always asked her to play it."[25] Lenin's mother, we shall remember, imbued him with a love for music, and later we shall see the connection for him of music and the softer feelings. Clearly, Inessa awakened strange and ancient emotions in Lenin. To her alone, aside from his immediate family, he used the "thou" form of address.

Lenin's love for Inessa, for so we must call it, persisted for ten years, with an occasional lover's quarrel, until her death in 1920. Yet his love did not prevent him from following his duty first. Inessa was treated publicly as just another revolutionary companion, and given tasks by Lenin to carry out ("slavishly," his enemies said). Only at her funeral did Lenin break down. As Balabanoff so poignantly describes it, "I never saw such torment, I never saw any human being as completely absorbed by sorrow, by the effort to keep it to himself, to guard it against the attention of others."[26]

Inessa was the one chink in his emotional armor. Otherwise, Lenin took care to avoid all sentimentality and softness in his relations. He told Valentinov that his views on the "sanctity" of love were exactly the same as those expressed by Turgenev in *Andrei Kolosov*. "These," Lenin said, "are not vulgar bourgeois views on the relations between men and women, but real, revolutionary ones." As Valentinov summarizes the story: "The narrator of the story calls Kolosov an 'uncommon' man who fell in love with a girl, then ceased loving her and left her. What, one might ask, is so uncommon about that? What is uncommon, the narrator tells us, is that Kolosov did this fearlessly: he made a clean break with his past and was not afraid of reproaches."[27] Lenin, who obviously saw himself as an "uncommon" man, who scorned, as he repeatedly put it, "petty feelings" of marital obligation, did not stay with Krupskaya out of moral scruple; assuming Inessa would have been willing to live with him, he would seem to have preferred his new-model marriage to Krupskaya to any romantic escapade with the intensely ardent and feminine Inessa. In this he showed his usual utilitarian approach to intimate matters.

Lenin and Krupskaya had no children, though it appears that they wished for them. Of the Ulyanov progeny, only the younger brother, Dmitri, had children of his own. The Bolshevik Party and the Revolution became Lenin's child. For example, in 1910, writing to Gorky of the squabbles in the Russian Social Democratic Party, Lenin declared, "Either—if all goes well—we lance the abscesses, drain the pus, and cure and raise the child. Or—if worse comes to worse—the child dies. Then we will live for a while without a child [that is, again set up a Bolshevik faction] and then we will give birth to a healthier infant."[28] In trying to restrain a group of workers who, before Brest Litovsk, were determined to go to the front and fight, Lenin used the same imagery: "You may go. But you will take my resignation with you. I have led the Revolution. I will not share in the murder of my own child."[29] And again, during the debates over Brest Litovsk, discussing the possibility of revolution in Germany, Lenin declared, "But Germany is only pregnant with revolution and with us a perfectly healthy baby has been born...."[30]

Lenin's parentage of the Revolution was equally acknowledged by his followers; that he was its "father" was never in doubt. As Trotsky lamented on the death of Lenin, "And now Vladimir Ilyich is no more. The party is orphaned. The workmen's class is orphaned."[31] The Revolution as one's child; marriage as a utilitarian union between new men and women: this is the ideal that emerges for their followers from the relationship of Lenin and Krupskaya. Only this time the utilitarianism is in the service, not of political economy, but of what I have called revolutionary asceticism.

I V

LENIN, with a few exceptions as noted, "loved no one but himself" (or, rather, loved only the Revolution). He is thus Freud's prototypic leader "with few libidinal ties." Was he, however, loved passionately by his followers? Adam Ulam, for example, casts doubt on such a conclusion. He describes how the other Bolshevik leaders reacted to the news of an assassin's wounding of Lenin in 1918 by first making sure that there was no supportive uprising and *then* going to see Lenin. Ulam comments, "This is in line with the Bolshevik unsentimental attitude in such matters and perhaps it would have been approved by Lenin himself, but it hardly bears out the tales of 'the boundless love' that his closest collaborators were said to have felt toward him." Ulam also cites the callous treatment of Lenin by his own closest lieutenants and would-be successors at the time of his fatal decline in 1924: "The legend they would try to preserve and enhance after his death. But for the man himself in his last illness they showed very little consideration."[32]

These are telling remarks. We must give less weight, presumably, to the adverse reactions of Lenin's political opponents, though we cannot dismiss them entirely. Thus Struve's comment that "the impression which Lenin at once made on me— and which remained with me all my life—was an unpleasant one" can be minimized, as well as his further statement, "A great number of people shared with me that impression of Lenin. I shall mention only two of them, and very different they were: Vera Zasulich and Michael Tugan-Baronovsky. Vera Zasulich . . . felt an antipathy for Lenin verging on physical aversion—their subsequent political quarrel was due not only to theoretical or tactical differences, but to the profound dissimilarity of their natures, quite understandable and expected."[33]

The possible lack of love among Lenin's own followers, however, calls for more extended explanation.

The evidence seems to support Ulam in his view that many in Lenin's inner group were not "bound" to him by "boundless love." A beginning explanation is offered by Wolfenstein when he says, "Tension exists because, just as the leader is one who, psychologically speaking, tries to become his own father, so also the leader projects onto his followers the ambivalent feelings he had toward his father. Thus he is able to view them as loving him, but he also finds in them the seeds of disloyalty and hatred. As he asserted his manhood against his father, so his followers will desire to challenge his authority."[34] Valentinov presents us with something of a case study in this process: "Though it is slightly ridiculous to say that I 'fell in love' with him," he tells us, "nevertheless this phrase better than any other expresses my attitude toward Lenin over a period of many months." Later, however, Valentinov disagreed with Lenin over a philosophical issue, and Lenin perceived in this disagreement the "seeds of disloyalty." He insisted that Valentinov either follow him blindly or be treated as an opponent. Valentinov then asked himself: "Was I really a Bolshevik, and if so, to what extent?" His answer was: "When it came to the voluntarism and the display of a strong will which had so attracted me in Lenin's "What Is to Be Done?" . . . I was a Bolshevik—*but only in this respect*. Yet this was not enough for continuing to consider myself bound by membership of the Bolshevik group. It was Lenin himself who had undermined my connection with it. . . ."[35]

Others, unlike Valentinov, not only "loved" Lenin, but were prepared to submit completely to his "strong will." These became the Bolshevik "hard core," ambivalent in their love for Lenin but obediently "bound" to him. As Wolfenstein has pointed out, part of the ambivalence came from Lenin's equally ambivalent treatment of them. And now we must add that Lenin's constant dictate to them was to be hard and "without sentiment": "Keep a stone in one's sling," he had said. Thus, paradoxically, part of the follower's love for Lenin required him "not" to love Lenin.

It is difficult to decide from this case whether the absence of "boundless love" between the revolutionary ascetic and his immediate followers is a necessary characteristic of all such relations, or just especially prominent in this situation because of the particular ideological dimensions. Other cases would have to be more closely examined. Provisionally, we must be willing to qualify the ideal type of "boundless love" by the existence in actuality of ambivalent feelings.

V

LET US LOOK more closely at the nature of the "love" that Lenin evoked. Even if one puts aside his political adulators, there is abundant testimony to the phenomenon itself. Lunacharsky, a faithful follower, and Gorky, an on-and-off observer, agree as to Lenin's seductive magnetic powers. As Lunacharsky explains and describes it, Lenin's "naive vitality," "breadth of his intellect," and "intense willpower" constitute his fascination. "This fascination is colossal: people who come close to his orbit not only become devoted to him as a political leader but *in some odd way they fall in love with him* [italics added].[36] Gorky, in a period of savage opposition to Lenin, paid honor to that power even in seeking to negate it: "Lenin is not an all-powerful magician, only a cold-blooded conjurer. . . ."[37]

What is the "odd way" Lenin made people fall in love with him? How was he a "conjurer" if not a "magician"? Word association, if nothing else, carries us to Thomas Mann's "Mario and the Magician," and we realize that we are talking about some strange hypnotic power. Hypnotic power, as is well known, is connected with the eyes. And the one fact that struck almost everyone who met the ordinary, prosaic, even plebeian-looking Lenin was the quality of his eyes. They were, it appears, his exceptional feature. Krzhizhanovsky, who met Lenin in St. Petersburg in 1893, wrote: "One had only to peer into the eyes of Vladimir Ilyich, into those unusual, piercing, dark dark-brown eyes, full of inner power and energy, to begin to sense that you were face to face with a far from usual type." Gorky talked of Lenin's "amazingly lively eyes." Trotsky tells of how a young delegate, Schotman, came back from a conversation with Lenin, constantly repeating "And how his eyes glitter; he looks right through one...."[38]

Lenin's eyes were only a part of his hypnotic power, but the power was certainly there. We can cite a number of statements by Valentinov, a close and sensitive observer of Lenin, to this effect. For example, describing Lenin's way of using his arms in speaking, Valentinov remarks, "This manner of Lenin's proved so infectious that some people who saw it constantly, for example Krasikow and Gusev, also started to put their fingers in the armholes of their waistcoats. *Lenin had a hypnotic influence even in this respect*" [italics added]. Other comments by Valentinov are: "Deference to Lenin's wisdom was combined with an *irresistible urge to obey him*" [italics added]; and "We must seek the explanation of that *mysterious and incomprehensible hypnotic influence of his* [italics added] which was noted by Potresov."[39]

"Mysterious and incomprehensible," "some odd way": These are the phrases used about Lenin's powers. In our theoretical discussion we have sought to make such powers less incomprehensible, less odd. We have suggested that the leader binds his followers to him and to one another because he has "few libidinal ties." As a result, he is free of transference to others, but in a position of enormous power to compel their transferences, and to attach them to himself by suggestion. Thus others follow him slavishly as the all-powerful father and leader.

The *detailed* nature of *Lenin's* power now requires further exploration, but first we will pursue a brief digression on one other aspect of his attenuated libidinal ties. Lenin, as we have suggested, had intense libidinal needs; the traumatic nature of the rupture with Plekhanov signals that fact. In place of Plekhanov, or any actual human being, Lenin substituted for *his* all-powerful and all-loving father-figure the ideology of Marxism. Although he insisted on numerous occasions that Marxism was a "guide to action" and not a "dogma," Lenin frequently betrayed his deeper feelings. At one point he shouted at Valentinov: "There is only one answer to revisionism: smash its face in! Neither Marxist philosophy nor the materialist conception of history, neither the economic theory of Marx

nor the labour theory of value, neither the idea of the inevitabil-
ity of the social revolution nor the idea of the dictatorship of
the proletariat—in short, not a single fundamental point of
Marxism is subject to revision!"[40] Perhaps even more revealing is Lenin's written statement of this view: "In this philosophy of Marxism, *cast from a single block of steel* [italics
added], you cannot eliminate a single substantial premise, a
single essential part, without deviating from objective truth,
without falling into the arms of bourgeois-reactionary false-
hood."[41]

Here Lenin had a love object that was all-powerful and all-
knowing, to which he could attach himself with total trust and
total affection. Unambivalently in love with the abstraction of
Marxism, which could never disappoint or betray him, Lenin
himself could be like "steel" toward others. This "hardness,"
frequently commented on by other scholars, emerged from his
lack of libidinal ties, made possible in part, as we now see, by
his own "hypnotic" subjection to those perfect "fathers" of
other times, Marx and Engels.

V I

ACCORDING TO Nathan Leites in his A *Study of Bolshevism*, Lenin bequeathed to his followers, especially in the
Politbureau, a code of behavior that centered around "hardness." I have tried to suggest that the key to the code of hardness and the other qualities associated with it, which we shall
discuss further, is the concept of the leader "with few libidinal
ties." The hardness itself is, of course, the positive of Lenin's
negative feelings toward softness and sentimentality. Earlier I
stated that Lenin's overt personality was consistent, with the
various parts interrelating and supporting one another. A
composite picture might show the following traits: hardness,
will, and energy combined with single-mindedness as to aim
(though enormous flexibility as to means); a stress on struggle,
"killing or being killed"; a black-white depiction of the enemy,
with every invective and means permitted against him; compul-

sive need for control over self and others, for discipline, for work, and for detail; and severe restriction of impulse, spontaneity, uncertainty, softness, and sentimentality, i.e., "emotions."

Lenin's hardness was obviously bought at a price, as we have already seen. Objectively, however, it made a good deal of sense. Like Stendhal and others before him, Lenin believed that revolutions could not be made with "kid gloves." Typical of many similar remarks were Lenin's statements that "Revolutions cannot be made with gloves and manicured fingernails . . . ,"[42] and that Jacobin Revolution is a "struggle to achieve the end in view, with no shying away from drastic plebeian measures, a struggle without kid gloves, without tenderness, without fear of resorting to the guillotine."[43] Lenin also believed, as he said to his sister Anna, "Our Russians are too soft"; and to Trotsky, "Russians are too kind ... lazybones, softies."[44] Much of Lenin's view, as we shall see, was confirmed by Russian literature. In this light, Lenin's hardness became Machiavellian: One executes an opponent to prevent further executions; hardness is actually "morally" right, a heavy duty that must be accepted. Thus, for example, one must be hard and approve the execution of the Tsar and his family, not because one enjoys killing, but to prevent a contender for the throne from serving as a rallying point in a civil war.

Clearly, Lenin's morality was not bourgeois morality, nor was it the morality of "intellectuals," whom Lenin despised for their "spineless sentimentality." Morality, Lenin claimed, is what is useful for the party. "In our opinion," he declared, "morality is entirely subordinate to the interests of the class war...."[45] "Our ethics is entirely subordinated to the class struggle. Ethics is that which serves to destroy a society based on the exploitation of man...."[46] In short, Lenin promulgated a new revolutionary morality, and it is in this context that his "hardness" must be seen.

Subjectively, Lenin was always vulnerable to "going soft." Krupskaya, for example, tells of a revealing incident in which Lenin, an ardent hunter, was suddenly confronted by a fox directly in front of him—and didn't shoot. When asked why, he replied sheepishly, "Well, he was so beautiful, you know." This from a man who was generally willing to shoot his opponents, or, rather, have them shot by others. That Lenin was not a sadist who, like Himmler, spared animals while torturing his fellow humans is clear from innumerable other glimpses of the sentimental side of his nature. Repression in Lenin was strong because of the threatening strength of the "soft" impulse. The justification for the repression, objectively, was that one could not "make" a revolution in Tsarist Russia in any other way.

Sustaining Lenin in his conviction of the necessity of hardness was his belief, almost paranoiac at times, that he was surrounded by traitors waiting to destroy him and his cause at the slightest sign of weakness. "Plekhanov betrayed us" is a typical comment. As Ulam puts it, "It was always clear to him that 'they' (the category including at times intellectuals, middle-class Socialists, and parlor radicals) were always ready to betray the cause, to turn into 'opportunists' prepared to abandon the revolutionary struggle and to negotiate with the class enemy."[47] Compromise, if we can believe Trotsky's memory, was perceived as soft and sexually seductive. Thus Lenin attacked Struve's "opportunism" in the following terms: "Naturally, Struve says to his Liberals, 'You must not use coarse German methods to our Socialism, but the finer French ones; you must *coquette*, *deceive* and *corrupt*, in the style of the Left French Radicals, who are *ogling* [italics added] Jauresism."[48]

Lenin, who constantly lied and betrayed others in the struggle for political power, appears to have projected his own feelings outward without much self-consciousness. As Richard Pipes describes him, as early as 1901, "He saw himself as the only genuine revolutionary—a leader with followers but no longer any allies. Around him were nothing but reactionaries, opportunists, traitors. 'We are moving in a tight band along a precipitous and difficult path, clutching each other's hand,' Lenin wrote that winter, 'We are surrounded on all sides by enemies, and we must always advance under their fire.' "[49] We can easily see why Lenin felt himself surrounded by traitors when we read his definition of trustworthiness: "Trustworthiness to him meant absolute certainty that an individual would carry out all orders [i.e., Lenin's], including those contrary to his conscience."[50] As we have seen, however, actions "contrary to one's conscience" was merely a bourgeois formula, for Lenin had redefined morality to mean anything that served the Revolution, which he, in turn, incarnated. To paraphrase a bit, "La Révolution, c'est moi" might have been Lenin's unconscious dictum; this, then, became his revolutionary morality.

VII

THE THEME of self-control, and control, is strong throughout Lenin's life, as is the fear of loss of control. Krupskaya frequently commented that Lenin was "a man of massive will, self-control."[51] Even in the last stages of his life, suffering from a stroke that left him paralyzed—the ultimate in loss of self-control?—he tried to bend the world to his will and to attend to all the details of a Soviet state which he no longer effectively controlled. If Krupskaya is right, however, Lenin was also a man of enormous impulsiveness, and his efforts at self-control involved a terrible battle with his other self. "Ilyich cannot bear long delays," she told Valentinov, ". . . he becomes restless and irritable, and roundly curses Russian sloth and slackness. Ilyich is a strong-willed man. . . . *He immediately puts into practice any desire that takes hold of him*" [italics added].[52]

Lenin's self-control, and its extension into a tight-knit, disciplined party of professional revolutionaries, i.e., other "controlled" individuals, is the picture with which we are all familiar. Underneath the somber exterior, however, lies the other, more impulsive Lenin, given to frequent rages and irritability. Lenin's "will" seems to sit in uneasy alliance with his equally vaunted "self-control." We are told that in his childhood he frequently threw temper tantrums, tended to fall and hurt his head, and refused to walk until the age of three.[53] In describing Lenin's party activities, Krupskaya refers to his being possessed by "rage"—her word—as a frequent form of behavior. Lenin himself wrote, "I admit that I often acted with frightful irritation and rage."[54]

It was part of Lenin's genius that to master the "frightful irritation and rage" he learned to exercise massive self-control.

We know from Freudian psychoanalysis that it is in the anal stage, when toilet training can become an issue, that the first struggles over "control" generally appear. In Eriksonian terms, the issue is joined between "autonomy and shame," and the child, just entering upon sphincter control, seeks to avoid parental control and regulation from without. Generally, he experiences "rage" at the effort by others to control what is so intimately "inside" him. Later, by introjection, he may take into himself compulsively the parental injunctions concerning cleanliness, regularity, and discipline. Unfortunately, we have no information on this stage of Lenin's early life, aside from the reference to his Spartan upbringing by his mother; we can only postulate it as an important formative time for his personality. Clearly, however, reached by one etiological means or another, Lenin in adulthood was given to rage, which he mastered by self-control, attempted control of his environment, and compulsive orderliness and discipline.

Lenin disciplined himself. In prison, for example, he forced himself rigorously to exercise in order to keep fit. At all times he practiced the usual ascetic control of neither drinking nor smoking; he extended his personal demand for discipline to his party, the workers, and to Russians in general; and he even gave credit to the capitalists in this matter: "The factory . . . is that highest form of capitalist cooperation which has united and disciplined the proletariat [and] taught it organization."[55] War, too, Lenin hoped, speaking of the "imperialist" war of 1914–1918, would "toughen the national character of Russia . . . tighten self-discipline . . . teach restraint."[56] Indeed, so successful was the Bolshevik use of the war in disciplining the Russian masses that one scholar tells us, "The fact that so many professional officers of the Tsar were ultimately enlisted in the Red Army cannot be ascribed solely to compulsion or the need for employment and livelihood. There was also the attraction for the military mind of Trotsky's 'New Model': an army where professional competence and discipline were to be the ruling consideration."[57]

Closely connected to Lenin's need for control and discipline is the related need for certainty. For Lenin, to be uncertain meant to be "out of control." Awaiting the sentence of exile to

Siberia, Lenin was all "nerves," but once the sentence was passed he recovered. "I have left my nerves in Moscow," he wrote his mother in 1897. "The reason for nerves was the uncertainty of the position and nothing else. But now that there is less uncertainty I feel well."[58] Control and certainty, I believe, were linked in his psyche; we have already noticed how Marxism, with its definite, controlled prediction of the future, gave Lenin the requisite feeling of certainty.

Lenin was able to convey his sense of total certitude to his followers. He held out before them the vision of a millennium, and imbued them with the faith that they would live to see the socialist revolution.[59] Lenin's certainty went hand in hand with his single-minded aim and his ability to be one of the great simplifiers of our time, as well as with his personal simplicity. He was, indeed, one of Jacob Burckhardt's "terrible simplificateurs," as he took Marxism, that "single block of steel," and pounded it into the minds and hearts of his listeners. A. N. Potresov, a Menshevik, recorded his first impression of Lenin in 1894: "A great force. But at the same time with a quality of one-sidedness, a kind of single role simplification, a quality of over-simplifying the complexities of life."[60] Again and again observers noted the polarization of simplification and complexities. "Life in its complexity is unknown to him," commented Gorky.[61] When Gorky later raised this subject with him, Lenin answered: "Who is not with us is against us.... You say that I simplify life too much? That such a simplification will ruin culture, eh?.... H'm. H'm.... The Russian masses must be given something very simple, something they can grasp. The Soviet and communism—it's simple."[62]

Lenin's oratorical power was based largely on his combination of hypnotic will power with simplification. Again it is Gorky who tells us that "It seemed to me that he spoke badly, but after a minute, I, and everybody else, was absorbed by his speech. I heard for the first time that it was possible to speak of complicated political problems so simply ... it is difficult to communicate the intense impression he made." The impression, Gorky adds, was compounded by the fact that "it seemed as if Lenin spoke not of his own will, but by the will of History."[63] Balabanoff, hearing Lenin the first time, noted the same features of his oratory, but wondered whether it sprang from his own personality or from contrivance: "He gave rise to a psychological question that renewed itself at every future encounter: Did his extremely simple way of expressing his views reflect his personal attitude, or was it a deliberately cultivated habit of concentrating his own attention and that of the audience on his arguments?"[64] Both, we are tempted to answer.

The same qualities distinguished Lenin's written work. Lunacharsky, for example, comments on "Lenin's strength as a publicist—his unpolished but extraordinarily clear style, his ability to present any idea, however complicated, in astonishingly simple form and to modify it in such a way that it would ultimately be engraved upon any mind, however dull and however unaccustomed to political thinking."[65] There is no need for multiple quotations; everyone agreed that Lenin's literary and oratorical powers rested to a great extent on his ability to simplify complexities, and indeed to ignore them completely. Moreover, this trait fitted in well with his elitist notion of a hard-core professional revolutionary party which would guide and be the consciousness of the mass of proletarians. If we can trust Balabanoff, Lenin's "sole objective was that his words become a credo to his listeners, a guide for their thought and action . . . his characteristic traits as a speaker were derived mainly from his way of dealing with the workingmen's movement. According to him, it was to be guided by an elite; there was no need for the lower strata to understand why they thought and acted one way or another."[66]

Complexity was for intellectuals, to whom Lenin was not writing or speaking. He wished his writings to be weapons, or rather tools, to bore into and hammer at his readers. His literary "style" was plebeian. Moreover, there is an anal touch to his repetition of a line from Heine: "Every word is a chamberpot and no empty one."[67] In opposition to the often vague, diffused, and sentimental style of the intellectuals, Lenin wrote simple, direct prose. Indeed, it was ascetic prose, befitting the personality behind it. As Trotsky puts it, "Lenin's literary and oratorical style is extremely simple, ascetic, as is his whole nature."[68]

Dress, speech, writing, and personality—all reflected tremen-

dous ascetic simplicity. There is a perfect fit between these
traits of Lenin and his conception of the need for an elitist,
disciplined, and centrally controlled party, led by himself, in
the service of a monolithic, all-certain ideology, Marxism. With
all aspects of life under control, freed from any danger of impulsive, spontaneous, undisciplined action—or thought—Lenin
could rest free from his nerves. Such is one psychological conclusion. Needless to say, these traits also helped make possible
Lenin's Bolshevik Revolution. History suggests that they were
at least as functional in the political world as they were in the
psychological.

VIII

LET US FINISH our brief survey of Lenin's "puritanical"
qualities. He was compulsively thorough and fastidious. As
Valentinov puts it, "He was order and neatness incarnate."[69]
He was also bound to the discipline of time and was extremely
punctual, as well as regulating others' allotment of time. Thus
it was very much in character when Lenin embraced Taylor's
time and motion studies as the key to increased efficiency and
productivity. Lenin hoarded space as well as time, writing in a
tiny script.

Work was an absolute necessity for Lenin. Believing in the
necessity of work for himself, he believed others should also
work hard; there were to be no parasites in his future society.
To his work Lenin brought the enormous energy for which he
was notorious, and with energy he associated the quality of
youth. "It is frantic energy, and yet more energy," Lenin wrote
in 1905, "that is required here. . . . Go to the youth, gentlemen.
That is the only means of salvation."[70]

The Revolution, in fact, meant a sort of continuous youth or
adolescence, a kind of revolutionary immortality. Thus Lenin
could say to Clara Zetkin shortly after the Revolution, "Yes,
dear Clara, we two are old. We must be satisfied with remaining young for a little longer in the revolution."[71] However,
there was ambivalence for Lenin in the old-young dichotomy.

In his early thirties he enjoyed being called "old man" (*starets*), as a tribute to his wisdom,[72] yet he also identified with continuing youth. For example, on the board of *Iskra* Lenin set himself, Martov, and Potresov off against the three "old" people, Plekhanov, Zasulich, and Axelrod. Trotsky captures some of the situation when he remarks that "Lenin embodies in himself the Russian proletariat, a youthful class, that politically is scarcely older than Lenin himself, withal a deeply national class, for the whole past development of Russia is bound up with it [i.e., is old], in it lies Russia's entire future; with it lives and dies the Russian nation."[73]

Salvation, then, took a different form for Lenin than it did for earlier puritans, and it was linked to youth and revolutionary immortality in a novel fashion, but it was reached by the same traits of hard work, avoidance of sloth, husbanding of time, compulsive thoroughness, and self-restraint. Weber's worldly asceticism has been turned neatly to revolutionary purposes.

IX

BEFORE SUMMARIZING the nature of Lenin's revolutionary asceticism, we must pause to underline the ambivalent elements to be found in it, the price he paid for his controls. The psychosomatic symptoms are many and go deep. Lenin, the man of energy, suffered from frequent bouts of fatigue, amounting to what one can only call fits of depression. For example, Valentinov informs us that he "first saw Lenin in a state of complete depression and indecision, and later on in a state of some kind of morbid exhaustion."[74] We get a hint of how personal relations made Lenin react with fatigue from Krupskaya's report that "Valdimir Ilyich used to get exceedingly tired" from his daily five- or six-hour talks with his former best friend, Martov. "He made himself quite ill with them," she states, "and incapable of working."[75] Valentinov confirms this interpretation when he describes Lenin's condition after the 1907 party congress in London: "The *rage*," Valentinov explains, "with which Lenin abused the liberal Cadets, called for armed uprising, and fought the Mensheviks, had sapped his strength to such an extent that he was half-dead when he returned to Kuokkala, in Finland. . . . He could hardly walk, had no desire to talk, and spent almost the whole day with his eyes closed. He kept dropping off to sleep all the time . . . the children from the neighbouring country cottage called him 'sleepyhead.' "[76]

The other side of the fatigue symptom was Lenin's insomnia. Krupskaya's *Memories* mention this fact incessantly, and it strikes an odd, naive note in her effort at hagiology when she confesses, "Those sleepless nights remain engraved on my memory."[77] Moreover, even when able to sleep, Lenin still fought his battles in his dreams. In relation to one particular episode, Krupskaya knowingly commented, "You will fall asleep and see Mensheviks in your dream and you will start swearing, and shout, 'Scoundrels, scoundrels,' and give the whole conspiracy away."[78] Thus apparently Lenin could swing rather abruptly from sleeplessness to fatigue.

We mentioned earlier how Lenin suffered from stomach disorders, which, surprisingly, disappeared in prison. In 1897 he wrote his mother from his Siberian exile: "People here also think I have grown fat during the summer. . . . All Petersburg illnesses vanish at once."[79] Richard Pipes suggests that it was Lenin's arrival at an ideological terminus—at certainty—that cured him. "This was a happy time for Lenin. Even though he spent two years in prison, and three in Siberia, he was confident of the future, entertaining no doubt about the ultimate triumph of the revolutionary cause. He felt himself a member of an irresistible movement and experienced none of the crises or fits of destructive rage so characteristic of him at other periods."[80]

More striking than Lenin's stomach disorders, which were often accompanied by headaches, was Lenin's case of what appears to be the shingles. It occurred in 1903, when he seemed to have lost out in the struggle for control of his beloved *Iskra*. As Krupskaya informs us, "Soon the Emancipation of Labour Group again brought up the question of moving to Geneva, and this time Vladimir Ilyich was the only one to vote against going there. . . . Vladimir Ilyich was so overwrought that he developed a nervous illness called 'holy fire,' which consists in inflammation of the nerve terminals of back and chest. . . . On the way to Geneva, Vladimir Ilyich was very restless; on arriving there he broke down completely, and had to lie in bed for two weeks."[81] Lenin did not seem to take easily to "losing" (and losing control?). As Gorky said, referring to a game of chess Lenin played, "When he [Lenin] lost he became cross, even despondent, like a child."[82]

Constantly preoccupied with his health, Lenin put his difficulties down to vague and ubiquitous "nerves," as did others around him. Thus Krupskaya, remembering the early days, comments that "the correspondence with Russia had a very bad effect on his nerves. To wait weeks . . . to be in a constant state of ignorance as to how things were progressing—all this was extremely incompatible with Vladimir Ilyich's character."[83] Toward the end of his life, in 1922, Lenin himself complained that "my nerves are still hurting," and a medical specialist agreed with him: Dr. V. I. Sokolov noted general nervousness, insomnia, and headaches, and diagnosed the case as "neurasthenia due to overwork."[84]

Lenin was eager to apply his own diagnosis to others, and we must suspect projection at work, as when he admonishes one of his supporters who was troubled at Lenin's actions in 1921: "A decadent petty bourgeois intellectual," Lenin wrote, "when he sees an untoward incident or injustice, whimpers, cries, *loses his head, his self-control* [italics added] . . . the proletarian . . . seeing something wrong goes about correcting it in a businesslike way . . . he carries it through firmly to the end." Lenin concludes, "I shall say because of our old friendship, you should cure your nerves."[85] It is clear from the context that "nerves" for Lenin meant loss of self-control (i.e., giving way to softness and sentimentality).

Lenin was in constant danger of giving way to his own impulses—either of rage or sentimentality—and it is the presence of the latter trait that makes him such a "humanistic" figure. This repressed, but basically irrepressible, side of him made him a dictator with a difference (different, for example, from Stalin). Lepeshinsky said of him, "He possesses a remarkably tender soul, not lacking, I would say, even a certain sentimentality,"[86] and M. Lyadov, in a memoir, remarks revealingly: "I remember Il'ich at a performance by Sarah Bernhardt in Geneva. We sat beside him in a box, and I was very surprised when I suddenly noticed that Il'ich was secretly wiping away his tears. The 'cruel' Lenin was crying over *La Dame aux Camélias.*"[87]

Music seemed to touch Lenin's heart most quickly and deeply, arousing his deepest emotions as far back as his early childhood. The focal point was his mother. As his sister, Anna, remembers: "Her [their mother's] favorite relaxation was music, of which she was passionately fond, and which she played with great feeling. And the children liked to fall asleep and, later in life, to work to the sound of her playing the piano."[88] Lenin's next strong emotional attachment to a woman, Inessa Armand, seems overdetermined in this respect, for we must recall the fact that she played for him constantly, especially Beethoven. "I can listen to Beethoven's *Sonata Pathetique* twenty or forty times," Lenin declared in this context, "and every time it holds my attention and delights me more and more."[89]

Lenin also liked to listen to the baritone Gusev, who often sang sentimental songs for him. Valentinov records one episode: "After one such party [of singing] I said to Gusev: 'Have you noticed the effect your song has on Lenin? He gets lost in some distant memory. I'm sure it's a matter of—*cherchez la femme.*' Gusev started to laugh: 'I think so too. Have you ever thought where Lenin's pseudonym comes from? Perhaps there was some Lena or Yelena?'" When asked, Lenin answered mockingly: "You'll soon grow old if you know too much."[90]

There is additional evidence of the effect of music on Lenin. His brother Dmitri recalls a visit with him to the Kazan opera in the winter of 1888; afterward, we are told, Lenin "'was in an extraordinary ecstatic condition,' and kept on and on singing the arias he had most liked."[91] Yet the music that so delighted Lenin was an increasing threat to him. It meant emotions: softness and sentimentality, libidinal ties. "Vladimir Il'ich loved music," Lunacharsky tells up, "but it affected him too strongly. I used to arrange good concerts at my house at one time ... more than once I asked Lenin to come to one of these evenings, but he was always otherwise employed. Once he said to me frankly: 'It is certainly very delightful to hear music, but it affects me too strongly, so that I feel oppressed. I stand music badly.'"[92]

The libidinal, even erotic, quality of music for Lenin is underlined by the musical imagery in his own description of his reaction to the end of his "infatuation" with Plekhanov (p. 116). "Outwardly," Lenin wrote, "it was as though nothing had happened; the apparatus must continue to work as it had worked till then, but *within a chord had broken, and instead of splendid personal relations, dry business-like relations prevailed* [italics added], with a constant reckoning according to the principle: *si vis pacem, para bellum* (If you desire peace, prepare for war)."[93]

Lenin's emotional reaction to music is paradigmatic for the whole analysis we are presenting here concerning his ambivalence toward libidinal ties and impulse. One famous, oft-repeated quotation that is prototypic for illustrating this ambivalence is Gorky's account of Lenin's reaction to Beethoven's music:

One evening in Moscow, when Lenin was listening to Beethoven sonatas ... he said: "I know nothing greater than the Appassionata; I'd like to listen to it every day. It's beautiful, *superhuman* [italics added] music. I always think proudly—it may be naive—what marvelous things people can do. ... But I can't listen to music too often, it affects the *nerves* [italics added], makes you want to say kind, silly things, to stroke the heads of the people who, living in a terrible hell, can create such a beauty. Nowadays you mustn't stroke anyone's head, you'd get your hand bitten off, you've got to hit them over their heads, without mercy, although, ideally, we're against the use of force. H'm, h'm, our duty is infernally hard!"[94]

This passage recalls to us Lenin's notion that one needed to keep "a stone in one's sling." It also suggests that Lenin conceived of himself along the lines of an Hegelian hero, whose "higher morality" forces him to transgress ordinary morality. His duty is different from, and harder than, that of the average citizen. Once again Gorky is worth quoting in this context. "Once in Gorki [the city]," Gorky recalls, "when he [Lenin] was caressing some children, he said, 'They will have better lives than we did; they'll not experience much that we lived through. Their lives will be less cruel.' Then Lenin added, 'Yet I don't envy them. Our generation had to fulfill a task of great historical significance. Forced on us by circumstances, the cruelty of our lives will be understood and vindicated. Everything will be understood, everything!'[95]

Do we understand Lenin's "cruelty" better, though perhaps in a way different from what he intended, when we place his fear of being bitten when he caressed the heads of little children in the context of his feeling about music and all it stood for? There is a caricature of Lenin's "hard duty" in the words of an Eichmann or a Himmler, who also felt that their moral duty forced them to commit seemingly inhuman acts, contrary to their softer sentiments. Caricature aside, an uneasy similarity exists in the account Gorky offers of an old friend of his, P. A. Skorokhodov, who was complaining about the "hardness" i.e., moral strain, of his work for the Bolshevik secret police, the Cheka, but then concluded: "But you know, Ilyich, too, has to suppress his emotions, and I am ashamed of my weakness."[96] We are left with the question: Once suppressed, once the chord is broken, is emotional harmony difficult to recapture?

Lenin himself wasted no time in such idle and introspective questions. When forced to deal with his "nerves," he turned to the therapy of nature—walking and mountain climbing were his tonics. More drastically, he sought his cure in increasing the amount of the very cause of his "nerves": a return to the struggle with even greater energy. In short, revolution itself became the deep therapy for Lenin's nerves.

X

WE HAVE ESCHEWED any attempt at a life history of Lenin. Instead, we have sought to delineate the characteristic traits, the pattern of behavior, that might throw light on our general subject of revolutionary asceticism. Before reaching a final summary concerning Lenin in relation to our major theme, we might pause briefly to indicate what a life-history approach to Lenin, if materials were available, might take as its "problem" areas.

The eminent scholar Bertram Wolfe presents the most pessimistic picture of such an attempt. Talking of the materials concerning Lenin's childhood, he concludes:

There is nothing to accord with the fashionable "psychological" explanations of the careers of the world's great rebels, nothing to document the formula of mother or father fixation, no unhappy family life, maladjusted childhood, youthful rebellion against domestic tyranny, no traces of a sense of inferiority due to failure at school in childish competitive sports, no sign of queerness or abnormality.[97]

While we agree that the paucity of material does not permit an adequate "psychological" explanation of Lenin's rebellion, in terms of a life history—Victor Wolfenstein is more sanguine than we in this matter—we would not accept the extreme view that there is "nothing."

Existing materials point to the following questions or problems as worth raising. Central to Lenin's development seems to be what we called his oedipal problem in relation to his father, later displaced probably onto his older brother Alexander, and related, of course, to his mother. Unfortunately, it is not sufficiently clear how Lenin resolved this problem, or exactly how intense it was.[98] In any case, crucial to such a resolution would be the problem of Lenin's identifications with his father and mother. For example, Lenin looked like his father, and like him he became a hard-working "teacher"—but this time of a nation. Like his father, too, Lenin apparently at first believed in religion, but, in accord with his mother's predilections, gave up his religious beliefs shortly after his father's death.

The father's death, especially for Lenin's brother Alexander, and thus probably at second remove for Lenin, seems to have been the pivotal moment in turning the Ulyanov family into revolutionaries. Alexander's attempted assassination of Tsar Alexander III, whose own father's "liberalism," i.e., efforts at reform, had been supported by Ulyanov *père*, seems likely, on the unconscious level, to represent the killing of the father-figure; some observers have interpreted Alexander's desire to be

punished by the death penalty as a reflection of his guilt feelings. In any case, the execution of Alexander, one year after the
father's death, was quite clearly of enormous emotional and
practical significance for Lenin. Any residual identification with
the father—and I am convinced that there was a great deal—
was complicated by identification with the martyred brother.
Alexander, however, was also committed to terrorism. For
Lenin, both personal disposition (as I have tried to show) and
ideological (that is, cognitive) development precluded such a
commitment. In this tangled skein, only one thing seems clear:
Tsarist society and Lenin's personal psychological dynamics
pushed and pulled him into becoming a professional revolutionary.

On a subterranean level, if not explicitly, Lenin was sustained in this commitment by his mother as well as his sisters.
Lenin's identification with his mother was complicated, we can
be sure, by the death of his father, bound to affect in some
fashion the sixteen-year-old Lenin's oedipal feelings. Moreover,
unconscious possession of the mother aside, any identification
with her was also complicated by Lenin's ambivalence about
softness and sentimentality (although, in fact, the mother was
hardly "soft"), which we have seen so forcefully expressed, and
repressed, in relation to music. In short, father and mother
identification raised for Lenin the problem of maleness and
femaleness, masculinity and femininity, aggressiveness and passivity, hardness and softness, and so on, but in exactly what
ways we are not sure.

The execution of Alexander made it certain that Lenin
would become a revolutionary. Out of that trauma Lenin
seemed also to emerge with an abiding hatred of the liberal
intelligentsia. Although he was one himself, Lenin felt, if one
believes the stories, that they had opportunistically deserted the
Ulyanovs in their hour of need, and turned "soft" and craven.
He seems never to have wondered why Kerensky senior, father
of the future head of the 1917 provisional government and
director of the Simbirsk gymnasium (i.e., high school), coura-
geously stood by him, and how such action by a liberal member
of the intelligentsia might qualify the general condemnation of
a whole spectrum of opinion and persons.

In any event, helped by Fyodor Kerensky and his own mother's appeals, Lenin was allowed to enter the University of Kazan. Very quickly, however, the sins of the brother caught up with him, for Lenin "accidentally" had become involved in some student protests and, as the brother of a former terrorist, was expelled. Lenin now spent the year 1887–1888 at Kokushkino, his mother's estate, where he began his revolutionary education. It is profitable to look at Lenin's life in the next few years in terms of a "conversion" experience. The prophet he now followed was Chernyshevsky. The effect of reading Chernyshevsky was ineradicable, turning Lenin into a professional revolutionary.[99]

Lenin also read another novel, Oblomov (1854) by Goncharov, and it is between the poles of these two novels that he began to shape his new character. An essay by Dobrolyubov, one of Chernyshevsky's young collaborators, had focused attention on Oblomovism, personified by the main character, calling it a disease common to Russians, characterized by weakness, indecision, apathy, and inactivity. Lenin was later to say, "I should like to take some of our party comrades—quite a lot of them—lock them up in a room and make them read Oblomov over and over again until they go down on their knees and say: 'We can't bear it any longer.' Then they would have to be put through an examination: 'Have you understood the essence of Oblomovism? Have you realized that it is also in you? Have you finally resolved to get rid of this illness?' "[100]

We can strongly suspect that Lenin, too, suffered from the illness of Oblomovism. Chernyshevsky was the doctor who prescribed the cure: hardness, hard work, the ascetic virtues in their utilitarian form, courage, and intransigence, all embodied in a "new man" and a "new woman" freed from the humbug of bourgeois morality and sentimentality. "It is the kind of book that influences you for your whole life," Lenin declared, and he called his first major piece of writing in the new key, in which he appealed for a Bolshevik-type party organization and ideology, "What Is to Be Done?" (1902).[101]

An analysis of Lenin's reactions to Oblomov and What Is to Be Done?, as well as the books themselves, would go a long way toward offering a psychological portrait in depth of Lenin.

This is not the place for such an analysis, and I shall content myself with the above, and with one additional remark to the effect that Lenin's fascination with these two books is extraordinarily strange in the light of his overt rejection of interest in sex and love, for both of these books are long novels about— sex, love, and romance!

Chernyshevsky, playing the positive to the negative pole of Goncharov's *Oblomov*, converted Lenin into a new-fashioned revolutionary. It was not until sometime between 1889 and 1892 that Lenin suffered his second conversion and became a *Marxist* revolutionary. We have already seen the psychological appeal of Marxism's steellike quality; a full life history would have to relate this appeal intimately, and functionally, to the "real" world surrounding Lenin, to the ideological polemics among the intellectuals, to the actual state of Russia's economic development, and to the revolutionary organizations existing at the time.

Lenin's development as a Marxist revolutionary took place after 1889 mainly in Samara, where he had been "rusticated," and then in Siberia (from 1897 on), where he was exiled. In such places, in the 1890s, Lenin ripened his latent powers and position. By July 1900, when he went abroad to join the Russian Social Democrats in exile in order to work for the underground back home, Lenin had prepared himself to progress from being a disciple to a leader, from a pupil to a teacher. We have already noted his public pronouncement, his ideological claim to be the new leader, in "What Is to Be Done?" and we have called attention to the traumatic split with Plekhanov over the control of *Iskra*. By 1903 Lenin had, at a fearful psychological price, renounced all libidinal ties, all softness. The division of the Russian Social Democratic party at the Party Congress of that year into "hards" and "softs," Bolsheviks and Mensheviks, was the outward symbolization of the internal change.

A life history of Lenin would probably conclude that by 1903 he had come to his maturity, set in the self-created mold of a Bolshevik revolutionary. This would not mean that changes and development in Lenin and in his interactions with the world around him were not yet ahead. There are still major problem areas: the Revolution of 1905, and Lenin's role therein; the nadir of his activities in 1910, when Lenin seemed on his way to languishing as a curious, quarreling, intransigent revolutionary exile, of no account, turning, perhaps in frustration, to an emotional involvement with Inessa Armand; the war of 1914–1918, which alone gave Lenin his chance; the Revolution of 1917, both in its February and October forms; and then the postrevolutionary Bolshevik rule, with Lenin as virtual dictator until his death, at the same age and of the same cause (cerebral hemorrhage) as his father before him, in 1924.

Did the postrevolutionary period, after Lenin's initial triumph and energetic, even frenzied, regrouping of the Bolshevik forces and positions in order to keep alive the precarious life of the new "child"—really a Caesarean birth, since Russia had not matured into the fully developed capitalist stage—witness a "return of the repressed" in Lenin? Did Lenin become even more the father figure, punitive and forbidding, unable to accept others as rebelling against *his* orders and views, and also unwilling to plan for a possible successor? And, on the other side of his character, was Lenin suddenly overwhelmed with the cruelty and lovelessness of the Soviet system that he had brought into being?

Questions such as these and the others we have raised above are evoked by the available materials and data. But Lenin was too repressed, too uninterested in his own intimate life, too busy with the outward necessities of his revolution, to leave us enough information necessary to answer such questions with any authority. We have plenty of external evidence as to the nature of Lenin in terms of what I have called a "revolutionary ascetic"; we have relatively little internal evidence to tell us how he got that way.

X I

LENIN, as our summary will now try to show, was an extraordinary example of a revolutionary ascetic. He embodied to an unusual degree the two parts of that character as we have tried to establish it as an ideal type: the "leader with few libidinal ties" and the "puritan" of Weber's work ethos. In addition, he shows better than any other revolutionary leader the terrible ambivalences that go into the making of such a character, the intense impulses of feeling that call forth even greater effort at repression and control.

Where does Lenin fit in terms of the "stages" of historical development of revolutionary asceticism outlined earlier? My thesis is that Lenin is the figure who marks the true linking of asceticism to revolutionary aims. He takes Victorian utilitarianism, combines it with the Russian tradition of conspiratorial revolution, and produces—Bolshevism!

Lenin's utilitarianism seems to have been inspired, consciously, by his reading of Chernyshevsky. As we have seen, the latter, an enthusiastic admirer of John Stuart Mill, based his psychology as well as his schemes for social regeneration on the utilitarian principles of enlightened self-interest. His "new man," social schemes aside, sounds suspiciously like James Mill. As we noted, when the heroine of *What Is to Be Done?*, Véra Pávlovna, asks, "Practical and cold men are therefore right in saying that man is governed exclusively by self-interest?," one of the "new men," Lopukhóv, answers calmly, "They are right. What are called elevated sentiments, ideal aspirations—all that, in the general course of affairs, is absolutely null, and is eclipsed by individual interest; these very sentiments are nothing but self-interest clearly understood."[102]

Trotsky, with his penetrating eye, puts the matter succinctly: "He [Lenin] was probably the most extreme utilitarian whom the laboratory of history has produced. But his utilitarianism was of the broadest historical scope."[103] Lenin's impact in Russia was extreme, largely because so many of his countrymen—even, or especially, the reformers and revolutionaries —were Oblomov-type men. In Goncharov's novel, in opposition to them, a "new man" was introduced, filled with energy and aims. He is Stolz—a proud man in the sense of being proud of himself—who is part German in his ancestry (like Lenin); even his Russian mother declares that she "was unable to detect any softness, any delicacy or tolerance, in the German character."[104] But it is Stolz's utilitarian character that we are interested in, and this is conveyed clearly in the following description, where we are told that he "lived on a fixed plan and tried to account for every day as for every dollar, keeping unremitting watch over his time, his labor, and the amount of mental and emotional energy he expended. It seemed as though he controlled his joys and sorrows like the movements of his hands and feet."[105]

The impact of a "new man"—actually a Benthamite transplanted to Russia—such as Stolz, or Lenin, on a Russia of Oblomovs was sharp and obvious. As René Fulop-Muller sums it up, "Had Lenin appeared in a West European State, his practical principles and civilizing schemes would perhaps have aroused little attention; but in Russia, utterly behind the times in modern civilization, this gospel of utilitarianism must have seemed in truth a new religion."[106]

It was, of course, in large part a religion of technology and science. Utilitarianism was placed at the service of industrialization. Lenin's definition of Communism as "Soviets plus Electrification" is highly revealing.[107] As early as 1893 Lenin attacked the Populists for refusing to see that the countryside was becoming mechanized, as a part of encroaching capitalism, and that one ought to welcome this development. In the paraphrase provided by Ulam, "No use lamenting the passing over of the old primitive peasant economy, of the substitution of machines for handicraft. Those were the facts, and benevolent facts at that. The progress of capitalism in Russia made the peasants live 'more cleanly' than before." Moreover, Ulam adds, Lenin's brand of utilitarianism led him away even from his revered mentor, Chernyshevsky: "*His* [Lenin's] Russia would not be like Chernyshevsky's, one vast choral society dedicated to healthful and innocent amusements. It would be, first of all a country of hard work, of strict industrial discipline and organization, where socialism would turn into a cult of production unmatched by the most exacting capitalism."[108]

Lenin's extreme dedication to industrialization emerges clearly once he is actually in power. Instead of destroying Tsarism, he tries to build Socialism, whose definition for him we have just given above. H. G. Wells, after a strange interview with Lenin around 1919–1920, came away saying that the

Lenin who scorned Utopia and Utopians had succumbed to "the Utopia of the electricians." "He is throwing all his weight," Wells reported, "into a scheme for the development of great power stations in Russia. . . . Can one imagine a more courageous project in a vast flat land of forests and illiterate peasants, with no water power, with no technical skill available, and with trade and industry at the last gasp?" Yet, Wells continued, Lenin "sees the decaying railways replaced by a new electric transport, sees new roadways spreading throughout the land, sees a new and happier Communist industrialism arising again. While I talked to him he almost persuaded me to share his vision."[109]

Others report how, in the midst of civil war in 1921, Lenin took the time to issue a specific order: "The peasants in the localities of Gor'kii and Ziianova are immediately to be supplied with electric light!"[110] (Does one irreverently think of the biblical, "And God said, 'Let there be light' "?) Earlier, in 1918, Lenin was making constant notes to himself, such as: "raise productivity"; "learn socialism from the big organizers of capitalism, from trusts"; "Tailors [sic] system, Motion study" [Frederick Winslow Taylor's labor-saving method]; "one-man management" of industrial plants; "piecework pay according to results"; "don't steal, don't be a slacker"; and, most revealing, "the Soviet government plus Prussian railroad efficiency plus American technology and organizations of trusts plus American public school education, etc., etc., plus plus equals socialism."[111]

Lenin's desire to industrialize Russia is beyond question. As Theodore Von Laue has pointed out, many nineteenth-century Russians saw themselves at the bottom of a "cultural slope" which, starting in West Europe and even America, stretched downward to the Urals.[112] The desire for "Westernization," for "modernization," though rejected by the Slavophiles, was intensely desired by many members of the intelligentsia, such as Lenin. For them, key parts of the modernization process were industrialization and science. Lenin's own family provided him with a strong context of science. His father had taken his degree in the faculty of mathematics and physics at the University of Kazan, inspired by the earlier work there of the great mathematician Lobachevski, and taught these subjects in the high school before becoming inspector of public schools in the province of Simbirsk. His brother Alexander was studying chemistry and biology before he decided to place his science at the service of revolution by making a bomb to blow up the Tsar.

Lenin, however, while giving lip service to natural science, did not enter upon its study. As we know, he entered the law faculty (interestingly, this was his father's initial attraction before he decided to study science). Lenin's science became Marxism, and there is a serious question as to his real comprehension and understanding of what was meant by modern science. A study of his "philosophical" debates with the empiro-criticists gives one real pause (cf. Valentinov's account).[113] Perhaps in embracing Marxism as a form of natural science, Lenin was inwardly rejecting an identification with his father and brother while outwardly affirming it. Thus, as early as "What Is to Be Done?" Lenin put forth his version of science: "The working class exclusively by its own efforts is able to develop only trade-union consciousness.... Modern socialist consciousness can only be brought to them from without... *can arise only on the basis of profound scientific knowledge* [italics added]. The bearers of science are not the proletariat but the bourgeois intelligentsia." The next sentence identifies for us the "bearers of science": "It is out of the heads of members of this stratum that modern socialism originated. . . ."[114] Not Lobachevsky but Marx and Engels are the "scientists" Lenin has in mind.

Thus Lenin's commitment to modern science is biased in the way we have just suggested. Yet, in gross terms, we can say that Lenin was a sincere advocate of technology and science as the means by which Russia could be modernized. In the service of these two gods he placed his utilitarian principles and what I call his revolutionary ascetic characteristics.

Moreover, Lenin's industrialized society was to be based on his own "industrious" nature. Disciplined hard work was the key to modernization. The desire to labor was to be internalized; thus, it would be "free" labor. Lenin proclaimed: "Communist labor . . . is unpaid labor for the good of society, labor rendered ... not in order to obtain the right to certain products ... but voluntary labor, labor beyond norms, labor which is being given without calculation of reward ... labor out of the habit of working for the common good and motivated by a consciousness (which has turned into habit) of the necessity of labor for the common good—labor as a requirement of a healthy organism." Such labor, Lenin declared, would emerge out of the "free and conscious discipline of the workers themselves."[115]

Any pleasure that stood in the way of work was simply to be abandoned. Lenin, who loved chess (and was emotionally bound up in the game, as we have seen), eventually gave it up because, as he said, "Chess gets hold of you too much, and hinders work." So, too, with his enjoyment of skating. As Lenin told Krupskaya, "When I was a schoolboy I used to go in for skating, but found that it tired me so that I always wanted to go to sleep afterwards. This hindered my studies. So I gave up skating."[116] We can assume that it was for similar or related reasons that Lenin "gave up" drinking, smoking, flirting, and similar distractions.

On the more positive side was his self-discipline through physical education. "You must value and take care of your health," Lenin told Valentinov, "It is always a blessing to be physically strong and healthy, to have powers of endurance— but for the revolutionary it is a duty." Then the Lenin who dutifully served his time in Siberia fantasied a bit: "Imagine you've been sent to the back of beyond, somewhere in Siberia, and that you have a chance to escape by boat—you wouldn't manage it if you can't row and your muscles are all flabby."[117] Lenin's stress on physical education was uncommon for a member of the intelligentsia, and his incitement of comrades to mountain climbing, walking trips, and bicycle tours was obviously part of the discipline necessary for the "new man." In this respect, physical education served the same revolutionary purpose as it did for Mao Tse-tung (as we shall see in the next chapter). For Lenin personally, it also served the rather unrevolutionary purpose of providing relaxation—a rest for his jangled "nerves." If we leave this qualification aside, we can say with surety that "play" served the same purpose as "work": It was to aid in the modernization of Russia.

Gorki summarized this ascetic side of Lenin when he wrote to H. G. Wells, "By nature he [Lenin] is a puritan."[118] Or when he wrote, "His personal life is such that in an epoch in which religion was dominant Lenin would be regarded as a saint." Or, once more, when he described Lenin's "heroism" as "something rare in Russia ... the modest, ascetic devotion of the honest Russian intellectual-revolutionary ... the heroism of a man who has renounced all the joys of earth for the sake of the difficult labor for the happiness of man...."[119]

XII

UTILITARIANISM and puritan asceticism—both were put by Lenin in the service of industrializing and modernizing Russia. But before this could be accomplished, it was necessary to revolutionize Russia. And this would only be done, according to Lenin, by professional revolutionaries. As such, they would have to be ascetics—and Jacobins. In this regard Lenin could turn to a tradition already existing in nineteenth-century Russian thought, and add the figures of men like Tkachev and Nechaev to the inspiration of Chernyshevsky. It was Nechaev who announced in anticipation of Lenin that the character of a real, i.e., professional revolutionary "excludes all romanticism, all sensibility, all enthusiasm, and all spontaneity; it excludes even personal vengeance.... Revolutionary passion becomes for him [the revolutionary] an unceasing habit and allies itself with cold calculation."[120]

To traits of unsentimentality and calculation the true revolutionary added an obsessive need for secrecy. At least in Tsarist Russia, he did not publicly play at being a revolutionary, but hid his true character. "If you want to be a revolutionist," Krupskaya records, "you must not make yourself conspicuous as one, but be able to use self-restraint. ..."[121] Thus the revolutionary had to take on the qualities of a conspiratorial personality, but Ulam is right when he remarks that, for Lenin, "the need for conspiracy was ... not only a matter of political conviction, it was an obsession."[122] As we have seen earlier,

Lenin was also obsessed with the fear of betrayal, a fear that went beyond the reality of Tsarist police spies and party informers and touched deeply on parts of Lenin's psyche. Possessed of these obsessive concerns with conspiracy and betrayal, Lenin, the professional revolutionary, set forth a "model character" that could persist long after the outward necessities that had helped call it forth.

The basic social structure that fitted best with the calculating conspiratorial personality was the so-called "ideological group." As described by Vladimir C. Nahirny, using the observations of revolutionist Vera Figner, all sentimental and libidinal ties were bound to the movement itself, and love or affection for particular persons in it was frowned upon. As exemplified by the Will of the People organization, Nahirny claims that "ideological groups require, first of all, that their members divest themselves of all personal ties and attachments. More specifically, they demand that their members obliterate completely the sphere of privacy and lay bare all their innermost feelings and desires.... There reigns thus a complete internal publicity and a total secrecy with reference to the surrounding world." Here is the injunction of one of the leading members of the Will of the People: "I enjoin you, brothers, to keep guard over each other ... in all the small concerns of everyday life. It is necessary that this guarding should enter into the conscience and thus turn itself into a principle, that it should cease to seem offensive, that personal considerations should be silenced before the demands of reason."[123]

Purge trials and confessionals after the Revolution attest to the long-range power of the injunctions of the conspiratorial ideological group. Such a group helped to establish the model and standards for Bolshevik party structure henceforth. Yet Lenin himself never accepted the command to "obliterate completely the sphere of privacy and lay bare all ... innermost feelings and desires...." His was an inner, as well as outer, secrecy, and only lesser comrades were expected to bare their sentimental failings. Perhaps because of Lenin's reservations, which set their own psychological model, perhaps for many other reasons pertaining to Russian culture, the Soviet Union never embraced "brainwashing" to the extent found in the

Chinese Communist system. Unlike the situation in China, one had to be a "traitor" before one confessed and was purged of one's lapses in the Soviet Union.

In another area of social structure, the family, Lenin also left a rather conservative heritage. His love for his family, especially his mother and sisters, is omnipresent, and it tended to overshadow in many ways his "new-model marriage" to Krupskaya. Even his attitude to so-called "free love" was highly puritanical. In his exchange with Inessa, and elsewhere, Lenin made it clear that he was opposed to bourgeois "free love," which he interpreted to mean "freedom from childbirth and freedom to commit adultery."[124] Inessa seems to have disagreed with his views. What Lenin approved of was "uncommon love," that is, the puritanical "free" relations of Chernyshevsky's "new man" wherein free meant free from sentimental but not ascetic ties. Thus it seems that Lenin's ideal family would out-Victorian the Victorian family. (Much of recent Soviet family life has borne out this interpretation.)

Lenin seems never to have contemplated following Chernyshevsky's rather vague and utopian hints as to dissolving the family and setting up communes. Lenin's whole character was opposed to such a notion, as when he confessed to Valentinov, "It is impossible to live in a house where the windows and doors are never closed, where they are completely open to the street and where every passerby considers it necessary to look in and see what you are doing. *I should go mad if I had to live in a commune*" [italics added].[125] Revolutionary as he might have been in other areas, Lenin was hardly revolutionary in relation to family life. Rather than a liberation of the family, he wished for what I shall call a further "purification."

The social structure on which Lenin concentrated his real interest and innovation was the party. Lenin created the Bolshevik party, the collective "hero" who was to play the role of Machiavelli's Prince and create the new state. We are forcefully reminded of Gramsci's views (see Chapter 2) in the remark of Lenin's fellow editor of *Iskra*, Potresov: "If the French king, Louis XIV, could say, *L'Etat c'est moi*, Lenin, without putting it into words, always had the feeling, *La Patrie c'est moi*, that in him the will of the movement was concentrated in one

man."[126] Lenin's party, built out of the prerevolutionary conspiratorial groups, was a resurrection of the Jacobin conception
developed in the course of the French Revolution. Marx briefly
believed in this conception around 1848, and then turned to the
impersonal laws of historical materialism. It was this 1848
Marx, however, whom Lenin mainly read, rather than the later,
less Jacobin Marx.[127]

What Lenin did, if we may oversimplify, was to combine
Nechaev with Marx to form his ideal of the Bolshevik party.
The Bolshevik was to be henceforth a professional, Jacobin
revolutionary, selflessly obeying orders from the party (which,
initially, meant Lenin, as Potresov confirms). The party itself
was to be centralized and tightly disciplined. In 1904 Lenin
revealed his ideas on the subject in a conversation with
Valentinov:

A revolutionary Social Democrat must be, cannot but be a Jacobin.
You ask me what Jacobinism means. First of all . . . the dictatorship of the proletariat. . . . Secondly—a centralized Party structure
in order that this dictatorship be brought about. . . . Thirdly . . .
real, strong discipline in the party. . . . The outcries of the minority
about "blind subordination" and "barrack discipline" reveal their
love of anarchistic phrases, their slackness—typical of intellectuals. . . . If you take away discipline and frustrate centralism,
where will the dictatorship find its support then? *Dictatorship, centralism, strict and strong discipline—all these are connected logi-
cally* [can we not also add *psychologically?*], *each complements
the others* [italics added]. All this taken together is the Jacobinism
which is being fought against . . . by Martov, Akimov, and all the
other Girondins. A revolutionary Social Democrat—this has to be
grasped once and for all—must be and cannot but be a Jacobin.[128]

To the task of establishing this Jacobin Social Democratic
rule Lenin threw all the resources of his formidable will and
character. A "leader with few libidinal ties," a professional
revolutionary ascetic, he used his hypnotic qualities, his simpli-
fications expressed in hammerlike prose, to draw to him the
members of his conspiratorial, ideological group. When World
War I, and chance, allowed him to come to power, his Bolsheviks became The Party: dictatorial, centralized, and disciplined, but now on the largest scale.

Lenin then placed this party in the service of his desires to

industrialize and modernize Russia. For his *revolutionary* asceticism, as we have suggested, Lenin could draw on the nineteenth-century intellectual tradition of Russia, epitomized in
Nechaev. For his *industrial* work ethos he could appeal to the
incipient utilitarianism and Victorianism of elements of late
nineteenth-century Russian society, as epitomized in Chernyshevsky—and in Lenin's father! Lenin uniquely marks the
successful and powerful fusion of these two psychological and
ideological sources—the asceticism of the professional revolutionary and the asceticism of the Victorian industrial entrepreneur. The result, as we have tried to show in detail, is a new
personality type: the revolutionary ascetic, who desires revolution in order to achieve modernization. One could call the stage
in which he exercises his calling Jacobin modernizing asceticism.
Lenin, much as he might have disliked the word, is its prototypic "hero."

CHAPTER 9

Mao Tse-tung

I

UNLIKE LENIN, who is almost a prototype of the revolutionary ascetic, Mao Tse-tung presents a far more difficult case. He appears at first to fit the ideal type only partially. Thus Mao *seems* a particularly apt illustration of the possible limits to our concept as it manifests itself in actual history.

There is no question that Mao Tse-tung, as much as Lenin, is a revolutionary, and that he has been the leader of a major successful revolutionary movement. There is also no question, as we shall try to show, that he exhibits traits that fit under our rubric of revolutionary asceticism. Moreover, numerous observers have pointed to the "puritan" quality of aspects of the Chinese Revolution. James Reston, back from a visit to Communist China, declares, "I had no sense of this enormous puritanical, evangelical atmosphere in China. . . . I happen to be a Scotch Calvinist, and though they deny they are a religious people, I have never heard so many Scotch Calvinistic admonitions given to a people since I went to Sunday school"; Maurice Meisner speaks of how the models set forth in *China Youth*, a Communist periodical, "might easily be mistaken for Calvinist-inspired moral tracts," and tells how the "new man" of Chinese Communism is expected to embody "the original bourgeois virtues," which are part of an "ascetic pattern of life demanded by

Chinese Communist ideology"; and Benjamin Schwartz tells us that "Maoist virtue, one might say, was to play the role of a kind of collectivistic Protestant Ethic."[1]

How strong is that "collectivistic Protestant Ethic"? How much of it is in Mao himself, as a deep personal need, and how much of it is for him a conscious manipulation of ascetic themes for their functional service in the revolution? We shall try to answer these questions, especially those relating to Mao, in some detail, but there are special difficulties which we should emphasize at the outset.

The first problem is one of a non-Western tradition. How strong is asceticism as a strand in Chinese culture? What sort of social checks exist to the expression of feelings? Here I can only step lightly. As I understand it, the Chinese tradition of eremitism had many ascetic features. The Confucian code encouraged many qualities of self-restraint and self-control. The question, of course, would be what psychological forces underlay these injunctions and ways of life, and to what ends were they directed? We shall address ourselves to this question a bit more fully in a moment. For now, we shall merely underline the fact that, as with Western culture and Christianity, we can only indicate the massive background to our particular problem, and suggest that an individual revolutionary ascetic must always be understood as resonating in some fashion to the ascetic and libidinal traditions of his culture.[2]

A second problem concerns the extent to which Mao embraced modernization, and thereby placed his traits of revolutionary asceticism in its service. To put it another way, did Mao deliberately, or even unconsciously, cultivate revolutionary asceticism as a means of modernizing his country? Once again the picture is not clear. Mao seems to have been an ambivalent modernizer, passing through different stages of dedication to the notion. In 1949, after coming to power, Mao seemed to want Chinese Communism to take the Soviet pattern as its model, and to push quickly toward industrialization. By 1955 he was hesitating in this commitment, and preparing to launch the Great Leap Forward of 1958, as much a matter of social mobilization as of technical progress. Nevertheless, in 1957 Mao was still holding to the goal of modernization reached through a kind of Protestant Ethic, as when he said, "To make China rich and strong needs several decades of intense effort, which will include among other things, the ... policy of building up our country through diligence and frugality."[3] Describing Mao in this mood, Stuart Schram talks of "Mao's concern, indeed his obsession, not only in 1958 but before and since, with rapid economic growth as the key to China's resurgence as a great power."[4]

Mao had other "obsessions" besides modernization, and these entered into a dialectic, the outcome of which is still uncertain, with the latter. Mao was intensely nationalistic; indeed, as Schram reminds us, he "was a nationalist (and a relatively conservative one) long before he was a Communist or revolutionary of any sort," and this nationalism was "psychologically primary."[5] Mao's nationalism, of course, was Chinese. And that meant that, unlike his counterparts in Russia, the West was not his model. He did not feel that China was at the bottom of a "cultural slope" (as we have seen Theodore Von Laue persuasively arguing in the case of Russia), needing to catch up and become exactly like the West.[6] Instead, economic growth was merely a means to allow China to shake off its humiliating subservience to the Western powers, and to assert more strongly its own version of culture, society, and the good life.

Yet Mao did not aim merely at a restoration of Chinese culture, now safe from Western intrusion. That would have meant resting with the policy of the self-strengthening movement of the 1860–1890s, which had proven itself insufficient. Mao was also a revolutionary who aimed at a total social and spiritual transformation of his country. Like Lenin, he wished for a "new man"; but it was a new man in Chinese dress. Thus Mao, like Rousseau's godlike legislator, wished to mold not only the laws but a two-sided new personality: Chinese "red and expert." To do this, he eventually advocated a "Cultural Revolution."

China, unlike many underdeveloped countries turning to revolution, already had a culture, one of the greatest in the history of the world. It did not suffer, therefore, from an "identity crisis." Rather, it was a question of asserting its already existent identity, though in developing form, befitting changed circumstances. Thus Mao's Cultural Revolution was not a matter of constructing a culture, but of reconstructing a personality. It differed from various "Western" countries, e.g., Russia, to whose existent culture the drive for modernization was intrinsic, as well as from newly formed countries, forced to construct a culture almost *de novo* on the basis of a modernization effort. China, in its Cultural Revolution, could presumably seek out a postmodernization solution without ever having to pass through the stage of classical modernization with all its attendant evils. Or such at least seems to have been Mao's aim.[7] (Another, of course, was to retain the "purity" of the Revolution, even if it was necessary to destroy the organizational structure.)

Thus, Marxist though he is, Mao did not yield to the emphasis on the primacy of the economic structure. Willed political power, and not economic "laws" of history, were to shape the new man. For example, one aim of Mao's Chinese Communists was land distribution, but reconstruction of personality was even more fundamental.[8] In the Cultural Revolution of 1966 we see all these elements come to a head. We also see the extraordinary ambivalence of Mao toward modernization, as understood in the West. And this ambivalence illustrates for us the complexity of dealing with revolutionary asceticism in Mao.

In short, there are special difficulties in treating Mao Tsetung as a revolutionary ascetic, standing in the historical development which sees revolutionary asceticism placed in the service of religion, then capitalist economics, and then revolution, the stages of which we have tried to trace earlier. Nevertheless, it is our thesis that Mao is a revolutionary ascetic, though most complicated and difficult to perceive, and that his revolution falls under the general explanations we have sought to establish for the phenomenon of revolutionary asceticism.

I I

WE SAID BEFORE that we would reexamine a bit more fully Mao's possible resonance with ascetic elements in his culture. To do this, and thus better to understand Mao's "fit" with his time and place, we must ask such questions as: What were the actual needs of China on the eve of the Revolution? What sort of leadership did it require? Without going into a detailed history of the period, but concentrating on the psychological situation, we can see that, certainly by the early twentieth century, the reigning dynasty, the Manchu, was increasingly perceived as an illegitimate authority. It combined the worst features of oppression toward its own subjects with subservience to foreign powers at home and abroad. Its privileges were no longer justified by its ability to defend its own people; its aura of sanctity was replaced by a penumbra of humiliation.

This situation has led scholars, such as Lucien Pye, to talk of a "crisis of authority," and to link this crisis with sentiments about aggression. Pye's overall thesis is that "the fundamental crisis of Chinese culture as it reacted to exposure to the modern world revolved around, first, a breakdown in the cultural concept of authority, and second and more fundamentally, a disruption of the mechanism by which the Chinese personality traditionally handled unconscious aggressions."[9]

Another scholar, Richard Solomon, has developed Pye's notion into a full-scale analysis of Chinese personality and culture, as well as an examination of Mao's efforts to work with and to change these factors.[10] According to Solomon, the Chinese "modal personality" involves strong dependency feelings (in comparison with, for example, American stress on independence and self-reliance), with the group taking precedence over the individual. Traditional child rearing stressed the need to avoid social conflict and to repress hostility and aggression. While the child was orally indulged and permissively toilet-trained, it was frequently beaten; thus Solomon postulates passiveness in the face of authority, as long as authority is legitimate, i.e., nurturant. This would be in line with the Confucian ethic of strict subservience of subject to emperor and son to father, with these authorities in turn living up to their rightful roles.

Aggressive feelings were to be strictly contained (Pye refers to the Chinese as "puritans about aggression").[11] One must "eat bitterness," and this fitted in with the Confucian code whereby inner feelings were not to be expressed. Even physical training and exercise were to be shunned as bordering on the aggressive. Contemplation and equanimity—the traits of Confucian gentlemen—were embraced as the ideal. If these injunctions were not heeded, then "Confusion" (*Luan*) would break out, "people would eat people," and chaos would reign.

According to Solomon, it was Mao above all others who perceived the absolute necessity of conflict and hostility for social change (of course, the context for Mao is the entire May 4th movement) and vehemently encouraged the display of aggressive feelings among the broad masses of Chinese people. He urged that feelings be liberated, that an "emotional storm" be provoked, and he organized rituals of mass hostility to implement these suggestions. Such letting out of aggression was facilitated by the campaigns against the landlords, as well as by the Japanese invasion. Only in this way could Mao free the Chinese modal personality from its dependency and passivity, and turn it to revolutionary anger and action.

Even this short summary of Solomon's most interesting work suggests the overlap with our theory of revolutionary asceticism.[12] The two are best seen as complementary rather than conflicting explanations. Solomon's notion that Mao encouraged the expression of hostility against previously inviolate authority coincides with our earlier point that the revolutionary ascetic offers his followers a new ego-ideal which "entitles" them to the release of their aggression (p. 37). As we have seen, the revolutionary ascetic first learns to break loose from libidinal ties in his personal experience, then stands free of them and their connection to the authority of the past, and is therefore able to free his followers from these same ties en masse by concentrating their love and dependency upon himself.[13]

So, too, as we shall see shortly, Mao advocated physical

education. We can now see that in the Chinese context it represented the expression of aggression as well as training in self-control. Solomon deepens our understanding of what is involved (and reminds us of the resonance of any particular tradition with our general concept of revolutionary asceticism). Similarly, Mao's emphasis on diligence and frugality also builds on the old Chinese child-rearing scheme wherein the child was expected to "repay" its socializing debt to the family by hard work.[14] In the Chinese context, of course, unlike in the West, hard work was not for individual gain. Hence we can perceive here a different causal explanation for Weber's "work ethic": It emerges from Confucian social relations rather than from Calvinistic internalized commands (which in the Weberian scheme are then linked in the West to "rational" pursuit of wealth). Nevertheless, the ascetic value of hard work in China is eminently present as a tradition available to revolutionary asceticism.

In such areas as work, physical exercise, and in more violent and storm-laden expressions of aggression, the need throughout is for *disciplined control*. There is always the danger of releasing impulse or effort without sufficient restraint, or, as Solomon puts it in discussing a specific problem, "a highly emotionalized style of politics" may be inappropriate "in a period where the Party's goals seem to require a rationalized approach to leadership and the promotion of technical innovation."[15] This is, in fact, the dilemma of Chinese modernization. Mao needed to call forth the expression of hostility for his revolution; he needed afterward to control its expression for the furtherance of his own claim to legitimacy of authority and of any efforts at modernization which his country was to take. In short, the problem of the functionalism of various traits of revolutionary asceticism both before and after the revolution takes on complicated, concrete, historical form.

Our thesis is that Mao, as a revolutionary ascetic, did play upon and develop various psychological chords present in Chinese culture and personality. Along with other qualities such as ideological shrewdness and organizational abilities, his traits as a revolutionary ascetic allowed him to offer the kind of leadership that China required in its "crisis of authority." Perhaps less of a prototype than Lenin, Mao still serves, when looked at closely in the context of Chinese culture, to illustrate the powerful functionalism involved in the component qualities embodied in our ideal type of the revolutionary ascetic.

III

THE ONLY WAY to test the validity of the assertions above is to go in search of Mao Tse-tung himself. Here, too, there are special difficulties that we (or at least I) encounter immediately. They are best handled frankly and briefly in a kind of "Apologia Pro Vita Mao."

The first difficulty concerns the paucity of material on Mao's personal life.[16] As with Lenin, we are in no position to attempt a full psychobiography. Fortunately, our intention is more limited. Though we shall present a slightly more general analysis of Mao as a revolutionary leader than we did with Lenin, our primary interest is in presenting portions of Mao's psychobiography in order to illustrate concretely, in a non-Western instance, the complexity surrounding what we have called "revolutionary asceticism."

A second difficulty arises from the unusual diffidence and difference of opinion among Chinese scholars themselves as to how to interpret recent Chinese history, and therefore Mao. This makes our reliance on secondary sources even more tentative than usual. But this situation, too, has its silver lining. If experts can argue so violently and on such fragmentary evidence, a relative amateur may gain courage, and, as a psychohistorian, advance hypotheses which the average Chinese expert would be unprepared or unwilling to consider on his own.

Thus I have been able to quiet my scholarly conscience. Most Chinese scholars have dismissed the effort at analyzing Mao's personality. As a typical example we can quote Jerome Ch'ên, who remarks that "Some attribute the intensity of Mao's hatred to the harsh treatment he suffered at the hands of his father.... I think rather that its origin is to be found in his reading of Darwin, Rousseau, J. S. Mill, and F. Paulsen, which

broadened his vision and encouraged him to break away from
obsolete tradition," and concludes, "In this study both the
Hegelian and the 'psychoanalytical' approaches are rejected."[17]
In contrast, I believe that *some serious and overt* effort at
understanding Mao's psychology is better than none. Other future scholars, with more adequate preparation in psychology
and Chinese studies, will surely be able to correct my gaffes;
meanwhile, I hope I shall at least have raised some of the right
questions. It is in this provisional sense, then, that we attempt a
partial psychohistorical analysis of Mao Tse-tung, seeking to
examine anew the complexity surrounding the exercise of revolutionary ascetic leadership, and to place our ideal type of the
latter back in the surrounding waters of phenomenological
history.

I V

IN SEEKING to analyze Mao, we have one enormous advantage over our investigation of Lenin. There does exist a key
personal document: the "autobiographical" interview with Mao
by Edgar Snow. Our first duty, therefore, is to look a little more
closely at this prime document.[18] Mao, at the time he talked to
Edgar Snow in 1936, was forty-three years old. Though he had
just achieved control of the Chinese Communist party (CCP)
(described by Snow as "the strongest Communist Party in the
world" outside of Russia) about a year earlier, his forces had
only managed to reach the Northwest intact after the heroic
Long March, there to preserve and develop themselves in preparation for an unknown future. At the time of the interview,
then, Mao had achieved partial success, but was by no means
the great and historic figure he has since become. Even Yenan,
as a sort of model Communist enclave, was to come later. Thus
it is the "Young Mao" (actually middle-aged) who tells us of
his life. (We shall stop our analysis of him more or less at the
point where he stops his narrative.)

Snow was an American journalist who had made his way
with great difficulty to the unknown and inaccessible Mao.

Clearly, Snow was sympathetic. His Chinese being limited, an interpreter was present. For accuracy, Snow's account was retranslated into Chinese, corrected by Mao, and then reretranslated into English. As Snow remarks, it is a straightforward account with no pretensions to literary excellence; as a result, it is perhaps more trustworthy than one which aimed at interpretation and elegance.

Why did Mao bother to tell his story to Snow? I have the feeling that Mao talked to Snow because the latter asked him to talk! Presumably, a Chinese person would never have probed into the intimate details of Chairman Mao's life, and, if he had, Mao would have felt insufficiently "distanced" from such an inquirer. Safe (so to speak) with the foreign Snow, Mao may also have felt flattered by this attention from the outside world.

Aside from such obvious reasons, what were the "purpose" and "meaning" of his autobiographical account to Mao? The ostensible reason given in the text is that it would serve to correct the false rumors circulating about him. On a deeper level, we can speculate that Snow's inquiry somehow played into a moment when it was important for Mao to take an overview of his own life—to seek to give it a shape and meaning, to rescue it from the chaos of recent events. This view is supported by the fact that Mao rejected Snow's initial idea of a list of questions, and responded, "Suppose that I just disregard your questions, and instead give you a general sketch of my life?" Thus it was *Mao* who volunteered the autobiography.

Autobiographies, at least ones such as Mao's, do not fit into a typical pre-1919 Chinese literary genre.[19] Thus, his very use of this Western genre (and one can compare here Gandhi's *Autobiography*) is itself an aspect of the modernization problem facing China. Next, it is clear that Mao's Communist ideology influences him both in the interpretation of specific events in his life and, more importantly, in his idea of how his *personal development* accords with *historical development*. The schema for the former comes largely from the latter. (Presumably, one must also allow for inspirations from the Chinese concept of the life cycle.) As a result, one overt purpose of his autobiography may also be said to be propaganda.

Propaganda or not, the account is enormously revealing from

a psychoanalytic viewpoint. Mao, of course, had read Marx; clearly, he had not read Freud. Thus, inadvertently, the account offers what is almost a classic case study of, among other things, an oedipal struggle of titanic dimensions. We can speculate that in the telling Mao achieved renewed "mastery" of the feelings involved, as he again worked through the story as he had come to arrange it in his mind. Told over a number of interviews, it was all recited from memory, without notes, and is a masterpiece of organization. Yet in spite of, or because of, that intellectual organization, Mao's account is also strikingly revealing on the psychological level.

For Mao himself, in middle age and poised on the edge of future defeat or success, the autobiography seems to have served to bring the personal and the political world into accord. As Snow tells us about all the Chinese Communists, they thought of their pre-Communist days "as a kind of Dark Ages . . . one's real life beginning only when one became a Communist" (p. 148). With Mao this seems only partly to have been the case. Like other Communists, Mao at first talked to Snow of "committees, organizations, armies . . . but seldom in terms of personal experience"; as Snow concludes, "he obviously considered the individual of very little import" (p. 121). But then the moment arrived when Mao decided to link his early, pre-Communist life in detail with his postconversion existence. In doing so, he showed himself to be the prototypic hero whose personal "mythic" existence qualified him to be leader of the CCP. Inadvertently, he also shows himself to be very human.

V

MAO starts his account in conventional fashion. "I was born in the village of Shao Shan, in Hsiang T'an Hsien, Hunan province, in 1893. My father's name was Mao Jen-sheng, and my mother's maiden name was Wen Chi-mei" (p. 123). Mao was the firstborn, followed by two other brothers. We are not told when the siblings were born, and they are mentioned only once again in the account when we are told that their wives were arrested in 1930 by a Kuomintang General, and then released. A sister, though not mentioned here by Mao, is acknowledged later when we are told of her execution. At the beginning there was also a grandfather who died before the birth of the youngest brother.

The father and the mother dominate the chapter labeled by Snow as "Childhood." Mao's father is a successful self-made man. Starting as a "poor peasant," he joins the army "because of heavy debts," then returns to his village, buys land, and rises gradually to be a "middle" and then "rich" peasant.[20] He is obviously a man of powerful character and ability, and, having achieved a measure of success, wishes his son to go beyond him.

As we know, Mao did go beyond him, but not in a way anticipated or desired by the father. There is an uncanny resemblance between Mao's relation to his father and that of Luther's to his (especially as depicted by Erikson).[21] Both fathers were self-made successes; both were "hard" men; both wanted their sons to have education—Mao in classics, Luther in law—that would further their social mobility *in terms of the direction* already set by the fathers; both obviously loved their sons, but did not know how to love effectively; and both bred a hatred and resentment in their sons that toppled not only *their* fatherly authority but the paternal authority of the highest political and religious figures.

The dominant image Mao seems to have of his father is that of a stern taskmaster. He drove not only himself—Mao unconsciously resents the fact that his father spent so much time at his business, and therefore not with him—but his family, or so Mao perceived it. Thus, wife and children—Mao at the age of six—were put to work on the farm. As soon as Mao started school and learned a few characters and the abacus, his father put him to work on the accounts at night as well. The picture darkens: The father, a "hot-tempered man," frequently beat both Mao and his brothers, gave them no money, and provided the most meager food. Later we shall see that Mao was also noted for his temper, which was a typical Hunanese trait. We can feel the intensity of Mao's resentment in his memory, which must be accepted as psychic reality though doubtful as actual reality, that "On the 15th of every month he made a concession to his labourers and gave them eggs with their rice, but never meat. To me he gave neither eggs nor meat" (p. 125).

There is a kind of mythical quality to this account. Jerome Ch'ên casts doubt on its authenticity when he says, "Since he [Mao] was working as an adult, he was eligible to receive eggs, fish, and a little meat for his food on the first and the fifteenth day of every month while his mother and brothers were not. On other days there were only rice and vegetables."[22] Obviously, for Mao the matter involved a deep emotional truth. Violating traditional Chinese reluctance to talk about emotions, partly out of a propagandistic desire to encourage the expression of hostility, Mao inadvertently reveals the depth of the hurt within him.

There is a terrible plaintive quality in this memory. Father and son are locked in a fated embrace which turns to hatred. As Siao-yu recalls, "Both father and son were very stubborn, always quarrelling, and never succeeding in coming to an agreement on any subject."[23] Reading the account, we sense a tragic, frustrated love on the part of the father (although one would never know this from Mao's explicit narrative), and a similar desire, made worse by a desire for *total* love, on the part of the son. Unable to have total love, Mao, like a jealous lover, seems to have turned totally against his father. Later we shall see the effect of all this for our thesis of revolutionary asceticism. But first we must say something about Mao's mother.

The mother is portrayed as the complete opposite of the father; Mao seems to have split his feelings totally.[24] In this he was supported by Chinese culture, which offers it as a typical family pattern. "My mother was a kind woman," he tells us, "generous and sympathetic, and ever ready to share what she had." She and the father, according to Mao, quarreled. At this point Mao sublimates his oedipal feelings into good Marxist dialectic and secures his mother as a *political* ally against his father: "There were two 'parties' in the family. One was my father, the Ruling Power. The Opposition was made up of myself, my mother, my brother and sometimes even the labourer" (p. 125).

Mao makes his family a model for the political world, and, of course, the political reality of 1936 colored his family memory of the early 1900s. Now emerges a debate on how to fight the "Ruling Power." In Mao's charming prose, "In the 'United Front' of the Opposition, however, there was a difference of opinion. My mother advocated a policy of indirect attack. She criticized my overt display of emotions and attempts at open rebellion against the Ruling Power. She said it was not the Chinese way" (p. 125).

The interesting fact is that Mao, in spite of his declared love for his mother, ends up rejecting her "Chinese way." The resolution occurs at the age of thirteen, a critical time for the oedipal feelings, when Mao openly challenges his father—and wins, in a way. Mao tells us:

When I was about thirteen my father invited many guests to his home, and while they were present a dispute arose between the two of us. My father denounced me before the whole group, calling me lazy and useless. This infuriated me. I cursed him and left the house. My mother ran after me and tried to persuade me to return. My father also pursued me, cursing at the same time that he demanded me to come back. I reached the edge of a pond and threatened to jump in if he came any nearer. In this situation demands and counter-demands were presented for cessation of the civil war. My father insisted that I apologize and k'ou-t'ou as a sign of submission. I agreed to give a one-knee k'ou-t'ou if he would promise not to beat me. Thus the war ended, and from it I learned that when I defended my rights by open rebellion my father relented, but when I remained meek and submissive he only cursed and beat me the more (p. 126).

This incident bears closer examination. Mao exhibits highly unfilial behavior, and we must bear in mind the unusual stress on filial piety in China. Indeed, we can hardly overemphasize this point. As John K. Fairbank has suggested, filial piety is so much the primary, old-style Chinese virtue, and the filial-paternal relationship so central to the system, that the rebellion of Mao against his father, while formally like that of Luther or other Western figures, has even greater significance.[25] As an illustration of what is involved, we can note that the legal codes specifically instructed fathers to destroy sons who were outrageously or willfully disobedient to parental instruction (though urging them not to kill their sons in an unusually cruel manner). Thus traditional Chinese social structure and ideology both reinforced the Freudian situation.

In this light, we can see how much guilt and tremulation must have accompanied Mao's outbreak. "My father's favourite accusations against me were of unfilial conduct and laziness" (p. 125). To this Mao now adds a forbidden curse on his father. The parental reactions are most interesting. The mother runs after him, to persuade him to return. The ambivalent character of his father's frustrated love for his son—so much like him that he is *too* much like him—is to pursue, "cursing at the same time that he demanded me to come back." Mao threatens suicide, a form of aggression turned inward, and in Chinese culture a way of shaming the opponent. The result is the one-knee *k'ou-t'ou*. Mao has learned how to rebel openly, yet with a shrewd sense of how to compromise.

Even more important for our purposes is Mao's resolution of his oedipal struggle. At this point we must, at least briefly, indicate the possible nature of an Oedipus complex in Chinese culture. According to Solomon, the classic oedipal struggle of the West is simply absent in traditional Chinese culture. Illustrating his point from the Confucian texts, Solomon shows how the good son, even when abandoned by his father (as was Oedipus), still exhibits the qualities of filial obligation. Moreover, his internal feelings are made to correspond with his external actions. This, of course, is the ideal, but Solomon seems to suggest it was also the norm in practice. Hence, according to Solomon, oedipal struggle and rebellion was not a theme in Chinese culture.[26]

To accept Solomon's thesis for traditional Chinese culture does not mean that we must deny the evident reality of an oedipal conflict in Mao's autobiographical account. In fact, we should expect that the throwing off of traditional authority, in both the family and the state, would call into being a new relation between father and son. It was because Mao experienced this to such a degree in his own life that he could symbolize for others (and his account, as noted, is partly propagandistic) the filial rebellion required by his political revolution. Indeed, many in Mao's generation were undergoing the same

conflict, and Ezra Vogel, criticizing Solomon, declares that "To
describe the resolution of oedipal problems in terms of the old
Hsüeh Jen-kuei solution [in the Confucian text it is the father
who goes off for a number of years, and then returns to kill his
unrecognized son in a challenge over marksmanship] ignores
the dominant thrust of the literature of the post-May 4th period
which was bitterly critical of submission to traditional authority
and romantic about youth leaving the traditional family."[27]

Thus we can hold to our notion of Mao's oedipal struggle,
and postulate that, in the main, he resolved it successfully,
letting go of his mother and identifying increasingly with his
father (though often in ways unsuspected by Mao himself, for,
of course, a "translation" had to take place). As Mao puts it in
a piece of sudden psychological insight, "I think that in the end
the strictness of my father defeated him. I learned to hate him."
Yet, as Mao admits, "At the same time it probably benefited me.
It made me most diligent in my work; it made me keep my
books carefully, so that he should have no basis for criticizing
me" (pp. 126–127).

Surely one can analyze this development in terms of Mao's
internalizing of his father's demands, of an "identification with
the aggressor." Whatever explanation one chooses, it is clear
that Mao *did* take on many of his father's attributes, such as his
outbursts of anger as well as his faith in hard work and diligence—ascetic virtues. In a curious passage, Mao admits this
development as a piece of self-knowledge. At the age of thirteen, just prior to the incident recounted above, Mao tells of his
response to the father's charge of laziness: "I used the rebuttal
that older people should do more work than younger, that my
father was over three times as old as myself, and therefore
should do more work. *And I declared that when I was his age I
would be much more energetic*" [italics added] (p. 126).

Clearly, Mao did not want to let go of his childhood, or its
treasured modicum of irresponsibility. When he did accept
adulthood, however, he did it with a vengeance, and his energy
and hard work were notorious in their drive. Moreover, he kept
his "accounts" well beyond merely his father's books, in the
process settling "accounts" with his father and all authority.
His constant, compulsive attention to numbers rivals that of

Benjamin Franklin, in a way to gladden Max Weber's heart.
Let me cite just a few of the examples throughout Mao's autobiography. At the very beginning we are given the *exact figures*
for Mao's father's acquisitions of land and rice: "As middle
peasants then my family owned fifteen mou of land. On this
they could raise sixty tan of rice a year" (p. 123). Why are
these specific figures so important as to be remembered by the
forty-three-year-old Mao? But it is not only such numbers that
Mao remembers. His attention to money is omnipresent. "During my years in normal school in Changsha I spent, altogether,
only $160 . . ." (p. 148); captured by the Kuomintang in
1927, and then escaping, he informs us that "I had seven dollars with me . . . when at last I reached the peasant guards
safely, I had only two coppers in my pocket" (p. 168). While
some of this attention to money may be attributed to the normal tight-fistedness of any peasant, much must be held ac-
countable to the father's account books—and his insistence
that Mao keep them.[28]

My thesis, then, is that Mao identified with his father more
than he knew. Further, my interpretation would be that Mao
found his mother's "softness" threatening to him. At the crucial
point of his Oedipus complex, around age thirteen, Mao appears to have been tempted to identify with the mother and her
qualities. Frightened by this possibility, he turned instead to a
strong if only partial identification with the father. Thus, psychologically one with the father, he could now "possess" his
mother successfully. In the process Mao also overtly rejected
"softness" and embraced his father's "hard" qualities.[29] At
this point he has taken on a number of the ascetic qualities;
however, as a *political revolutionary* he is still in embryo.

VI

ACCORDING to his own account, Mao "was the family
scholar" (p. 127). His father, who had had two years of
schooling and could read just enough to keep books, wanted
him "to master the Classics, especially after he [the father]

was defeated in a law suit due to an apt Classical quotation used by his adversary in the Chinese court" (p. 127). Mao, however, like so many youths in his generation, turned against the Classics. They stood for the "old" China, the China of fathers and authority, and worse, of parental authority that was failing in the face of the challenge of Western power and knowledge.

Instead of the Classics, Mao enjoyed "the romances of Old China, and especially *stories of rebellions*" [italics added] (p. 127).[30] He adds:

It occurred to me one day that there was one thing peculiar about these stories, and that was the absence of peasants who tilled the land. All the characters were warriors, officials or scholars; there was never a peasant hero. I wondered about this for two years, and then I analyzed the content of the stories. I found that they all glorified men of arms, rulers of the people, who did not have to work the land, because they owned and controlled it and evidently made the peasants work it for them (p. 128).

I suggest that this passage attests to Mao's increasing identification with the peasants. On the level of the unconscious, his father was a man of arms who had secured his land through military service. Mao was made to work for him, just like the peasants. Moreover, what seems at first to work against my theory of the identification with the father is able, in the "illogical" way of emotions, to come to terms with that identification as well, for Mao's father was originally just a peasant. Thus Mao could affirm his father in one part of his story while rejecting him in another part.

Mao looked ahead to reform, as well as behind to romance, in his reading. For example, he read a book called *Words of Warning*. "The authors," he says, "a number of old reformist scholars, thought that the weakness of China lay in her lack of Western appliances—railways, telephones, telegraphs and steamships—and wanted to have them introduced into the country. My father considered such books as a waste of time. He wanted me to read something practical like the Classics, which could help him in winning lawsuits" (pp. 127–128). Once again we see Mao's personal development and the development of China brought into correspondence. China is "weak" and needs to strengthen herself with Western appliances, a policy largely opposed by the ruling power. Mao is "weak" compared to his father, and needs to strengthen himself with Western knowledge, a desire opposed by *his* ruling power.

Eventually Mao, to continue *his* studies, a pursuit opposed by his father, ran away from home (a recurring pattern, for he had done this before at age ten). At sixteen he enrolled in a school in Hsiang Hsiang *hsien* (county), where his mother's family lived (in the process lying about being a native of that county). Needless to say, he tells us the precise amount (fourteen hundred coppers) that he paid for room, board, and so on. This school taught "natural science and new subjects of Western learning," and finally Mao's father agreed to let him enter "after friends had argued to him that this 'advanced' education would increase my earning powers" (p. 132). Fight though he might, the father was outwardly gradually losing his son.

Mao was not happy at the new school. He, who had complained about being the son of a "rich" peasant in his own village, now found himself the poor peasant among rich sons of landlords. "I was more poorly dressed than the others," Mao complains, and "Many of the richer students despised me because usually I was wearing my ragged coat and trousers" (p. 132). To add to his isolation, Mao claims he was disliked because he was not a native of Hsiang Hsiang. Despised by all except the teachers, Mao confesses that "I felt spiritually very depressed" (p. 132). Other sources suggest additional reasons for Mao's spiritual depression. As Lucian Pye summarizes, "He was a big strapping lad, large for his age, and over six years older than any of his classmates. Those who remember him at this period picture a youth who could not deal easily with his equals, who was always challenging his teachers, and who displayed all the aggressive bullying tactics of his father."[31] Was it also possible that Mao, for the first time distant from home—"this was the first time I had been as far away from home as fifty li [about sixteen miles]" (p. 132)—in possession of his new freedom, found himself, as others before him, homesick? Was his victory having a bitter taste? Reading between the lines, one suspects as much.

One other event that occurred during this period must be

mentioned. Shortly after quarreling with his father and then running away from home, Mao reports, "At this time an incident occurred in Hunan *which influenced my whole life*" [italics added]. The incident concerns a severe famine, during which the starving people finally "attacked the Manchu yamen [official headquarters], cut down the flagpole, the symbol of office, and drove out the governor." Retribution from on high soon followed. "A new governor arrived, and at once ordered the arrest of the leaders of the uprising. Many of them were beheaded and their heads displayed on poles as a warning to future 'rebels'" (p. 129).

Why did this episode influence Mao's "whole life"? His explanation is as follows:

This incident was discussed in my school for many days. It made a deep impression on me. Most of the other students sympathized with the "insurrectionists," but only from an observer's point of view. They did not understand that it had any relation to their own lives. They were merely interested in it as an exciting incident. I never forgot it. I felt that there with the rebels were ordinary people like my own family and I deeply resented the injustice of the treatment given to them (p. 130).

On the unconscious level, an additional element offers itself. Mao's account cries aloud for "castration" interpretation: the rebels cutting down the flagpole, "symbol of office," and being "beheaded" for their audacity. Well might Mao understand that it did have a relation to his life, and that the injustice of the treatment was resented because, on the symbolic level, it was treatment meted out to *him*.[32] Such an interpretation does not deny the overt, public explanation given by Mao; hopefully, it enriches it by indicating the personal passion fueling his resentment.

The paragraph immediately following the one quoted above continues the theme. In it Mao tells of a conflict between members of a secret society and a local landlord. Instead of submitting, the secret society members rebelled, and "withdrew to a local mountain called Liu Shan, where they built a stronghold." Only after long efforts were they suppressed, and their leader captured and beheaded. This time Mao draws a more invigorating moral. "In the eyes of the students, however, he [the rebel leader] was a hero ... " (p. 130).

In this light, can we speculate further on why Mao, at his school at this time, "felt spiritually very depressed"? Consciously, he felt isolated and despised, a poor, uncouth youth. Unconsciously, was he also having to come to terms with the possible outcome of his rebellion against his father: symbolic castration? The result, as we know, was that Mao conquered his fears and went on to be one of the most successful rebels in history. In this conquest of his own fears, he also conquered for the Chinese people. Our grounds for such an hypothesis is Mao's extraordinary attention to the theme of rebellion and retribution by beheading (in itself a commonplace of Chinese criminal procedure, but in Mao's account of special symbolic value), and his otherwise relatively inexplicable statement that the incident "influenced my whole life."

Lastly, we note that a pattern of rebellion is unfolding in Mao's account. He "runs away"; the secret society leader "withdraws to a mountain stronghold." Neither, of course, is totally original; for example, the tradition of bandits (or rebels) retreating to the mountains is omnipresent in Chinese history. Mao is therefore within a great tradition. Yet it is the fact that he makes this tradition his own, giving it new glory and dimensions in the Long March and in the retreat to the mountains of the Northwest, bringing into correspondence his personal adaptation and the external needs of the Chinese Communist party in 1934–1936, which must hold our attention.

VII

IN 1913, aged twenty, his "spiritual depression" apparently behind him, Mao walked one hundred twenty li (forty miles) from his home to enter school in "Changsha, the great city." Mao was the small-town boy attracted to the excitements of the big metropolis. Later, as we know, Mao's ambivalent feelings about urban life manifested themselves with significant consequences for China. At this moment in his development, however, he was eager for the intellectual stimulation of the city.

During the next five years at Changsha, Mao underwent what social scientists are fond of calling "political socialization." In this he was at one with his entire generation of students. In those five years, too, Mao found himself, or, to use the Eriksonian phrase, solved his "identity crisis." The resolution and maturity he reached then were still present in 1936, when he looked back over his life for Edgar Snow. Only later, when in full power after victory in 1949, did Mao show significant signs of what psychoanalysts call "the return of the repressed." Even then, I believe, this great man was growing creatively, at the same time as he was regressing in some areas. But this is another theme, beyond the scope of this present effort.

In Changsha Mao read his first newspaper, "a nationalist revolutionary journal which told of the Canton Uprising against the Manchu dynasty" (p. 135). He learned also about Sun Yat-sen. At this point Mao's life cycle, with its personal rebellion, becomes caught up in the historical cycle of China, with its great revolution stretching over thirty-eight years (1911–1949).

Inspired, Mao wrote his first article, which was also his "first expression of a political opinion" (p. 135), and posted it on the school wall. Avidly reading more newspapers, Mao became aware of "Socialism," which was really "social-reformism." He wrote enthusiastically to several of his classmates on the subject, although with little response. Mao's reading of newspapers and writing of articles was to continue increasingly throughout his life. Even this early, we can see how vital to his personal political socialization and to his political socialization of others was that "revolutionary" product of modernization, the newspaper. Along with pamphlets, it became Mao's major vehicle for communication. Like Luther's before him, Mao's revolution may be said to have been made in large part by the printing press, a development aided by the introduction of a simple, more vernacular style of language espoused by the new culture movement.[33]

We can also see that Mao's initial chosen skill as a revolutionary was the literary one. Having rejected, ostensibly, the

Classics, he was still a scholar of the pen. At the beginning, then, as well as later, it was by the power of his written word that Mao hoped to lead men into revolution. As we shall see shortly, he added to his literary leadership an extraordinary ability for organization, a rare and powerful combination. But the writing came first.

Mao's political agitation was not restricted to writing articles. In another telling incident, he recounts how his fellow students "demonstrated their anti-Manchu sentiments by a rebellion against the pigtail. One friend and I clipped off our pigtails, but others who had promised to do so, afterward failed to keep their word. My friend and I therefore assaulted them in secret and forcibly removed their queues, a total of more than ten falling victims to our shears" (pp. 135–136). Two comments are in order here. The first is that Mao was already showing his leadership ability and his willingness to use force in the process. The second is that, inasmuch as the wearing of the queue was a sign of subservience to the Manchu, Mao was symbolically as well as literally rebelling against the reigning authority.

Mao went even further in the direction of revolution than merely cutting off his pigtail. He also joined a revolutionary army. By accident he had witnessed his first battle in Changsha itself, where he "stood on a high place and watched the battle" (p. 137). Then, along with many other students, he enlisted. Once again we have another curious incident in Mao's life. Unlike the other students, Mao "did not like the student army; I considered the basis of it too confused. I decided to join the regular army instead, and help complete the revolution" (p. 138). Is this an expression of Mao's scorn for the amateurish students, who also scorned him? A dislike for "intellectuals," which was to recur many times, culminating in the Cultural Revolution? Or, more likely at the time, an imitation of and identification with his father, who had also joined the "regular army"?

The people Mao liked most in the army were "a Hunan miner in my squad, and an ironsmith" (p. 138). These were workers, and perhaps Chairman Mao's memory in 1936 is colored by ideological motives. In any case, he tells us he also got on friendly terms with the platoon commander and most of the soldiers. "I could write, I knew something about books, and they respected my 'Great Learning'" (p. 139). Mao is still, therefore, a superior, a "leader," by virtue of his literary training. The ambivalence involved for him in identification with peasants and workers is illustrated by the rest of his rather odd account. "My salary," he says, "was seven dollars a month—which is more than I get in the Red Army now however—and of this I spent two dollars a month on food." (Again we have Mao's compulsive and rather formidable memory for monetary details; how deep must be the emotion behind his earlier comment, "He [father] gave us no money!") "I also had to buy water," Mao continues. The reason offered is most revealing. "The soldiers had to carry water in from outside the city, but I, being a student, could not condescend to carrying, and bought it from the water-pedlars" (p. 138). Mao, though rejecting the student army in favor of the regular army, still retains his superior identification as a student. Can we not perhaps see that his awareness of the tenaciousness of "bourgeois" habits might predispose him to be sympathetic to others later on, and to recommend brainwashing rather than beheading as the cure? In this Mao would be in accord with the Confucian idea that man is perfectible, rather than bedeviled by original sin, and that therefore instruction or indoctrination is the correct way to deal with him.

VIII

DURING his years in Changsha, Mao thrashed about for his true path. His vacillation about a career seems extraordinary for the future "authoritarian" leader of the CCP, but quite normal for an uncertain, rebellious boy. Mao is unexpectedly candid about his tribulations—or is this part of the self-image he wishes to project for himself and followers?—and we must match his self-revelation by not imposing our images of the later Mao on the young boy of Changsha.

After his six months service in the army, Mao tells us he

"decided to return to my books" (p. 139). It is a strange return. First he saw an advertisement in the papers for a police school, and registered there. Before starting, however, he read another advertisement, about a soap-making school, which "told of the great social benefits of soap-making, how it would enrich the country and enrich the people" (p. 139). Mao decided to register in this school. What a wonderful picture is now conjured up for us: Mao Tse-tung, if destiny had so ordered, as China's "soap-maker" king instead of Chairman of the CCP!

It was not to be. A friend urged him to enter law school, and Mao, swayed by the promise of becoming a mandarin, wrote to his family for permission and tuition. While waiting for their reply, he read an advertisement about a commercial school and decided to register there. Then he wrote of his decision to his father. "He was pleased," Mao informs us. "My father readily appreciated the advantages of commercial cleverness. I entered this school and remained—for one month" (p. 140). The reason given for Mao's short sojourn in commercial school was that most of the courses were in English—and Mao knew no English! How clever of him not to have found this out ahead of time!

The whole situation is presented by Mao in a straightforward tone, as if his vacillations were the most natural thing in the world.[34] He offers no indication as to how his father reacted to his changes of mind (although we can guess). Perhaps we may sympathize a bit with the parent, at the same time as we recognize that Mao's behavior was most likely a form of testing, teasing, and taunting his father. Hitler, for example, got back at his father by failing in school; Luther by entering the monastery; and Mao by alternately doing and then undoing what his father wanted in the way of his schooling. We must add, of course, that Mao was not only testing his father; he was testing himself as well.

Mao's next experiment was in the First Provincial Middle School. Having entered at the head of the list of candidates (by exam), Mao found he did not like the school. "Its curriculum was limited and its regulations were objectionable.... I had also come to the conclusion that it would be better for me to read and study alone" (p. 141). Thus after six months Mao

left the school and spent the next half year reading in the
Hunan Provincial Library. During this period of self-education,
he tells us that:

I read many books, studied world geography and world history.
There for the first time I saw and studied with great interest a map
of the world. I read Adam Smith's *The Wealth of Nations* and
Darwin's *Origin of the Species*, and a book on ethics by John
Stuart Mill. I read the works of Rousseau, Spencer's *Logic*, and a
book on law written by Montesquieu. I mixed poetry and romances, and the tales of ancient Greece, with serious study of
history and geography of Russia, America, England, France and
other countries[35] (pp. 141–142).

Another curious incident is reported by Mao as occurring at
this time. He tells us that he was living in a guild house for
natives of his district:

Many soldiers were there also—"retired" or disbanded men from
the district, who had no work to do and little money. Students and
soldiers were always quarreling in the guild house, and one night
this hostility between them broke out in physical violence. The
soldiers attacked and tried to kill the students. I escaped by fleeing
to the toilet, where I hid until the fight was over (p. 142).

To our image of Mao as soap-maker we must now add the
picture of Mao hiding in the toilet! These are hardly heroic
portraits, and we must wonder why Mao paints them for us and
for his countrymen. Is the conflict of students and soldiers
(perhaps symbolic of Mao and his father) so strong that Mao
is literally *compelled* to recall the episode? Or does he mention
it, in quiet good humor, to show as an example that even a
person starting with very human frailties could rise above them
to be a great Communist?

Whatever the explanation, this incident was in some way
important, as was the six-month reading period. Indeed, the
latter may have served, in Erikson's sense, as Mao's "mora-
torium." In any case, after the months in the library Mao seems
to have found his initial vocation. "Meanwhile," he says, "I
had been thinking seriously of my 'career' and had about decided that I was best suited for teaching." The decision taken,
Mao asked for his family's confirmation. "I wrote of my intention to my family and received their consent" (p. 142).

We note a number of significant elements here. Mao, a twenty-year-old boy, having "run away" from his family, constantly "runs back" to them for approval. As for the "hot-tempered" father who gave no money, eggs, or meat, he has either aged gracefully, or become weak, or been partly misrepresented by Mao earlier, for he certainly has gone along with his son's career jumping. Lastly, we must add to our story the role of *teachers* in Mao's development, for they have played an important part from the beginning, although we have purposely neglected them until now.

The first teacher mentioned by Mao plays a negative role. Mao identifies him with the harsh father. We encounter him in the local primary school when Mao was around eight, and are told that this teacher "belonged to the stern-treatment school. He was harsh and severe, frequently beating his students." Then follows a significant result that sets a pattern we have noticed before:

Because of this I ran away from the school when I was ten. I was afraid to return home, for fear of receiving a beating there, and set out in the general direction of the city, which I believed to be in a valley somewhere. I wandered for three days before I was finally found by my family. Then I learned that I had circled round and round in my travels, and in all my walking had got only about eight li from my home. . . . After my return to the family, . . . to my surprise, conditions somewhat improved. My father was slightly more considerate and the teacher was more inclined to moderation. The result of my act of protest impressed me very much. It was a successful "strike" (pp. 124–125).

"Running away" works, as does "opposition" to oppression. A cynic, or a psychoanalyst, might comment that, psychologically, Mao's "running away" from his father (the teacher is a father substitute, but Mao later ran away from his father directly) only led him in circles "round and round," and never really away. A historian would have to add that Mao's psychological circles certainly had linear implications for China and world history!

The next teacher mentioned by Mao had a more positive effect. He, too, was in the local primary school, but he was a "radical," as Mao explains, "because he was opposed to Buddhism, and wanted to get rid of the gods. . . . I admired him and agreed with his views" (p. 131). At the Hsiang Hsiang county school, where Mao had gone in opposition to his father's wishes, he tells us that he was liked by his teachers, "especially those who taught the Classics, because I wrote good essays in the Classical manner" (p. 132). There was also a teacher here, returned from being a student in Japan, who made a strong impression on Mao. A teacher also introduced Mao to the school in Changsha, and another teacher there, according to Mao, "helped me very much; he was attracted to me because of my literary tendency" (p. 141).

Teachers obviously saw promise in the rebellious, curious Mao. And Mao came gradually to identify with teachers in a positive fashion. In choosing to be a teacher, Mao was not, on the unconscious level, rejecting his father completely. Rather he was reaffirming the authority reposing in the good, nurturing father by becoming like that figure. Having split his father's image into a harsh "teacher" and a supporting, "giving teacher," Mao identified with the latter.

This development became confirmed for Mao in the figure of Yang Ch'ang-chi, the teacher of ethics at the Changsha Normal School.[36] One might never guess Yang's full role from Mao's understated recital (leaving us with the suspicion that Mao passes lightly over his most intimate memories, screening them from us, perhaps, with his overrevealing "incidents"):

[Yang] believed in his ethics very strongly, and tried to imbue his students with the desire to become just, moral, virtuous men, useful in society. Under his influence, I read a book on ethics translated by Ts'ai Yuan-p'ei and was inspired to write an essay which I entitled "The Energy of the Mind." I was then an idealist and my essay was highly praised by Professor Yang Chen-ch'i, from his idealist viewpoint. He gave me a mark of 100 for it (pp. 143–144).

Mao only admits here that he was "later to become intimately related" to Yang; further on he tells us that he married Yang's daughter.

Mao forgets to tell us one other thing. According to his boyhood friend, Siao-Yu, Yang (who, probably as a joke, was nicknamed "Confucius" in the First Normal School, a strange name for one admired by Mao, who supposedly confided to a friend that he "hated Confucianism from the age of eight") took cold baths, saying, "Every day one must do something difficult to strengthen one's will. Cold water not only strengthens the will; it is good for the health!" Later Siao adds, "In rejecting traditional customs, he advocated living in a new, 'democratic' and 'scientific' manner. He thought that breakfast should be omitted and urged his students to go in for deep breathing, meditation and year-around cold baths." Yang seems to have been Mao's teacher in ascetics as well as ethics, a conclusion confirmed for us by Siao's final comment that "Mao Tse-tung ... and a number of other students accepted Yang as their model."[37]

Yang Ch'ang-chi obviously played a major role in young Mao's development. It is permissible for us to guess at the psychological springs of the relationship. Yang, his teacher, gave Mao his first sustained ego-ideal—idealism, in this case—at a time in late adolescence when Mao was most in need of such ideological sustenance. Psychologically now Mao's "father," Yang also became Mao's actual father-in-law (at least posthumously; Yang died in January 1920, before the marriage itself). We are reminded here of Karl Marx's similar admiration for a substitute father figure, Ludwig von Westphalen, and his marriage to the latter's daughter Jenny. A series of teachers, as we have seen, were "tried out" for the fatherly role by Mao, who then, in his own good time, chose a real "teacher-father" and identified with him fully by also deciding to be a teacher.

History conspired to turn Mao into a teacher of a very special sort, as we know. Changsha, however, was the real sustained beginning. As at all his schools, Mao disliked the constricting rules. "There were many regulations in the new school and I agreed with very few of them." In the light of the future problem concerning the modernization of China, it is interesting to note one of Mao's disliked regulations. "For one thing," he tells us, "I was opposed to the required courses in natural sciences. I wanted to specialize in social sciences" (p. 143). Poor in natural science, he was also weak in mathematics and drawing. Fortunately, his good marks in social science saved him, and after five years at Changsha he graduated in 1918 with a degree. In the process of acquiring his degree, Mao had also acquired some other knowledge that eventually changed his projected career as a teacher (or changed him into another sort of teacher). To these developments we must now turn.

IX

MAO'S initial gestures in the direction of becoming a revolutionary had been literary. Now he began to exhibit unusual organizational skill and initiative. Feeling the need "for a few intimate companions," Mao tells us he inserted an advertisement in a Changsha newspaper inviting contacts. "I specified youths who were hardened and determined, and ready to make sacrifices for their country." The initial response consisted of "three and one-half replies." Gradually, however, Mao built up a hard-core group of students around him, and this society, as he informs us, "was to have a widespread influence on the affairs and destiny of China" (p. 145).

From this original group we see the emergence of Mao as a revolutionary and, what is more, as a revolutionary ascetic. A quotation from Mao will supply our evidence:

It was a serious-minded little group of men and they had no time to discuss trivialities. Everything they did or said must have a purpose. They had no time for love or "romance" and considered the times too critical and the need for knowledge too urgent to discuss women or personal matters. I was not interested in women. My parents had married me when I was fourteen to a girl of twenty, but I had never lived with her—and never subsequently did. I did not consider her my wife and at this time gave little thought to her. Quite aside from the discussions of feminine charm, which usually play an important role in the lives of young men of this age, my companions even rejected talk of ordinary matters of daily life. I remember once being in the house of a youth who began to talk to me about buying some meat, and in my presence called in his servant and discussed the matter with him, then ordering him to buy a piece. I was annoyed and did not see this fellow again. My friends and I preferred to talk only of large matters—the nature of men, of human society, of China, the world, and the universe (pp. 145–146).

Let us analyze this passage. Mao and his companions had no time for love, and Mao especially was not interested in women. We can speculate that at this stage in his life a "loving" woman, such as his mother, was a distinct threat to Mao. Such libidinal ties might constrict his activity by weakening and undermining his hardness and determination, and by distracting him from total dedication. Thus Mao had begun to embrace some of the characteristics of what I have called displaced libidinal leadership. This was unquestionably the image he projected as leader of the CCP and then of China. Apparently devoid of personal ties, Mao could offer total love to his people.

In fact, as we know, Mao fell in love personally at least once, and within a few years of his youthful dismissal of the tender emotion he married the girl, Yang Ch'ang-chi's daughter.[38] We also know that his feelings could be intense, as his "hatred" for his father indicates (and hatred is often the opposite side of love). Clearly, Mao was extremely ambivalent about strong libidinal ties. How can we equate this side of Mao with a picture of him as a leader with "few libidinal ties"?

First, I suggest we must amend, or deepen, our picture of the displaced libidinal leader. It is not the absence of feeling, but the overwhelming threat of *too much* feeling, that causes him to harden himself against all emotion. Mao was only partially successful in this effort. He did try to cut himself off from his family by hating his father and removing himself from his mother (the other aim of running away?). As for Mao's wife, Yang K'ai-hui, she, too, was a revolutionary. We can guess how much time together they might have had from numerous accounts of other such "revolutionary" comradeship marriages.[39] According to André Malraux, however, Mao "loved her, and refers to her in a famous poem as 'my proud poplar' (a play on her name)."[40] In 1930 Yang K'ai-hui was executed by the Kuomintang. What shield did Mao find necessary to build around his heart? The fact that he later remarried twice, the second time to an actress, Chiang Ch'ing, tells us very little about his feelings.[41]

It is interesting to note in this connection that Snow had placed the subject of Mao's love-life on his list of original inquiries: "How many times have you been married?" According to Snow, Mao smiled at the question, and Snow adds, "The rumour later spread that I had asked Mao how many wives he had" (p. 122). Mao's public image seems to have taken two forms. The first is that of Mao as the dedicated hardened revolutionary, ascetic and relatively libidoless, though with a faint rumor to the contrary. We have analyzed the function of this sort of image in Chapter 3. The second is of Mao the breaker of the traditional Chinese family pattern, with his espousal of freely chosen romantic love. As early as 1919, in his articles on Miss Chao's suicide, he sounded the note of "freedom to choose [one's] own love." This was the spirit that animated the decree regarding marriage of the First Session of the Central Executive Committee of the Chinese Soviet Republic: "Free choice must be the basic principle of every marriage; the whole feudal system of marriage, including the power of parents to arrange marriages for their children, to exercise compulsion, and all purchase and sale in marriage contracts, shall henceforth be abolished."[42]

Later, as we know, when Mao came to complete power in China and the whole "feudal system," including marriage, was overturned, "free choice" in marriage was sublimated once again, but this time to the dictates of Mao and the CCP, and not of individual parents. "Mao Tse-tung is my father; the Communist party is my mother" was the song taught to babies in the kindergartens. Once of age, they were taught that love, as a widely circulated official booklet puts it, is "a psychosomatic activity which consumes energy and wastes time." As Jacques Marcuse reports, quoting the magazine *Chinese Youth Fortnightly*, neither physical nor sentimental attractions are to play any part when marriage is contemplated. Instead, what counts is "a shared political consciousness which can lead to greater joint efforts in building Socialism and increasing production."[43] Shades of Mao's "united front" with his mother! Shades of Mao's family-arranged marriage for him! All this, however, was to be in the future. Young Mao of 1918 claimed to have no time for love or women, though in theory he believed in freedom of love.

In place of being interested in women, Mao and his companions "became ardent physical culturists." (We have already

noted the inspiration of his teacher, Yang Ch'ang-chi.) Mao
explains their regimen:

We slept in the open when frost was already falling and even in
November swam in the cold rivers. All this went under the title of
"body training." Perhaps it helped much to build the physique
which I was to need so badly later on in my many marches back
and forth across South China, and on the Long March from Ki-
angsi to the North-West (p. 146).

In fact, it was not only the body but more importantly the
mind that was trained by Spartan living. In his 1917 article, "A
Study of Physical Culture," Mao's first complete and authentic
text written before 1923 which is available in the West, Mao
explained how physical education (and I emphasize the ascetic
part of it) was the necessary foundation for revolutionary regeneration. "Our nation is wanting in strength," he begins. The
cultivation of physical and mental tranquillity, the contemplation advocated by Buddha and Lao Tzu, is not the way to
obtain it. Instead "rude and savage" exercise is the path to
strength, for exercise is the basis even of the intellectual knowledge that gives a man and a country power: "Physical education not only strengthens the body but also enhances our
knowledge. . . . Physical strength is required to undertake the
study of the numerous modern sciences, whether in school or
through independent study [cf. Mao's self-education?]. He who
is equal to this is the man with a strong body. . . ." And the
psychic significance of asceticism and displaced libido is
strongly sounded in Mao's declaration that "we often observe
that the weak are enslaved by their sentiments and are incapable of mastering them. Those whose senses are imperfect or
whose limbs are defective are often enslaved by excessive passion, and reason is incapable of saving them. Hence it may be
called an invariable law that when the body is perfect and
healthy, the sentiments are also correct. . . ."[44] Thus it was not
just physique, honed by spartan, ascetic training, that prepared
Mao for the Long March and for guerrilla warfare in general;
the correct "sentiments," the control and mastery of passions,
were equally essential.

As part of the correct "sentiments," one other psychic con-
tribution to Mao's Long March abilities concerns his reliance

on the peasants for sustenance. For example, Mao tells us that while at Changsha Normal School he read an account in a newspaper—the ubiquitous source of ideas in Mao's life!—of two Chinese students traveling across China. That summer Mao decided to journey through five counties, accompanied by another student named Siao-Yu (in Siao-Yu's version of the trip it is his idea, and Mao accompanies him!). "We walked through these five counties without using a single copper," Mao recalls with pleasure. "The peasants fed us and gave us a place to sleep; wherever we went we were kindly treated and welcomed" (p. 144). This note of peasant sustenance and friendliness occurs throughout Mao's account (on another occasion he is escaping from the Kuomintang, and "On the road I met a peasant who befriended me, gave me shelter and later guided me to the next district" [p. 168]). What is its "meaning"?

Some of his remarks merely reflect the standard rhetoric of revolution. However, on the deepest personal level, it signifies Mao's feeling that the peasants are like his mother: "Kind ... generous and sympathetic ... ever ready to share...." They are nurturant. On the more obvious level, they offer Mao the emotional sustenance for a belief in guerrilla warfare. Combined with his personal asceticism and its denial of need and desire, the reliance for nourishment and care on the peasants— the one acceptable outlet for his dependency feelings— provided a powerful faith and trust underlying Mao's chosen method of fighting. On the more rational level, Mao's perception of the peasants became the basis for his transformation of Marxist-Leninist ideology in the direction of a peasant revolution. Neither the 1934 Long March, nor the 1927 "Report of an Investigation into the Peasant Movement in Hunan," would have had the same meaning for Mao if his psychological perception of the peasants had not been so personal in nature.

X

ASCETICISM, as was stated in Chapter 3, is only one device by which the adolescent controls the libidinal feelings that threaten to overwhelm him. Another defense is intellectualization. Here, as Anna Freud reminded us, "the *thinking-over* of the instinctual conflict" can be safely undertaken. "The task which asceticism sets itself is to keep the id within limits by simply imposing prohibitions; the aim of intellectualization is to link up instinctual processes closely with ideational contents and so to render them accessible to consciousness and amenable to control."[45] The demand for revolution outside, therefore, may be aided by the revolution already taking place inside.

In his adolescent intellectualization, Mao showed the same vacillation as in his career choice. As we have already noted, he was strongly influenced by the "idealism" of his future father-in-law, Yang Ch'ang-chi, who was himself a disciple of the English idealist T. H. Green (and, shades of our ascetic work ethic, also of Samuel Smiles, the nineteenth-century English author of such works as *Self-Help* and *Lives of the Engineers*). Even before this Mao had come under the influence of two great reformers, Liang Ch'i-ch'ao and K'ang Yu-wei. As with his entire generation, the famous magazine of the literary renaissance, *New Youth*, exerted its sway over Mao's mind, and its editors and contributors, Ch'ên Tu-hsiu and Hu Shih, became dominant figures in Mao's intellectual development. (In the case of Ch'ên the influence also became personal, and we shall explore this aspect briefly a little later on.) Thus, in the spring of 1918 when he graduated from Changsha Normal School, Mao could say, "At this time my mind was a curious mixture of ideas of liberalism, democratic reformism, and Utopian Socialism" (p. 147).

It is not to our purpose here to trace Mao's intellectual odyssey in detail. That is well done, for example, by Stuart R. Schram in his *Political Thought of Mao Tse-tung*. We are concerned only with two facts: Mao's initial, youthful vacillation as to ideology, and his eventual "total" commitment to communism as the "intellectualization," to use Anna Freud's term, wherein his instinctual drives were effectively "bound" for the rest of his life. Interestingly, one of Mao's earliest intellectual flirtations was with an ideology that *seemed* to offer the minimum of binding and restraint: anarchism. In fact, of course, anarchism offers intense *inner* controls (often ascetic) with the minimum of *external* bonds. In any case, as he wrote a friend, by 1920 Mao had become convinced of "the impossibility of a society without power or organization." He summed up his position by saying, "For all the reasons just stated, my present viewpoint on absolute liberalism, anarchism, and even democracy is that these things are fine in theory, but not feasible in practice . . ." (p. 216).

The ideology that linked theory and practice for Mao was Marxism. The Russian Revolution showed Mao the practice, and his readings—for example, *The Communist Manifesto* and Kautsky's *Class Struggle*—gave him the requisite theory. In coming to this position, Mao first rejected the "democratic" teachings of Hu Shih, the Deweyan pragmatist. He then submitted himself to the positive influences of Ch'ên Tu-hsiu, the editor of *New Youth*, and Li Ta-chao, who joined the editorial board of the paper in the fall of 1918. Ch'ên, in the May 4th period, was a "radical Westernizer" who by 1919 had established contact with the Comintern and begun to make the arrangements that led to the formation of the CCP. Li Ta-chao played a leading role in its organization.

These two men became the guiding spirits for Mao, leading him into communism. As Schram puts it, talking of Ch'ên and Li:

Without doing too much violence to the truth, one can say that the former was above all a Westernizer, who turned to Communism as the most efficient method for modernizing Chinese society, whereas the latter was a nationalist, who saw in the Leninist theory of imperialism a justification for his chauvinistic views. Mao owes something to both, but more to Li than to Ch'ên.[46]

Mao, in his own account, says:

Under Li Ta-chao, as assistant librarian at Peking National University [a post secured for Mao by his future father-in-law, Yang Ch'ang-chi] I had rapidly developed toward Marxism, and Ch'ên Tu-hsiu had been instrumental in my interests in that direction too. I had discussed with Ch'ên, on my second visit to Shanghai, the Marxist books that I had read, and Ch'ên's own assertions of belief had deeply impressed me at what was probably a critical period in my life (p. 157).

In any case, whosoever's influence, Ch'ên's or Li's, was greater, I think Schram is right in arguing that:

While Mao is a deeply convinced Leninist revolutionary, and while the categories in which he reasons are Marxist categories, the deepest springs of his personality are, to a large extent, to be found in the Chinese tradition, and China's glory is at least as important to him as is world revolution.[47]

All in all, then, Mao is a "nationalistic" revolutionary at the same time as he is Leninist. It is in this light that we ought to understand his ideological commitment, his intellectualization of impulse, as when he tells us, "By the summer of 1920 I had become, in theory and to some extent in action, a Marxist, and from this time on I considered myself a Marxist" (pp. 156–157).

XI

"IN MY LAST YEAR in school my mother died," Mao tells us, "and more than ever I lost interest in returning home" (p. 149). The death of Mao's mother in 1919 freed him from the last ties binding him to home; it may also have freed him to love and marry another woman. Mao was also appointed the next year (1920) to the post of director of the primary school attached to the First Normal School, and this undoubtedly also made it financially possible for him to marry Yang K'ai-hui. In any case, in 1921 Mao married the daughter of his former ethics teacher, Yang Ch'ang-chi. In his autobiography he announced this fact immediately after stating that he now had a fixed ideology: "From this time on I considered myself a Marxist. In the same year I married Yang K'ai-hui" (pp. 155–156).

Even before his marriage, in 1918, as we have already noted, on the recommendation of his future father-in-law, Mao had also secured his first real job. He had been given the position of library assistant by Li Ta-chao, the university librarian at Peking National University. It was obviously a fateful appointment. Mao was now exposed to Li's ideas as well as his personality, and was caught up in the center of the movement to reform and radicalize China. As at school, however, Mao initially felt that he was being scorned and marked off by his lowly position:

My office was so low that people avoided me. One of my tasks was to register the names of people who came to read newspapers, but to most of them I didn't exist as a human being. Among those who came to read I recognized the names of famous leaders of the renaissance movement, men like Fu Ssu-nien, Lo Chai-lung, and others, in whom I was intensely interested. I tried to begin conversations with them on political and cultural subjects, but they were very busy men. They had no time to listen to an assistant librarian speaking southern dialect (p. 150).

Mao's isolation and ignominy did not last long. He had now found his true calling in life, and had begun to find his place in the changes taking place in China. By the end of 1920 his wavering as to a life plan was over. At the age of twenty-seven Mao had passed through the pains of his instinctual, vocational, and intellectual growth, and emerged into maturity. He had embraced many of the controlled ascetic and libidinal qualities extolled in his article on physical culture, but allowed himself the luxury of falling in love and marrying. He had dallied over a number of careers, and then chosen first to be a teacher, and then, moved by fate and history, to be a revolutionary. He had quietly explored a number of ideological positions, and then settled firmly and irrevocably on Marxism. Thus the mold of Mao's personal development had largely set. It remained now for Mao to test his personality in the fires of China's experience after 1920.[48]

XII

MOST OF OUR ANALYSIS of Mao is now finished. His personal history henceforth becomes submerged in the public history of the Chinese Revolution, or, rather, mingled with it. However, before entering on a brief recital of Mao's role in the evolution of the CCP and the Chinese Revolution, one other personal episode can profitably be looked at for our purposes. Once in Peking, Mao became more and more involved in politics. He journeyed with other students to Shanghai, but did not leave with them for France. Instead, Mao turned *back* to China, visiting Confucius' grave and Mencius' birthplace. (Unlike Chou En-lai, Mao never left China, except for two short sojourns in Moscow.) Eventually returning to Changsha, this time as a teacher, Mao involved himself in the activities of the Hsin Min Hsüeh Hui (New People's Study Society).[49]

This society had a program, as Mao informs us, "for the 'independence' of Hunan, meaning, really, autonomy". Disgusted with the Northern Government, and believing that Hunan could modernize more rapidly if freed from connections with Peking, our group agitated for separation" (p. 154). It is curious that future nationalist Mao should start out as a separatist of sorts (one is reminded of Adolf Hitler's separatist *putsch* in Bavaria; he, too, became a rabid "nationalist"). As for the word "modernize," Mao intends by it reform rather than, say, industrialization. In fact, as he tells us, the separatists aimed at a "bourgeois democracy."

Was there a "personal" as well as "political" aspect to Mao's involvement in this Hunan separatism (which is, like all regional affiliations in China, a very complex problem not yet well understood)? We have certain hints to this effect in Mao's earlier statements. His sensitivity to regionalism was first made apparent at the Hsiang Hsiang school, where he tells us that he was disliked because he was not a native of the district. More importantly, as a library assistant at Peking University he felt that he was not listened to because he was "speaking southern dialect." Is it too speculative to believe that Mao, along with many of his provincial compatriots, sought his first tentative political identity as Hunanese? And only when this failed did he go on to a greater Chinese identity? Psychologically, Mao's Hunanese separatism must be important; politically, it was a dead end. Paucity of information on the subject prevents us from further speculation.

In any case, the separatist movement failed. The way it failed, and, moreover, the psychological meaning of that failure for Mao, is important. Led by a militarist called Chao Hêng-t'i,

Mao's group attacked the provincial parliament—and won.
"However," Mao explains, "when Chao Hêng-t'i seized control
he betrayed all the ideas he had supported.... Our society
therefore turned the struggle against him." The theme of betrayal is critical here. In this particular case it is linked to the
betrayal of "democracy," and Mao draws the stringent conclusion, "From this time on I became more and more convinced
that only mass political power, secured through mass action,
could guarantee the realization of dynamic reforms" (p. 155).
But everywhere in Mao's account betrayal is present as a
possibility.

Mao usually remarks on betrayal in the context of a listing of
names in some society or organization. In this respect his autobiography is almost a "Who's Who" of the Chinese Revolution.
Thus, talking about Yu Sha-t'ou, who was made commander of
the Communist First Army, Mao tells us that "soon afterwards
he deserted and joined the Kuomintang. He is now working for
Chiang Kai-shek at Nanking" (p. 168). Mao continues,
"Cheng Hao was made commander of the remaining troops,
about one regiment; he, too, later on 'betrayed' " (p. 169). As
Mao tells of these betrayals, he exhibits remarkably little affect.
Clearly, at a time of constantly shifting allegiances, betrayal
had become a commonplace. Yet at the deepest level of being
we can assume an affect of basic anxiety and distrust. Defense
against these threatening feelings might naturally take the form
of withdrawal of affectionate feeling, helping to produce what I
have earlier called the leader with few libidinal ties. I think
Mao reacted in this manner.

As for the "Who's Who" aspect of Mao's account, that could
serve a number of functions. It could place Mao in the context
of leadership in the Revolution; it could show his familiarity
with the other "great men" of his time; it could be the mere
reminiscing of an "elder statesman" about his companions; and
it could be the discharge of an historical duty. There is one
special aspect to this "naming," however, that we need to note.
It emerges in Mao's listing of the first society he helped organize: the Hsin Min Hsüeh Hui (New People's Study Society)
of his Changsha days. He tells that it had from seventy to
eighty members, and of these "many were later to become

famous names in Chinese Communism." I select for my purposes: "Ho Hsien-hôn, who became high judge of the Supreme Court in the Central Soviet regions and was later killed by Chiang Kai-shek; Kuo Liang, a famous labour-organizer, killed by General Ho Chien in 1930 . . . Ts'ai Ho-sheng, a member of the Central Committee of the Communist Party, killed by Chiang Kai-shek in 1927 . . . ," and so the list goes on (including, of course, a "betrayer": "Yeh Li-yûn, who became a member of the Central Committee, and later 'betrayed' to the Kuomintang") (pp. 146–147).

In many ways, then, Mao's list is a "death" list, an obituary column of the Revolution. And Mao, of course, is the survivor. This extremely important aspect of Mao's psychology has been well explored by Robert Lifton in his book, *Revolutionary Immortality: Mao Tse-tung and the Chinese Cultural Revolution*,[50] and we need not do more than call renewed attention to Mao's survival "guilt" and the transcendence of that guilt in his quest for immortality.

XIII

THE REST of Mao's account is mainly public history. In May 1921 Mao went to Shanghai to attend the foundation meeting of the CCP. He specifically notes that "there was only one other Hunanese at the historic first meeting in Shanghai" (p. 157). Mao quickly became the secretary of the Hunan branch of the party, spending his time organizing students and workers ("the work of the Communist Party was then concentrated mainly on students and workers, and very little was done among the peasants") (p. 158).

There are a few curious lacunae about Mao's role in these early Communist years. For example, Mao tells us that he did not attend the Second Congress of the party in 1922. "I intended to attend. However, I forgot the name of the place where it was to be held, could not find any comrades, and missed it" (p. 159). This is incomprehensible.[51] Mao's memory, as all those lists attest, was fabulous. At the Congress

itself, the momentous decision was taken to have the CCP col-
laborate with the nationalists; eventually this led to Communists participating in the Kuomintang as individual members. Why should Mao have missed this meeting?

Similarly, Mao tells us how in the winter of 1924, "I returned to Hunan for a rest. I had become ill in Shanghai, but
while in Hunan I organized the nucleus of the great peasant
movement of that province" (p. 159). What could have been
the nature of Mao's illness, the only such "mortality" of which
he gives evidence in his autobiography? We are told nothing. I
have the strong suspicion that Mao's absence from the Second
Congress and his illness in Shanghai would be personally revealing as well as politically self-serving, but we shall probably
never know in what way. In his autobiography he gives only
these tantalizing hints.

Mao, like all the other Communists after 1922, worked in
collaboration with the Kuomintang. Here the issue of who was
using whom, and who was betraying whom, must have been
acute. Yet Mao's pattern of a one-knee *k'ou-t'ou* probably
made the compromise easier for him than for others, and therefore accompanied by less psychological affect than might be
expected.

Mao's turn to the peasant is of the greatest significance, and
we have tried to suggest the personal aspects of this relationship. Mao states that "Formerly I had not fully realized the
degree of class struggle among the peasantry, but after the May
30th Incident [1925], and during the great wave of political
activity which followed it, the Hunanese peasantry became very
militant" (p. 160). By 1927 Mao was ready to write his
famous "Report of an Investigation into the Peasant Movement
in Hunan," which he does not even mention in his account! In
any case, as is too well known to need further discussion, Mao
had opened a new chapter in Marxist-Leninism as well as in
communist revolutions by advocating not only the *use* of the
peasantry as a revolutionary force (this was already in Lenin),
but the idea that the peasantry was also the *source* and *basis* of
the CCP itself.

This "revolutionary" idea as to revolution brought Mao into
conflict not only with members of his own party, but ultimately

with the Russian Communist party. In 1926 this meant Boro-din, the chief Russian adviser to the CCP. Later it shaped Mao's relations to Stalin and then to Khrushchev (along with many other factors). Our only interest here is in raising the question of Mao's feelings about the *parent* Russian organiza-tion and ideology, as these feelings worked themselves out in time, and as they took their origin from the psychological pat-terns in relation to authority that we have tried to discern in the youthful Mao. We can, of course, do no more than raise the issue.

Mao's relations to the peasantry, the Kuomintang, and the Soviet Union are part of the tactics and strategy of his climb to political power. In the process Mao had to break with one of his "teachers," Ch'ên Tu-hsiu, and eventually to replace him as leader of the CCP. Psychologically, it was necessary for Mao to free himself from Ch'ên's tutelage, and thus to be able to grasp titular power for himself. Once in power, except for relations with the Russians, and possibly the post-Great Leap Forward developments, Mao's "authority" problem, *at least in its origi-nal form*, was a thing of the past.

Ch'ên, as we recall, was editor of the *New Youth*, studied so avidly by Mao, and one of the two key founders of the CCP (Li Ta-chao was the other). In his magazine Ch'ên had announced that "It is the youth who must save this great revolution from the powers of the past." As Lifton summarizes it, "The modern student was even given a blueprint for the identity change asked of him: the 'old youth'—weak, effeminate, devoid of militancy, seeking only wealth and high position—was to be supplanted by the 'new youth'—courageous, strong, free of parental domi-nation, idealistic and patriotic."[52]

Mao took Ch'ên's teachings literally, even to the point of throwing off Ch'ên's "parental domination." (In this, of course, he was in correspondence with the reality of the party's disown-ing of Ch'ên in 1927.) As Mao retells the story of the tortured relationship, in 1921 Ch'ên had "been instrumental" in Mao's conversion to Marxism. "I had discussed with Ch'ên . . . the Marxist books that I had read, and Ch'ên's own assertions of belief had deeply impressed me at what was probably a critical period in my life" (p. 157). By about 1925, however, when

Mao was writing pamphlets emphasizing his new conception of
the peasantry, matters had changed: "Ch'ên Tu-hsiu opposed
the opinions expressed [in one of Mao's pamphlets]...,
which advocated a radical land policy and vigorous organization of the peasantry, under the Communist Party, and he refused its publication in the Communist central organs. I began
to disagree with Ch'ên's Right opportunist policy about this
time, and we gradually drew further apart, although the struggle between us did not come to a climax until 1927" (p. 161).

The climax came about, according to Mao, as follows:

When the Fifth Conference was convened in Wuhan in May, 1927,
the Party was still under the domination of Ch'ên Tu-hsiu. Although Chiang Kai-shek had already led the counter-revolution and
begun his attacks on the Communist Party in Shanghai and Nanking, Ch'ên was still for moderation and concessions to the Wuhan
Kuomintang. Overriding all opposition, he followed a Right opportunist petty-bourgeois policy. I was very dissatisfied with the Party
policy then, especially towards the peasant movement.... But
Ch'ên Tu-hsiu violently disagreed. He did not understand the role
of the peasantry in the revolution and greatly underestimated its
possibilities at this time. Consequently, the Fifth Conference, held
on the eve of the crisis of the Great Revolution, failed to pass an
adequate land programme. My opinions, which called for rapid
intensification of the agrarian struggle, were not even discussed, for
the Central Committee, also dominated by Ch'ên Tu-hsiu, refused
to bring them up for consideration (p. 162).

Here we must pause to note that Mao's account may not be
quite accurate. As Schram explains the 1925 pamphlet episode:

In his autobiography, Mao claims that Ch'ên Tu-hsiu opposed the
publication of his article on the classes of Chinese society because
it called for "a radical land policy and vigorous organization of the
peasantry, under the Communist Party." Nothing of the kind is
stated or implied, even in the revised version of 1951. On the other
hand, the earlier article on the peasantry does end with the statement that the peasants should "struggle" against the landlords and
"overthrow them altogether" in special circumstances, where they
are particularly reactionary and evil. In making the statement regarding Ch'ên's attitude in 1926 Mao perhaps confused these two
articles. But Ch'ên's principal objection to both articles was probably that they were simply too crude.

It is possible that Mao's notion that Ch'ên blocked discussion of his opinions in 1927 may also be more "psychic" than "actual" reality.

In any case, the counterrevolution by Chiang Kai-shek, starting in April 1927 when he decimated the workers' organizations in Shanghai and killed Li Ta-Chao, brought actuality to a head. Again we follow Mao's account:

Many Communist leaders were now ordered by the Party to leave the country, go to Russia or Shanghai or places of safety. I was ordered to go to Szechuan. I persuaded Ch'ên Tu-hsiu to send me to Hunan instead, as secretary of the Provincial Committee, but after ten days he ordered me hastily to return, accusing me of organizing an uprising against T'ang Sheng-chih, then in command at Wuhan. The affairs of the Party were now in a chaotic state. Nearly everyone was opposed to Ch'ên Tu-hsiu's leadership and his opportunist line. The collapse of the entente at Wuhan soon afterwards brought about his downfall (p. 163).

Discussing these events in retrospect with Snow in 1936, Mao claimed that "objectively," Ch'ên was an "unconscious traitor":

Ch'ên was really frightened of the workers and especially of the armed peasants. Confronted at last with the reality of armed insurrection he completely lost his senses. He could no longer see clearly what was happening, and his petty-bourgeois intincts betrayed him into panic and defeat. He did not show other Party leaders the orders of the Comintern, nor even discuss them with us (p. 165).

Mao describes the end for Ch'ên:

On August 1, 1927, the 20th Army, under Ho Lung and Yeh T'ing, and in co-operation with Chu Teh, led the historic Nanchang Uprising, and the beginning of what was to become the Red Army was organized. A week later, on August 7, an extraordinary meeting of the Central Committee of the Party deposed Ch'ên Tu-hsiu as secretary. I had been a member of the political bureau of the Party since the Third Conference at Canton in 1924, and was active in this decision (p. 166).

Four crowded years later, in 1931, the first All-Chinese Congress of Soviets proclaimed the establishment of the Chinese Soviet Republic, and elected Mao president.

In the person of Ch'ên, Mao had carried through his identification with his teachers to the point of "cannibalistically" assimilating them. In its way, this is the ultimate tribute. Politically, Mao had learned Marxism from Ch'ên and then broken with him on the issues of collaborating with the Kuomintang, basing Communist policy on the cities, and relying mainly on the workers rather than the peasants. Henceforward, Mao's ideology in these matters was set, and his policies ultimately became the policies of the CCP. It was his elevation to leader of the CCP that permitted him to implement his policies. I have tried to suggest here that, on the personal level, his elevation to leadership involved a complex and ambivalent displacement of his earlier mentor, Ch'ên Tu-hsiu. It goes without saying that, on the nonpersonal level, the situation just described is the classical Marxist one of controversy over the correct "party line."

XIV

THE NANCHANG uprising not only deposed Ch'ên Tu-hsiu but, more importantly, led to the formation of the Red Army. And the Red Army made the "New Youth" into "New Men." Mao's initial role in this momentous development was to organize the movement in Changsha which later became known as the Autumn Crop uprising. Recruits for the Hunan army came from the peasantry, miners, and the insurrectionist troops of the Kuomintang. As Mao described this little army, "Discipline was poor, political training was at a low level, and many wavering elements were among the men and officers" (pp. 168–169). Hemmed in by the Kuomintang, it nevertheless managed to break through and, a thousand strong, climb up Chingkanshan to safety.

As Snow describes it, "Chingkanshan was a nearly impregnable mountain stronghold, formerly held by bandits" (p. 169). "Running away" to a mountain is a pattern of Chinese history, and of Mao's personal inspiration, that we have already noted, and it will repeat itself in 1934. We are reminded of Mao's hero of the secret society who also withdrew to a local mountain (and was beheaded). And we recall Mao's boyhood fondness for reading "the romances of Old China, and especially stories of rebellions." The enemies of Mao and the CCP were quick to label his army as "Red Bandits," and bandits *did* join the army at Chingkanshan, as Mao himself tells us.

But Mao's "bandits" did not remain "primitive rebels," in the sense so intriguingly spelled out by E. J. Hobsbawm in his book of that name.[54] They were given a new discipline and educated in unifying ideology. Mao's description of this process is as follows:

> Gradually the Red Army's work with the masses improved, discipline strengthened, and a new technique in organization developed. The peasantry everywhere began to volunteer to help the revolution. As early as Chingkanshan the Red Army had imposed three simple rules of discipline upon its fighters, and these were: prompt obedience to orders; no confiscations whatever from the poor peasantry; and prompt delivery directly to the Government, for its disposal, of all goods confiscated from the landlords. After the 1928 Conference emphatic efforts to enlist the support of the peasantry were made, and eight rules were added to the three listed above. These were as follows:
> 1. Replace all doors when you leave a house;
> 2. Return and roll up the straw matting on which you sleep;
> 3. Be courteous and polite to the people and help them when you can:
> 4. Return all borrowed articles;
> 5. Replace all damaged articles;
> 6. Be honest in all transactions with the peasants;
> 7. Pay for all articles purchased;
> 8. Be sanitary, and especially establish latrines a safe distance from people's houses (p. 176).

The new discipline laid the basis for guerrilla warfare (or as Mao calls it, "partisan warfare"). Giving to the peasants, as many of the old bandits had done, Mao's men no longer preyed on the peasantry, as had the bandits. Armed with an ideology preaching the giving of land to the peasants, the Communist armies were in a special position to be "like the fish that swim in the ocean of the peasantry." This partisan-peasant relationship became the tactical basis on which Mao and his cohorts fought their way to power.

Fundamentally, Mao's role in the military was political and

organizational. He informs us that at one point he became the actual "commander" of the Chingkanshan army, and there is some evidence that he was a competent strategist. More generally he served as political commissar, holding this or similar positions in a bewildering array of Communist army formations. Like others, Mao was instrumental in setting up the earliest Soviets, where consolidation of a military situation with a political-social organization could be effected. At the time he was against a terrorist policy of raiding and killing landlords, and for this policy was branded by his opponents as "reformist." With his commitment to a "compromise" policy, Mao also espoused "slow but regular development" as against the "putschists." He opposed pitched battles and attacks on cities, and favored patient conversion of the peasants and establishment of model Soviets.

At the beginning Mao's policies brought him into conflict with the CCP leadership, and he was even dismissed in 1927 from the Politbureau. Gradually Mao's views, and the practical results flowing from them, prevailed. By 1931, as we noted, he was president of the Chinese Soviet Republic, and in 1935 was at last named president of the Central Committee of the Party.

Mao does not tell us about his political rise in the 1930s (and the details are still not clear to this day). Aside from two personal episodes, the rest of his autobiography is about the campaigns of the Red Army and the efforts of Chiang Kai-shek to exterminate them. The first episode, which we have already noted, concerns his arrest by the Kuomintang and his seemingly miraculous escape, including a peasant befriending him. The second personal episode follows:

My name was known among the Hunanese peasants, for big rewards were offered for my capture, dead or alive, as well as for Chu Teh and other Reds. My land in Hsiang T'an was confiscated by the Kuomintang. My wife and my sister, as well as the wives of my two brothers, Mao Tse-hung and Mao Tse-tan, and my own son, were all arrested by Ho Chien. My wife and younger sister were executed. The others were later released. The prestige of the Red Army even extended to my own village, Hsiang T'an, for I heard the tale that the local peasants believed that I would be soon returning to my native home. When one day an aeroplane passed overhead, they decided it was I. They warned the man who was then tilling my land that I had come back to look over my old farm, to see whether or not any trees had been cut. If so, I would surely demand compensation from Chiang Kai-shek, they said (pp. 179–180).

Interestingly, the one member of Mao's family whose death or eventual fate is never mentioned is Mao's father. From Mao's account we have no idea of how or when he died. This is rather unfilial behavior, especially in China, as we have pointed out.

As for the Red Army, we are told about its victories over Chiang Kai-shek's increasingly large extermination campaigns. It is David defeating Goliath. In 1934, however, Chiang's pressure became too great, and the famous Long March began. For the first time in his autobiography Mao becomes lyrical. It is worth quoting the whole passage:

Through many, many difficulties, across the longest and deepest and most dangerous rivers of China, across some of its highest and most hazardous mountain passes, through the country of fierce aborigines, through the empty grasslands, through cold and through intense heat, through wind and snow and rainstorm, pursued by half the White armies of China, through all these natural barriers, and fighting its way past the local troops of Kwangtung, Hunan, Kwangsi, Kweichow, Yunnan, Sikong, Szechuan, Kansu and Shensi, the Red Army at last reached northern Shensi in October, 1935, and enlarged the present base in China's great North-west (pp. 187–188).

Mao's analysis of the meaning of this march, in his concluding autobiographical paragraph, is even more revealing:

The victorious march of the Red Army, and its triumphant arrival in Kansu and Shensi with its living forces still intact, was due first to the correct leadership of the Communist Party, and secondly to the great skill, courage, determination and almost *super-human* [italics added] endurance and revolutionary ardour of the basic cadres of our Soviet people. The Communist Party of China was, is, and will ever be, faithful to Marxist-Leninism, and it will continue its struggles against every opportunist tendency. In this determination lies one explanation of its invincibility and the certainty of its final victory (p. 188).

"Super-human"; this is the quality in Mao himself that we have been trying to understand in terms of what we have called revolutionary asceticism. It is time for us to analyze the manner in which this particular element in Mao's personality takes its place in the complexity of his whole character.

XV

ANYONE who has observed children, once Freud has pointed the way, can see that they go through feeding problems, toilet training, an Oedipus complex, and so on, with important psychological as well as physical results. The passage of some children through these stages is so smooth and "natural" that it is hardly perceptible. For others, such as Mao, the turmoil can be enormous, often with enormous consequences for good and evil. When the personal turmoil is matched with historical turmoil, the result can literally be revolutionary.

Whatever else occurred in Mao's development we can see the presence of a tremendous father-son conflict. Based on Mao's own perceptions, *this* conflict is the dominant motif in his life. (I have suggested that a partial resolution took place in terms of Mao's successful identification with, as well as transcendence of, his father.) Mao's own parental struggle merged with the fate of China. The problem of rightful authority for China became intertwined with the problem of the rightful authority to be accorded his father by Mao. The problem of how China should be controlled became involved with the problem of how Mao should control himself.

This epic struggle over authority and control colored, often in subtle ways, all the other views and actions of Mao's life. Not the only psychological dynamic in Mao's personality, it strikes me as the most significant (and the one on which he gives us the fullest report). I have tried to sketch out its relation to many areas: Mao's ambivalence about being a student and a "bourgeois," a Hunanese, a classicist; his feelings toward the peasants; his attitude toward money; his concern with betrayal and with survival; and so on.

In this context we can analyze Mao as a revolutionary ascetic, our leader with few libidinal ties. Was he a true revolutionary ascetic? First, let us examine the counterevidence. Mao *did* marry, not once but thrice (not counting his first marriage, arranged by his family); at the time he was talking to Snow he had had three children by his "first" wife, Yang K'ai-hui, and several by his "second" wife.[55] Moreover, Snow reports that "Mao impressed me as a man of considerable depth of feeling. I remember that his eyes moistened once or twice when speaking of dead comrades, or recalling incidents in his youth..." (p. 78). Schram, discussing a recent poem dedicated by Mao to Yang K'ai-hui, concludes that he is "still capable of deep sentiment," and the writing of poetry in general is evidence of his feel for emotions. On a more trivial level perhaps, we learn that Mao was an inveterate cigarette smoker, not denying himself this pleasure (or necessity). And Snow adds that Mao has "a lively sense of humour and a love of rustic laughter" (p. 74).[56] Lastly, we can add that the young Mao, according to all the accounts we have seen, simply did not have charisma, as defined by Max Weber.

Whence, then, the claim of asceticism and displaced libido? Our emphasis and evidence have been as follows. Fundamental to his personal development was Mao's identification with his father, and this meant embracing the virtues of hard work, energetic activity, and frugality. Mao attached these personal traits to China's need for rejuvenation, and advocated physical culture as the required cure. In his prescription, physical culture as such was also the prerequisite for thought control. The ultimate development of this line of thought can be seen in the mental and physical ability to withstand the rigors of partisan warfare, and especially of the Long March.

It can also be seen in two other areas: the Red Army and the program of thought reform. Snow's description of the Red Army is to the point. He called it, in 1936, "the only politically iron-clad army in China" (p. 278). The allusion to Cromwell's army is borne out by the additional statement that "very few of the Reds smoked or drank: abstention was one of the 'eight disciplines' of the Red Army." Moreover, we are told, "the majority of the soldiers as well as officers of the Red Army were unmarried. Many of them were 'divorced'—that is, they had left their wives and families behind them." Indeed, according to Snow, most of these "Red fighters were still virgins" (pp. 278–281). In spite of his "inveterate smoking" (and, others would add, wenching), Mao, as their leader, had to share, or at least appear to share, most of their controls and disciplines.

Thought reform, which came into being mainly after the triumph of the "puritanical" Red Army, added a disregard for "feelings" (or at least traditional feelings) to the Army's asceticism. Mao himself, in a speech of 1942, laid down the basic tenets: "Two principles must be observed. The first is 'punish the past to warn the future' and the second, 'save men by curing their ills.' Past errors must be exposed *with no thought of personal feelings or face*" [italics added].[57] By denying personal feelings, we can "save" the man by converting him, as Mao had been converted, to the true faith and behavior. Similarly, in an essay, "In Opposition to Liberalism," Mao's bad example is "failing to start an argument in principle with a person . . . letting things slide for the sake of peace or cordiality, all because he is an old friend, a fellow villager, a fellow student, a close friend, *someone beloved* [italics added]. . . ." Robert Lifton's comment on this passage is apt:

Mao is referring here mainly to the principles of personal loyalty, propriety, and harmony carried over from the filial identity of traditional Chinese culture. All these principles are then viewed in terms of individual character, and "liberalism" is extended to include "refusing to consider correction of your errors even when you recognize them, adopting a liberal attitude toward yourself." Liberalism becomes equated with laxity, softness, and self-indulgence. Here, the traditional Chinese considerations for "human feelings" —that special tolerance for individual frailty which gave balance to an otherwise rigid Confucian system—is under fire; and so is the modern liberal ethic which also urges respect for individual differences.

"Sentimentalism" has essentially the same significance as the personal side of "liberalism," and refers mainly to a reluctance to sacrifice personal loyalties, and especially those of family, to political (Communist) considerations. This is primarily an attack upon traditional practices, although a modern liberal can also be guilty of sentimentalism in connection with his concern for other people as individuals.

Even more apt for our purpose is Lifton's further statement that "In this sense, all of Thought Reform is an attempt to emulate Mao Tse-tung's own example and 'out-grow' one's class characteristics by changing from one class to another."[58]

Mao not only "outgrew" his class characteristics. To a large extent, he also "outgrew" his sentimental feelings. I have already suggested that, in finally identifying with his father, Mao rejected the "softness" represented by his mother. Just as with Lenin and his followers, "hardness" and "masculinity" became the prime virtues. Well could the young Mao have said what his youthful Red Guards are reputed to have said much later: "Demolition bombs and hand grenades will be thrown.... Let what is called 'human affection'... get out of the way.!"[59]

Thus, though married and with children, the image that Mao projected—and that is what is critical for our ideal type of revolutionary leader—and to a large extent embodied, was of the leader with few libidinal ties. Fear of betrayal, both of himself and of the Revolution, a recurrent experience in his life, must have enforced in him a rigorous suppression of feeling. And that feeling, as Snow and Schram have pointed out, ran deep and strong. The Freudian injunction that the strength of the repression indicates the power of the impulse holds doubly true. In Mao's case, the repression was not only unconscious, out of personal needs, but extremely conscious as well, out of stringent political requirements.

These political requirements, as we have already suggested, corresponded with elements of traditional Chinese culture. Numerous scholars underline the fact that warm affection plays almost no role in Chinese family life, with the exception of the mother-son relation. As Francis Hsu puts it, in contrast to the American stress on emotions, there is the "tendency of the Chinese to underplay all matters of the heart."[60] Where the expression of sentiment is allowed, it is in terms of proper forms and correct rituals.

Hence Mao's displaced libidinal quality, in itself only a matter of degree, could draw upon the existing style of Chinese life. How atypical Mao was is difficult to say. If one can believe his childhood friend Siao-Yu, who later broke with him, Mao was unusually notable for his absence of sentiments—"no sentiments whatever" is the accusation of a number of their friends, and one young lady fortune teller supposedly predicted, "You could kill ten thousand or even a hundred thousand people without turning a single hair."[61] Whatever the truth of Siao's memories, we do know that Mao learned to control or eliminate most personal affections and place them in the service of revolution—the displacement of libido we have talked about—and to steel himself, and his followers, to whatever political action was necessary.

One of those actions was to try to break up social relations, especially the family, as they had traditionally existed. Where grandparents, in-laws, parents, and children had all lived under one roof, the Communists sought to alter this arrangement, for example, "by assigning places of work, by stimulating population movement, by the work-study program and measures."[62] Again we must see that this accorded with the lack of stress on affection in Chinese families, manifesting itself in the fact that a peasant father might often go off to labor elsewhere for two or three years, with such actions occurring long before Communism was ever heard of in China. Of course, the Maoist intent in breaking up the family was to break up the Confucian authority pattern, with its inhibition of aggression. While some "affection" might indirectly be liberated for use by the Communists, the concurrent aim was to place the newly freed aggression in the service of the revolution.

Similarly, Mao tightened the screw on the repression of sexual feelings, even seeking to eliminate its presence in literary works. But this "puritanism" must be seen in its Chinese context, as when the anthropologist Francis Hsu attacks Westerners for mistakenly designating the Communist actions as "a Chinese puritanism forced upon the people by the new government. Nothing is further from the truth. Puritanism involves repression of sex, which is commensurate with the individual-centered approach to life. The new Chinese pattern is merely a more widespread and striking expression of the compartmentalization of sex, which is today, as in centuries past, still rooted in the situation-centered approach to the problems of existence."[63]

At every point, then, we see that Mao's revolutionary asceticism corresponded with aspects of Chinese culture (and must be interpreted in that context) as well as with needs of the revolution. Yet it is nonetheless a new development, both revolutionary and ascetic (which here includes displaced libido). Siao-Yu reports Mao as saying, "In order to reform a country one must be hard with one's self and it is necessary to victimize a part of the people."[64] The ideal was total hardness and control over oneself, as grounds for total control over one's followers. Mao, as we have tried to show, realized this only partly for himself, and his similar aim for China has also had only partial success.[65] This is merely to say that revolutionary asceticism is an ideal type, and that Mao and China are historical realities. The ideal type hopefully enables us better to understand some aspects of Mao's leadership of a fundamentally *Chinese* revolution, which is nevertheless a *revolution,* and thus subject to the same psychological relationships, historically exhibited by revolutions in general, whose pattern we have attempted to conceptualize.

CHAPTER 10

Conclusion

I

THE RELATIONS of leader and led are a constant subject of history, though their particular form and content are constantly changing. We have sought to examine a part of this relation, which we have placed under the rubric "revolutionary asceticism," as an ideal type. Our guides in this new revolutionary underworld have been Max Weber and Sigmund Freud. Taking Weber's notions of asceticism and charisma, and Freud's notions of displaced libido, masochism, sadism, and narcissism, we have tried to comprehend the way in which revolutionary asceticism serves the needs of the leader functionally in both the personal and political arena, and on both the conscious and unconscious level; then we have tried to do the same thing, rather more sketchily, for his followers.[1]

If we have been successful in this effort, the human-all-too-human qualities of Rousseau's godlike legislator should now be, to a large extent, comprehensible to us. The passions that move him, as well as some of his followers, should be apparent. Moreover, we should be able to understand these passions, not only in a more comprehensive surface fashion, but in a much deeper sense than before. Machiavelli's Prince, Rousseau's legislator, even Hegel's world hero trampling over existing morality: All of these we should be able to regard in a new and more revealing light.

We have also studied the revolutionary ascetic as an emerging historical figure in the period since the Puritan Revolution of 1640. Here our thesis has been that traits of asceticism and displaced libido, originally placed in the service of religion, were displaced first to the service of economic activity, and then to the service of revolutionary activity. Originally exhibited in the monastery, as Max Weber has shown, these traits emerged into the public realm as "worldly asceticism." By the late eighteenth century the caricature of the utilitarian confirmed the prevalence of the worldly ascetic. Characters such as Bounderby in Dickens' *Hard Times* epitomized the successful entrepreneur, self-made, breaking with his family, spurning all the softer emotions that stood in the way of success.

Prepared for by the utilitarian and Victorian entrepreneur, translated into a Russian model by Chernyshevsky and others, the revolutionary ascetic emerged full-blown in Europe at the end of the nineteenth century, and quickly became an international figure in the twentieth century. The revolutionary ascetic is a professional revolutionary who devotes his whole life, and love, to his profession (just as one of Weber's ascetic businessmen does to his business). In part he is a fusion of Weber's ascetic with a charismatic leader; of Freud's sadomasochist with a narcissist with few libidinal ties. From another aspect he is simply the professional doing his job according to ordinary functional necessity.

His key problem is control: of himself, of his followers, and of society at large. We have tried to analyze that problem of control primarily in terms of the Freudian concepts of libido, i.e., love, and aggression. Control, of course, is another way of saying power and authority, and these terms supply the terminal points to the line leading from individual psychology to political science. In our analysis we have been concerned with both the creativity involved in the revolutionary ascetic's achievement of self-control, and thus the ability to break with an old world in order to create a new one, and the danger that he (and his followers) will mistake conscious self-control, and then control of others, for the truer self-control that only knowledge of the unconscious can permit.

I I

THE UNCONSCIOUS is peculiarly the domain of psycho-analysis. Psychohistory tries to utilize psychoanalytic concepts and insights in regard to traditional materials in history and the social sciences, and reciprocally to reexamine psychoanalysis in the context offered by such materials. This present work on revolutionary ascetics has taken a few strands in psychohistory —some particular character traits—and sought to examine their role and function as manifested in leaders and led at selected moments in modern history. By setting up an ideal type, partly cogitated in pure thought and partly derived from the historical examples, we have tried to establish a definite character type: the revolutionary ascetic. The pure revolution-ary ascetic is a creature of imagination, like Hamlet or Iago, not to be met with as such in real life. Yet the pure type will call our attention more forcefully than otherwise to reality it-self.

In analyzing the pure type of revolutionary ascetic, and then its visible and partial representatives such as Cromwell, Robes-pierre, James Mill, Chernyshevsky, Lenin, and Mao, we have employed mainly libidinal theory. By and large, this has not led us to any significant reexamination of the psychoanalytic theory involved, except as employed by Freud in his effort to explain group psychology. As for other parts of psychoanalytic theory, such as concepts of sadism, masochism, asceticism, and so on, we can only claim to have discovered a paucity of psycho-analytic literature on the subject of asceticism, and thus point to a problem worth pursuing.

There are, of course, other ways of approaching the analysis of revolutionary leaders. The emphasis could have been on aggressive impulses, the other basic "instinct" along with libido recognized, though rather grudgingly, by Freud, and accorded increasing importance and prominence today. Only in passing have we mentioned puritan aggressive feelings, or Mao's ag-gressive impulses toward his father, and a good deal more could be made of the topic. So, too, we could have put more stress on object loss and its consequences, and the nature of real and symbolic object ties. Once again, it must simply be stated that this would be a supplementary (though not, I trust, contradictory) means of understanding the phenomena.[2]

As for predecessors in the analysis of revolutionary personalities, they have exhibited a strong tendency to look at their subjects in terms of the role of the Oedipus complex. Revolutionaries are seen as rebels against the father who, once in power, experience the "return of the repressed." This is undoubtedly true and important for some revolutionaries. Mao Tse-tung seems to me to fall most nicely under this heading. Nevertheless, I do not see the Oedipus complex as crucial to the formation of revolutionary ascetics. It *may* be the source of feelings of object loss, or pose the threat of too close libidinal ties, which need then to be totally rejected; but other etiologies for the development of asceticism and displaced libido, as I have tried to show, are just as likely to be present (and some of them conscious). In short, while acknowledging the tremendously important role of the Oedipus complex—Mao, again, is our best example—I have sought here to avoid overemphasis on what one of my friends has described as "oedipal-schmedipal."

I I I

CLEARLY, there have been revolutionary ascetics in the past. Will there be revolutionary ascetics in the future? To answer that question requires an estimate first as to the possibility of revolutions in the future, and a guess as to what types they might be.

The classical Marxist view of revolution, as promulgated in the nineteenth century, was that revolution would occur in the advanced, industrialized countries of the West. It would be proletarian, and it would be the "last" revolution. In fact, a successful proletarian revolution has not occurred in such countries as Great Britain, Germany, or the United States. Instead, as we have seen in our study of Lenin, revolution came to backward Russia in 1917 as the means of transforming her more rapidly into a modernized country. Later in the twentieth century, revolution has come to a whole host of underdeveloped and peasant countries, often as a means of nation building as well as modernization: China, Algeria, and Cuba come readily to mind as fitting parts of this picture.

By definition, once colonial, nation building, and modernizing revolutions have brought peoples into advanced industrial status (assuming the effort to be successful), we shall presumably have run out of the most promising potential revolutionary situations. If there are to be future revolutions, they will have to occur under different conditions; we have already seen that they have not yet occurred in the advanced industrial nations of the West, as predicted by the Marxists.

Will they nevertheless occur in the near future? If we take America as a possible model, the initial answer seems to be "no." As Barrington Moore, Jr., a scholar sympathetic to revolution, has asserted in a brilliant analysis of the conditions for revolution in America, old-style leftist revolution in America appears to be simply a chimera (rightist dictatorship, he believes, is the more likely outcome of an attempted left-wing takeover).[3]

But what of a new-style revolution, the so-called aesthetic (or counterculture) revolution which will serve as prelude to a political-social revolution?

In such an aesthetic revolution, as manifested, say, in America, the revolutionary impulse differs profoundly from the Russian or Chinese Communist revolutions which have engaged our attention in the persons of Lenin and Mao (or from the Cuban, Algerian, or Egyptian revolutions, if we had studied them as well). While these were modernizing and nationalistic, the recent (and perhaps continuing) American revolutionary impulse is nonnationalistic and nonmodernizing; indeed, we might say it is antinationalistic and antimodernization. Whereas in the past those in America who opposed the values of modernization were politically on the right, today they appear to be mainly on the left. It is a unique situation.

What is the nature of this aesthetic revolution? It is pro-

foundly antiascetic. It involves a rejection of the so-called puritan ethic, with its demand for hard work, restraint of impulse,
deferral of gratification, and general self-control. A possessor
of these former virtues is now widely looked upon as being
uptight. Swingers and TV advertisers alike exhort us to live
while we can, to take our pleasures now, and pay later (if at
all).

In back of their exhortations, of course, stands another, intellectual revolution: the Keynesian revolution. In somber and
highly technical language, the Keynesians pioneered the transition from production to consumption values. Saving was shifted
from the balance column of virtues to that of vices; deferment
of gratification was equated with a lag in utilization of produc-
tive resources. In other words, the puritanical is necessarily the
opposite of the affluent society.

The aesthetic revolution, then, with its removal of repression
and control in innumerable areas of personal behavior—sex,
clothes, manners, and drugs—is merely the public expression of
a long-term secular development. Its front-runners are the
young people, especially those in the more affluent universities
and colleges of America, who have formed out of the materials
at hand what they proudly proclaim as a new "life style" (as
opposed to the old-fashioned "way of life").

In this life style it has been a Wilhelm Reich and a Charles
Reich who have served as the revolutionary apostles, exhorting
their followers not to asceticism but to self-indulgence, not to
hardness and unsentimentality but to love. In Wilhelm Reich's
view, the strong man is he who acts out and gratifies all of his
appetites, rather than repressing them. Norman Brown en-
courages us to "polymorphous perversity."[4]

It is no surprise, then, that in France, which seemingly stood
on the brink of political revolution in May 1968, the students
began their demonstrations with a demand for sexual permis-
siveness! More serious demands quickly followed, but the sexual
was symptomatic of much else in the movement. Cohn-Bendit,
the student leader, after detailing the sexual demands, devoted
an entire book to his analysis of the May Days primarily in terms
of an attack on the Leninist-type control manifested in the offi-

cial French Communist party, in a passioned plea for the
"spontaneity" of the student-worker's movement, and in a
eulogy of anarchism.[5]

Leaders of any sort are in theory an anathema to radical
militants of today. Thus for them, by definition, a revolutionary
ascetic leader is out of the question. Yet the reality of the
radical movement often undercuts its rhetoric. Posters of Castro, Guevara, and Mao, as found ubiquitously in the late
1960s, indicate the latent attraction of the leader. Much of this
hero worship, of course, has been playacting: The same "militants" who put up pictures of Mao often indulge heavily in
drugs, whereas in China Mao has forbidden consumption of
opium as debilitating and antirevolutionary.

Will the attraction of leaders remain largely in the category
of playacting? If leaders do emerge, will they be revolutionary
ascetics? The "new revolution" has clearly been caught in a
dilemma, for all the available evidence shows that successful
political revolutions in the past have tended to require leaders
who are hard, controlled types, with pronounced traits of displaced libido and asceticism. In America of the late 1960s and
early 1970s, there were signs of the emergence of revolutionary
ascetic types, though not yet true leaders, in the radical movement. Thus in the Students for a Democratic Society (SDS) it
was the Leninist-like Progressive Labor party, complete with
short haircuts and uptight morals, that won out against the
"aesthetics," i.e., hippies and "freaks," in the fight for control
of the movement. Word had it that the Weathermen—the ultra-
radical branch of SDS—had been practicing physical culture
(such as fifteen to twenty miles of running) in the hills of
Vermont.

More significantly, I suspect, repression and consequent jail-
ing of revolutionary aesthetes—a situation partly brought on by
confrontation tactics, still half in the realm of playacting, of the
young radicals—produced one of the prime conditions for
forming revolutionary ascetics. Once jailed, aesthetic revolutionaries could see little likelihood of a successful career in the
Establishment, even if they had wished to return. Once beaten
up, their anger often congealed into total hatred of the "system" they saw as standing behind the policeman. For such

reasons many of them became, at least spiritually, professional revolutionaries (merely waiting for the right moment to become active again).

As such, I suspect, they may well also be future revolutionary ascetics. Let me offer one representative example. It comes from the prison letters of a black man, George Jackson, placed in Soledad Prison at the age of eighteen (for presumed criminal rather than political acts). When a prison guard was killed, Jackson was one of three black convicts accused of murdering him, and this event suddenly made him a political hero—one of the Soledad Brothers. From the depths of his experience, Jackson exclaimed: "I have trained away, pressed out forever the last of my Western habits. . . . I have no habits, no ego, no name, no face, I feel no love, no tenderness for anyone who does not think as I do. . . . Control over the circumstances that surround my existence is of the first importance to me."[6] Julius Lester, reviewing the book, tells us that Jackson (since killed in an attempted escape) "trains himself to sleep only three hours a night. He studies Swahili, Chinese, Arabic and Spanish. He does push-ups to control his sexual urge and to train his body. Sometimes he does a thousand a day. He eats only one meal a day." Lester then concludes with an ominous threat: "There will also be some critics (white) who will compare this book to *Soul on Ice*, since both came out of prisons. George Jackson makes Eldridge Cleaver look like a song-and-dance man on the Ed Sullivan show. In fact, after reading this book, whites will long for the good old days when all they had to think about was Stokely Carmichael and H. Rap Brown."[7]

Jackson's case and Lester's words form a particularly dramatic instance of what I have in mind, and describe what happened to some whites as well as blacks in America. Jackson's prison regime and feelings are strangely reminiscent of Lenin's. Will someone like Jackson be the future Lenin of a new American revolution? Or are the Jacksons of America in the 1970s merely the Tkachevs and Nechaevs, heralding a Lenin to come? In short, will revolutionary ascetics emerge to dominate a revolution in the developed, highly modernized countries of the West?

The answer, I believe, depends in part on whether the advanced industrial nations, such as America, remain affluent. An aesthetic revolution requires an affluent society, or one that is perceived to be affluent. The revolutionary in such a situation finds it uncongenial to embrace the "hard" virtues that seem historically necessary to make a political revolution. ("Make love, not war" is a poor recipe for revolution.) One could advance, therefore, the argument that the line leading from asceticism and displaced libido in the service of religion, then economic enterprise, and more recently revolutionary activity is on the point of being broken. Of course, individuals with a strong display of ascetic and displaced libidinal traits may still surface, but they would no longer be able effectively to place these traits in the service of political revolution. Instead, perhaps a different sort of man, a "loving" man aware of the need for control of his "baser" human passions, but conscious of the chameleonlike way such control can increase rather than bridle his impulses, might emerge into prominence in new sorts of "revolutions" in the future.

But to say this is to assume the continuation of affluence in the advanced nations. Recent events suggest other possibilities: zero-growth, or, indeed, a decline toward greatly lowered standards of living. In such a "new" situation, the old-fashioned "virtues" of the revolutionary ascetic may once again become highly functional. In short, the question of whether the ideal type—a revolutionary ascetic—will emerge into significant actuality can only be answered in terms of specific historical circumstances; these we can guess at, but not predict.

In the end, we must return to our original assertions. There are many kinds of revolutionary personalities. To understand any of them, we must also understand the revolutionary context in which they operate. Of particular interest to us has been the revolutionary ascetic. His (or her) traits seem highly functional in many of the revolutions of the past, and increasingly so as we moved from the seventeenth century to the twentieth century in Europe. We have analyzed these traits in detail, and seen how they came increasingly to be employed in the service of "modernizing" revolutions. We have also tried to see how effectively our analysis could be extended to non-Western revolutions, such as the Chinese.

Our assumption has been that men do make their history, only under circumstances not under their own control (and here we paraphrase Marx). In the effort to gain control over their circumstances, some men seek to control themselves in an ascetic and displaced libidinal fashion. They are what we have called revolutionary ascetics. In seeking to fathom their "super-human" nature, we have sought to understand some of the ways in which human character and historical circumstance intertwine. The result, we hope, has been a more "human" comprehension of some who have aspired, for many and complicated reasons, to lift their fellow men and women to new heights, and sometimes, in the process, failed to understand what was deepest in themselves and their followers.

NOTES

NOTES

CHAPTER 1

1. E. J. Hobsbawm, "Revolution Is Puritan," *New Society*, May 22, 1969, p. 807.

2. André Malraux, "Two Interviews," *Encounter* 35, no. 3 (September 1970):24.

3. If this is not the case in a particular revolution, such as the American, then this points our attention to the question of what sort of revolution mitigates against the appearance of puritanical tendencies. Cf. my paper, "Leadership in the American Revolution: The Psychological Dimension," delivered at the Library of Congress Symposia on the American Revolution, Washington, D.C., May 10, 1974 and published in *Leadership in the American Revolution* (Washington, D.C.: Library of Congress, 1974).

4. It goes without saying that revolutions are not merely the product of "correct" revolutionary leaders; revolution arises out of complex causes, only one of which is the character of its leaders.

5. See Max Weber, *The Protestant Ethic and the Spirit of Capitalism*, trans. Talcott Parsons (New York: Scribner's, 1958). Weber's thesis has occasioned much controversy—see, for example, *Protestantism, Capitalism and Social Science: The Weber Thesis Controversy*, ed. Robert W. Green, 2d ed. (Lexington, Mass.: D. C. Heath, 1973)—but for our specific purposes his general thesis serves admirably.

6. S. Freud, "Group Psychology and the Analysis of the Ego," in *The Standard Edition of the Complete Psychological Works of Sigmund Freud* ed. James Strachey (London: Hogarth Press, 1953–1974), 18:69–143.

7. In his important article, "Some Observations on Ideological Groups," *American Journal of Sociology* 67 (1961–62):397–405, Vladimir C. Nahirny speaks of "displaced affectivity" (403). As he notes, "It is one of the most striking and general features of ideological groups that they frown upon and oppose vehemently any display of personal affective attachments among their members" (398).

8. Few analysts after Freud have given the attention to asceticism that the topic would seem to warrant. One of the few occasions when Freud mentions the subject is in his "On the Universal Tendency to Debasement in the Sphere of Love (Contributions to the Psychology of Love II)"

(1912), where he comments: "It can easily be shown that the psychical value of erotic needs is reduced as soon as their satisfaction becomes easy. An obstacle is required in order to heighten libido; and where natural resistances to satisfaction have not been sufficient men have at all times erected conventional ones so as to be able to enjoy love. This is true both of individuals and of nations. In times in which there were no difficulties standing in the way of sexual satisfaction, such as perhaps during the decline of the ancient civilizations, love became worthless and life empty, and strong reaction-formations were required to restore indispensable affective values. In this connection it may be claimed that the ascetic current in Christianity created psychical values for love which pagan antiquity was never able to confer on it. This current assumed its greatest importance with the ascetic monks, whose lives were almost entirely occupied with the struggle against libidinal temptation" (*The Standard Edition of the Complete Psychological Works of Sigmund Freud*, ed. James Strachey [London: Hogarth Press, 1953–1974], 11:187–188). A glance at Alexander Grinstein's *Index of Psychoanalytic Writings*, 13 vols. to date (New York: International Universities Press, 1956—), indicates the paucity of articles and books on the subject, compared to those on seemingly more trivial subjects. Unfortunately, even the few items listed, in obscure German periodicals or out-of-print books, were unobtainable to me. In general, however, most of the psychoanalytic attention given to asceticism has been in terms of its connection to sadomasochism.

9. Sigmund Neumann, "The International Civil War," *World Politics*, April 1949, pp. 333–334 n. 10.

10. Paraphrase taken from an article by Perez Zagorin, "Theories of Revolution in Contemporary Historiography," *Political Science Quarterly*, vol. 88, No. 1 (March, 1973): 23–52. Who would add to Johnson's list "a change of governmental policy as well." Zagorin's article, along with Lawrence Stone, "Theories of Revolution," *World Politics* 18, no. 2 (January 1966):159–176, gives an excellent overview of work in the field. See, too, Bruce Mazlish, Arthur D. Kaledin, and David B. Ralston, eds., *Revolution: A Reader* (New York: Macmillan, 1971).

11. See James N. Rosenau, "Internal War as an International Event," in *International Aspects of Civil Strife*, ed. James N. Rosenau (Princeton, N.J.: Princeton University Press, 1964), pp. 45–91, and Chalmers Johnson, *Revolution and the Social System* (Stanford, Calif.: Hoover Institution Studies No. 3, 1964).

12. Karl Griewank, "Emergence of the Concept of Revolution," trans. Heinz Lubasz from *Der Neuzeitliche Revolutionsbegriff* (Weimar: Hermann Böhlaus Nachfolger, 1955), pp. 171–182, in *Revolutions in Modern European History*, ed. Heinz Lubasz (New York: Macmillan, 1966), p. 16.

13. Ibid., p. 61.

14. Crane Brinton, *The Anatomy of Revolution* (New York: Vintage Books, 1965).

CHAPTER 2

1. The version we have used is Niccolò Machiavelli, *Discourses on the First Decade of Titus Livius*, trans. Ninian Hill Thomson (London, 1883), I, ix, p. 42, quoted in J. H. Burns, "The Fabric of Felicity: The Legislator

and the Human Condition" (Inaugural Address Delivered at University College, London, March 2, 1967), p. 8.

2. Jean Jacques Rousseau, *The Social Contract*, chap. 7, "The Legislator." We have used the translation by G. D. H. Cole in the Everyman edition (London: J. M. Dent & Sons, 1947), p. 320.

3. *The Republic of Plato*, trans. Francis Macdonald Cornford (New York and London: Oxford University Press, 1945), p. 318.

4. Rousseau, *The Social Contract*, p. 34.

5. Ibid., p. 4.

6. Ibid., p. 6.

7. When asked to draw up constitutions for Corsica and Poland, Rousseau recognized this fact.

8. Antonio Gramsci, *The Modern Prince and Other Writings*, trans. Louis Marks (New York: International Publishers, 1968), pp. 137, 138.

CHAPTER 3

1. Sigmund Freud, *Group Psychology and the Analysis of the Ego*, in *The Standard Edition of the Complete Psychological Works of Sigmund Freud*, ed. James Strachey, 24 vols. (London: Hogarth Press, 1953–1974), 18:123 (hereafter referred to as *SE*).

2. Sigmund Freud, *Totem and Taboo*, SE, 13:89.

3. Cf. Ives Hendricks, *Facts and Theories in Psychoanalysis* (New York: Delta Books, 1958), p. 117.

4. Without clinical analysis it is difficult to tell for sure how narcissistic a particular leader is, and how strongly he has displaced his narcissism to an abstraction. In each individual case, therefore, one must examine public utterances and private observations in order to speculate on the narcissistic component of that revolutionary.

5. Quoted in George Rudé, ed., *Robespierre* (Englewood Cliffs, N.J.: Prentice-Hall, 1967), pp. 86, 133.

6. See, for example, Rudé, *Robespierre*, p. 84.

7. Robert Darnton, *Mesmerism and the End of the Enlightenment in France* (Cambridge, Mass.: Harvard University Press, 1968), p. 3. G. B. Shaw refers to this magnetic or hypnotic power as Awe, and gives an interesting personal account of it in his *Everybody's Political What's What* (New York: Dodd, Mead, 1944), pp. 286–287: "This power is called Awe. It enables a head master to control masses of schoolboys who could mob him and tear him to pieces as de Witt was torn by a Dutch mob in 1672 if they were not restrained by Awe. The statesman has to exploit it because he has to give authority not only to superior persons who naturally inspire it, but to ordinary Yahoos who can be made to produce an illusion of superiority by unusual robes, retinues and escorts, magnificient liveries and uniforms: in short, by making animated idols of them. Uniforms, vestments, robes, maces, diadems, retinues, pageants, processions, cannon salutes, and codes of etiquette are artificial Awe producers to give authority to persons who are not natural Awe producers.

"The reaction against the factitious Awe has produced the Roundhead, the British Quaker, and the American diplomat who appears at court among costumed peers and royalties in coat and trousers instead of in breeches, swordless and plain Mister; but these iconoclasts are powerless

against the genuine natural Awe inspirer. I am as irreverent and even de-
risive as any sane thinker can be; but I can remember an occasion (I was
over twenty at the time) on which I was so overawed by a Jewish Rabbi
that I could hardly speak to him. There was no reason for this: we had
never met before, and had less than five minutes conversation on an ordinary matter of business which gave no occasion for embarrassment on either
side of any sort; but he terrified me by some power in him, magnetic or
mesmeric or hypnotic or whatever you like to call it, which reduced me to
a subjection which I had never experienced before, and have never experienced since. I was simply discouraged by him. Since then my observation,
and the stories I read about the dying-out of primitive tribes at the impact
of civilized invaders, have convinced me that every living person has a magnetic field of greater or less intensity which enables those in whom it is
strong to dominate those in whom it is relatively weak, or whose suscepti-
bility to its influence, called shyness, is excessive. I have ranked this as a
scientific fact in the fourth part of *Back To Methuselah*; but it will not be
accepted as such by the professional biologists until one of them has succeeded in making a guinea pig overawe a dog in a laboratory. Someday an
intelligent biophysicist will perhaps find out how to measure this force as
we now measure electricity. Meanwhile there is no denying that it exists
and must be recognized and even exploited by every practical ruler.
"In my Utopia I therefore fell back on Awe, both natural and artificial,
as a means by which my Coming Race kept the Yahoos in subjection."

8. Frank E. Manuel, *The Prophets of Paris* (Cambridge, Mass.: Harvard
University Press, 1962), pp. 188–189. A comparison with the similar behavior of Charles Manson at his recent trial seems pertinent, though Manson can hardly be equated with Enfantin as a political thinker or, indeed,
as an historical figure.

9. Quoted in Alan Bullock, *Hitler, A Study in Tyranny* (New York:
Harper & Row, 1962), pp. 373–374.

10. Sigmund Freud, "An Autobiographical Study," *SE* 20:42.

11. It may pain some analysts to read this comparison: needless to say,
nothing pejorative is intended concerning *their* use of transference and
countertransference. The reason for making the comparison is, of course,
simply to secure an important insight into the nature of political mesmerism.

12. As Trotsky wrote, "At times it seemed as if I felt, with my lips, the
stern inquisitiveness of this crowd that had merged into a single whole.
Then all the arguments and words thought out in advance would break and
recede under the imperative pressure of sympathy, and other words, other
arguments, utterly unexpected by the orator but needed by these people,
would emerge in full array from my subconscious. . . . In a semiconscious-
ness of exhaustion, I would float on countless arms above the heads of the
people to reach the exit . . ." (quoted in E. Victor Wolfenstein, *The Revolutionary Personality: Lenin, Trotsky, Gandhi* [Princeton, N.J.: Princeton
University Press, 1967], p. 262).

13. *Webster's New World Dictionary*, College Edition (Toronto: Nel-
son, Foster, & Scott, 1957).

14. Max Weber, *The Protestant Ethic and the Spirit of Capitalism*,
trans. Talcott Parsons (New York: Scribner's, 1958), pp. 118–119.

15. Ibid., pp. 158–159. Cf. Michael Walzer, "Puritanism as a Revolutionary Ideology," *History and Theory* 3, no. 1 (1963):81.

16. Weber, *The Protestant Ethic*, p. 180.

17. Otto Fenichel, *The Psychoanalytic Theory of Neurosis* (New York: W. W. Norton, 1945), p. 359.

18. Ibid., p. 364

19. Ibid.

20. Anna Freud, *The Ego and the Mechanisms of Defense* (New York: International Universities Press, 1965), pp. 168–169. The other quotes that follow are on pp. 170, 176, and 177.

21. Cf. Peter Blos, *On Adolescence* (New York: Free Press, 1962), p. 117, for a recognition of the fact that adolescent asceticism and intellectualization are themselves influenced by the cultural and social context in which the youth finds himself.

22. Indeed, it is interesting to compare at some length Weber's theory of charismatic leadership with our own concept of revolutionary asceticism. The first thing we note is that charisma, that extraordinary quality of a person which brings authority that is neither bureaucratic nor hereditary, like the classic asceticism per se is a notion—and phenomenon—that originates in the religious domain, and then is taken over into the political realm by Weber. In fact, Weber borrowed the term "charisma" (meaning "gift of grace" in the original Greek) from Rudolf Sohm, a church historian.

In one respect classic asceticism, in Weber's view, facilitates the acquisition of charisma. As Weber informs us, "Numerous forms of chastisement and of abstinence from normal diet and sleep, as well as from sexual intercourse, awaken, or at least facilitate, the charisma of ecstatic, visionary, hysterical, in short, of all extraordinary states that are evaluated as 'holy' " (H. H. Gerth and C. Wright Mills, eds., *Max Weber: Essays in Sociology* [New York: Oxford University Press, 1958], p. 271). On the other hand, and more fundamental, is the fact that charisma, in Weber's *sociological* formulation, is perceived as being antirational. On his own terms, when religious asceticism becomes "worldly" among the puritans, and thus is in the service of rational capitalist activity, Weber must place it in opposition to charisma. As he puts it, "charisma, and this is decisive, always rejects as undignified any pecuniary gain that is methodical and rational (ibid., p. 247). At this point, psychologically, we must split with Weber's concept of charisma, for our concept of revolutionary asceticism *assumes* that its component of classic asceticism will be placed in the service of methodical and rational goals.

Agreement between our concept and Weber's is greater on two other points. His theory of charisma and our concept of revolutionary asceticism are both conceived of as being about revolutionary forces—"its attitude is revolutionary," Weber says of his charisma (ibid., p. 250)—which tend to attack the institutions of established societies, and to do so in the name of an "illegitimate" and strange spiritual power. And both point toward the phenomenon of "displaced libido." As Weber puts it, "In order to do justice to their mission, the holders of charisma, the master as well as his disciples and followers, must stand outside the ties of this world, outside of its routine occupations, as well as outside the routine obligations of family life" (ibid., p. 248).

There is really very little quarrel between Weber's charismatic leader and our revolutionary ascetic. In fact, quite the contrary: Weber has given us our starting point here as in so many areas. His stress, however, is sociological. He himself is keenly aware of this when he declares about his theory of charisma: "In the latter field of phenomena lie the seeds of certain types of psychic 'contagion' and it is thus the bearer of many dynamic relations of social processes. These types of action are very closely related to phenomena which are understandable either only in biological terms or are subject to interpretation in terms of subjective motives only in fragments and with an almost imperceptible transition to the biological. But all these facts do not discharge sociology from the obligation, in full awareness of the narrow limits to which it is confined, to accomplish what it alone can do" (Max Weber, *The Theory of Social and Economic Organization*, trans. A. M. Henderson and Talcott Parsons [New York: The Free Press, 1964], p. 106).

On our side, we have been seeking to add to "the narrow limits" of sociology the insights of Freudian psychoanalysis, in order better to understand the "psychic 'contagion' " mentioned by Weber.

23. Fred Weinstein and Gerald M. Platt, *The Wish To Be Free: Society, Psyche, and Value Change* (Berkeley: University of California Press, 1969), pp. 116–117.

24. Isaiah Berlin, "Introduction" to Franco Venturi, *Roots of Revolution* (New York: Grosset & Dunlap, 1966), pp. xxiii–xxiv.

25. Ivan Goncharov, *Oblomov*, trans. Ann Dunnigan (New York: The New American Library, 1963). Nathan Leites, *A Study of Bolshevism* (Glencoe, Ill.: Free Press, 1953).

26. Quoted in Lewis S. Feuer, "Lenin's Fantasy," *Encounter* 35, no. 6 (December 1970):23. A slightly different translation is found in Lenin's "Philosophical Notebooks," *Collected Works*, trans. Dutt (Moscow, 1961), 38:372–373. As Feuer remarks, "We might call the fear that one's avowed goals are an illusion the 'revolutionary anxiety.' Since he is pitting himself against the established norms and values of society, the 'revolutionary anxiety' arises in moments of doubt" (Feuer, "Lenin's Fantasy," p. 28).

27. Philip Mason, *Prospero's Magic* (London: Oxford University Press, 1962), pp. 126–127.

28. Robert C. Tucker, "The Theory of Charismatic Leadership," *Daedalus* 97, no. 3 (Summer 1968):741–742.

29. A. N. Potresov, *Posmerty sbornik proizvedenii* (Paris, 1937), p. 301, in ibid., pp. 741–742.

30. This last is a moot point needing further investigation; as Hegel reminds us, "No man is a hero to his valet." Folk wisdom, too, confirms that "familiarity breeds contempt." But does this hold only for noncharismatic leaders?

CHAPTER 4

1. Max Weber, *The Protestant Ethic and the Spirit of Capitalism*, trans. Talcott Parsons (New York: Scribner's, 1958), p. 19.

2. Ibid., p. 121. The quotes that follow, unless otherwise noted, are also from *The Protestant Ethic*, and the reference is simply placed in the text, after the quote.

3. Erik H. Erikson, *Young Man Luther* (New York: W. W. Norton, 1958).

4. I would like to qualify Weber's insight by suggesting that the matter

as to magical thinking is a bit more complicated than as presented. In talking of Baptism, Weber comments that: "In so far as Baptism affected the normal workaday world, the idea that God only speaks when the flesh is silent evidently meant an incentive to the deliberate weighing of courses of action and their careful justification in terms of the individual conscience. The later Baptist communities, most particularly the Quakers, adopted this quiet, moderate, eminently conscientious character of conduct. The radical elimination of magic from the world allowed no other psychological course than the practice of worldly asceticism" (Weber, *The Protestant Ethic*, p. 149).

I would like to suggest that the introduction into Calvinism of what I have called "elitist asceticism" is, psychologically, a form of magical thinking. It is a sort of "sympathetic magic," in which the doing of an act is understood not to be directly related causally to another act, but only symbolically so. Yet it assures the success of that latter act. For example, in one primitive society the women place resin on their fingers while going about their daily tasks, in order to insure that nothing slips through their fingers; this is done so that game will not "slip" through the nooses of their men hunting in the fields. One cannot help feeling that the Calvinist elect, in their practice of worldly asceticism, were also insuring that their salvation did not slip through God's fingers!

5. E. J. Hobsbawm, "Methodism and the Threat of Revolution in Britain," in *Labouring Man* (London: Weidenfeld and Nicolson, 1968), pp. 23–33. Elie Halévy's views were put forth in his *History of the English People in the Nineteenth Century*, vol. 1, *England in 1815*, trans. E. I. Watkin and D. A. Barker (New York: Barnes & Noble, 1968). See also E. P. Thompson, *The Making of the English Working Class* (New York: Vintage Books, 1966).

6. Sigmund Freud, *Civilization and its Discontents*, in *The Standard Edition of the Complete Psychological Works of Sigmund Freud*, ed. James Strachey, 24 vols. (London: Hogarth Press, 1953–1974), vol. 21 (hereafter referred to as *SE*).

7. For Weber's concern over this problem, see Arthur Mitzman, *The Iron Cage: An Historical Interpretation of Max Weber* (New York: Alfred A. Knopf, 1969).

8. Sigmund Freud, "A Seventeenth-Century Demonological Neurosis" (1923), SE, 19:72–105.

9. See, for example, Ernest Jones, *Papers on Psycho-Analysis* (Boston: Beacon Press, 1967). Karl Abraham, "Contributions to the Theory of the Anal Character," in *Selected Papers* (London: Hogarth Press, 1948); and Norman Brown, *Life Against Death: The Psychoanalytic Meaning of History* (Middletown, Conn.: Wesleyan University Press, 1959).

10. See, for example, an old-fashioned work, Louis Schucking, *The Puritan Family*, trans. Brian Battershaw (London: Routledge & Kegan Paul, 1969), and a more up-to-date treatment, John Demos, *A Little Commonwealth: Family Life in Plymouth Colony* (New York: Oxford University Press, 1970).

11. While sex seems to be accepted today, rather blatantly, as a topic for discussion, anality is regarded with great disfavor and seen as unforgivably reductionist. Still, it must be remembered that human beings do empty their bowels, and that cultures do provide acceptable modes and promote particular feelings about this biological process that have, as a

moment's reflection will confirm, powerful psychosocial consequences. Whether any particular analysis of anality in an individual or a culture is correct is, of course, another matter.

12. Cf. Fred Weinstein and Gerald M. Platt, *The Wish To Be Free* (Berkeley and Los Angeles: University of California Press, 1969).

CHAPTER 5

1. Max Weber, "Religious Rejections of the World and their Directions," from *Max Weber*, ed. H. H. Gerth and C. Wright Mills (New York: Oxford University Press, 1958), p. 340.

2. For the literature on the Puritan Revolution, see, for example, Perez Zagorin, *The Court and the Country* (New York: Atheneum, 1970), and its citations. See also J. Bronowski and Bruce Mazlish, *The Western Intellectual Tradition* (New York: Harper & Brothers, 1960), chap. 9.

3. Michael Walzer, "Puritanism as a Revolutionary Ideology," *History and Theory* 3, no. 1 (1963):59–90; and *The Revolution of the Saints* (New York: Atheneum, 1968).

4. Walzer, *The Revolution of the Saints*, p. vii. The quotes that follow are identified by page numbers from this same book.

5. William N. Chambers, "Party Development and Party Action: The American Origins," *History and Theory* 3, no. 1 (1963):98.

6. Robert Walcott, "The Idea of Party in the Writing of Later Stuart History," *The Journal of British Studies* 2 (May 1962):54.

7. E. J. Hobsbawm, *Primitive Rebels* (New York: W. W. Norton, 1959).

8. Walzer, "Puritanism as a Revolutionary Ideology," pp. 64–65. The following quotes are from the same article.

9. What Walzer sees as specific for the puritans is perceived by H. R. Trevor-Roper as general for all Europeans. Trevor-Roper reminds us that "Ever since 1618 at least there had been talk of the dissolution of society, or of the world, and the undefined sense of gloom of which we are constantly aware in those years was justified sometimes by new interpretations of Scripture, sometimes by new phenomenon in the skies" ("The General Crisis of the Seventeenth Century," in *Crisis in Europe 1560–1660*, ed. T. Aston [London: Routledge & Kegan Paul, 1965]).

10. Cf. Anna Freud's notion of fear by the ego of the instincts, in *The Ego and the Mechanisms of Defense* (New York: International Universities Press, 1936), chap. 12.

11. Walzer himself offers this quotation, though without my interpretation; see "Puritanism as a Revolutionary Ideology," p. 79.

12. Ibid., p. 85. See, incidentally, the analysis of puritan attitudes to witchcraft, along the same lines that I am advancing, in John Demos, "Underlying Themes in the Witchcraft of Seventeenth-Century New England," *American Historical Review* 74, no. 5 (June 1970):1311–1326.

13. Erik H. Erikson, "Reflections on the American Identity," in *Childhood and Society* (New York: W. W. Norton, 1963), p. 292.

14. Erik H. Erikson, *Gandhi's Truth* (New York: W. W. Norton, 1969), p. 373. This view coincides with the position of G. G. Coulton, who emphasized that in the Middle Ages there was much greater hatred and fear of the body, bodily functions, women, etc.—one thinks of the

prevalence of celibacy—than after the sixteenth century. Thus the puritans exhibit by contrast a much greater acceptance of the flesh and its desires.

15. Maurice Ashley, *The Greatness of Oliver Cromwell* (London: Collier-Macmillan Ltd., 1969), p. 30.

16. The quote is from W. C. Abbott, ed., *The Writings and Speeches of Oliver Cromwell*, 4 vols. (Cambridge: Cambridge University Press, 1937–1947), 1:20. The mourning effect may have been softened by the lavish entertainment of James I by Cromwell's uncle, Sir Oliver, as the new king passed through Huntingdon on his way to London a month later. Christopher Hill, *God's Englishman: Oliver Cromwell and the English Revolution* (New York: Dial Press, 1970), in a facetious dash at psychological interpretation, comments on the effect of this predominantly feminine upbringing of young Oliver: "We may speculate on the effects of this petticoat environment; by all accounts . . . he grew up to be a rough, boisterous, practical-joking boy, with no effeminate characteristics" (p. 39).

17. Abbott, *Writings and Speeches*, 1:65. As with almost all quotations about Cromwell, there is always the danger that like or dislike of the man—usually the latter—will color inordinately all contemporary references to him. However, we must use, though with caution, the material we have.

18. Ibid., 1:25.

19. Ibid., 1:132.

20. Ashley, *Greatness of Oliver Cromwell*, p. 38.

21. Abbott, *Writings and Speeches*, 1:39.

22. Ibid., 1:124.

23. Ibid., 1:34.

24. Ibid.

25. Ibid., 1:79.

26. Ibid., 1:64. John Simcott, Cromwell's own doctor at Huntingdon, confirmed the melancholia, and suggested hypochondria as well. Cf. Hill, *God's Englishman*, p. 46.

27. Sir Charles Firth, *Oliver Cromwell and the Rule of the Puritans in England* (London: Oxford University Press, 1953), pp. 38–39.

28. Abbott, *Writings and Speeches*, 1:96–97.

29. Ibid.

30. Ashley, *Greatness of Oliver Cromwell*, p. 38.

31. The contemporary observation on Cromwell's behavior at the death of his daughter is quoted in Frederic Harrison, *Oliver Cromwell* (London: Macmillan, 1888), p. 25. The letter to his wife is quoted in Firth, *Oliver Cromwell and the Rule of the Puritans in England*, p. 8.

32. Bronowski and Mazlish, *Western Intellectual Tradition*, p. 169; see also Gustave Bychowski's interpretation in "Oliver Cromwell and the Puritan Revolution," *Clinical Pathology* 7 (1945):281–309. In chapter 9, "Providence and Oliver Cromwell," in *God's Englishman*, Hill offers a good analysis of the function of a belief in Providence, and especially Predestination, in girding up the loins of its believers. While Hill gives hints as to the psychological effects, his analysis stays mainly on the "ideological" surface, thus standing as a necessary complement to our more psychological approach.

33. Cromwell's behavior illustrates the basically nonrevolutionary ascetic quality of the English Revolution as a whole. Affective ties, for example, tended to persist, and not to be displaced completely onto an ideological

abstraction. Perez Zagorin, following Guizot, remarks perceptively in *The Court and the Country*, "The English Revolution did not devour its own children. Neither side resorted to systematic and ideologically buttressed destruction of political enemies, and there was no 'Red' terror while the revolutionary governments were in power and no 'White' terror at the Restoration" (p. 9).

34. Clarendon, *Selections from "The History of the Rebellion and Civil Wars" and "The Life by Himself,"* ed. G. Huehns (London: Oxford University Press, 1968), p. 381.

35. Charles Firth, *Cromwell's Army* (London: Methuen, 1902), pp. 36–37. With army pay only a penny a day more than the remuneration of agricultural laborers, we can understand the need for impressment.

36. Ibid., pp. 276–283.

37. Thus in Manchester's (the Commander-in-Chief) regiments of foot, only half were commanded by independents, and the other half by Presbyterians.

38. Hill, *God's Englishman*, p. 65.

39. Ibid., p. 64.

40. Firth, *Cromwell's Army*, p. 363.

41. Perez Zagorin, A *History of Political Thought in the English Revolution* (London: Routledge & Kegan Paul, 1954), pp. 10, 8.

42. See, for example, the excellent account in William Sargant, *Battle for the Mind* (Baltimore: Penguin Books, 1957).

43. Robert Lifton, *Thought Reform and the Psychology of Totalism: A Study of Brainwashing in China* (New York: W. W. Norton, 1963), p. 28.

44. Ibid., pp. 473–474.

45. Ibid.

46. Russian "thought reform," insofar as it exists, has set itself very different goals and been of a very different nature; see, for example, Arthur Koestler's *Darkness at Noon*, trans. Daphne Hardy (New York: Macmillan, 1941).

CHAPTER 6

1. In English there is especially J. M. Thompson, *Robespierre*, 2 vols. (New York: Basil Blackwell, 1935), and in French especially G. Walter, *Robespierre*, 2 vols. (Paris: Gallimard, 1961).

2. For example, he had not signed the registration of his wife's death, or attended her funeral, presumably because he was too distraught. The reality as to why he left is confused—Walter seems to show that it was not due to debt (*Robespierre*, 1:24)—but, in any case, it does not matter in comparison to the rumors which must have surrounded his desertion of his family. Psychologically, one possibility is that in some strange way he "blamed" his children for the death of his wife, but we have no evidence to back up such a speculation.

3. Robespierre's close call to illegitimacy must be seen in the context of the times, when many marriages were entered into after the conception of a child and condoned by society. However, this pattern seems to have been generally restricted to rural and lower-class persons. See, for example, Ed-

ward Shorter, "Illegitimacy, Sexual Revolution and Social Change in Modern Europe," *The Journal of Interdisciplinary History* 2, no. 2 (August 1971):237–272.

4. Quoted in Reginald Ward, *Maximilien Robespierre: A Study in Deterioration* (London: Macmillan, 1934), p. 18.

5. Thompson, *Robespierre*, 1:5–6.

6. Ibid., 1:23.

7. Ibid, 1:14.

8. For details see Walter, *Robespierre*, 1:54–61.

9. Ibid., 1:81–90.

10. Ibid., 1:95.

11. Ward, *Robespierre*, p. 37.

12. Max Gallo, *Robespierre the Incorruptible. A Psycho-Biography*, trans. Raymond Rudorff (New York: Herder & Herder, 1971), which came into my hands after I had finished this chapter, is in part such an attempt, though, as its subtitle indicates, it aims at psychobiography rather than psychohistory. Though written in a novelistic manner, it is psychoanalytically informed. Its general thesis is that Robespierre "was pathologically sensitive because of his childhood wounds" (p. 66), i.e., over his father's "guilt" and thus his own, and felt a constant sense of humiliation and lack of self-esteem. By identifying with the Revolution, he sought to restore the latter. All of his speeches show his personalizing of the Revolution. Also, Robespierre wished to be a martyr, and thus worked for his own ultimate doom, which he kept predicting.

13. George Rudé, ed., *Robespierre* (Englewood Cliffs, N.J.: Prentice-Hall, 1967), pp. 81, 82. Gallo analyzes Robespierre's habits of dress as follows: "His careful elegance, the time he spent powdering, clothing and contemplating himself, proved his self-love. It was a form of narcissism which confirmed the importance which he attached to cutting a dashful figure and his determination to mask his body. His way of denying his body by covering and masking it with silk, lace, and powder, hiding it behind a social appearance, was his unconscious way of expressing self-love and denying man's carnal, animal aspect" (p. 62).

14. Thompson, *Robespierre*, 1:183. Thompson's comment is that "It may be that one day Maximilien took Eléonare's hand in his—the symbol of betrothal in Artois: but in spite of the episode of the Saintonge, everything suggests that he was at this time too devoted to his career, and to his reputation, to commit any social indiscretion, even that of matrimony." The assertion about the mistress is based on the "testimony" of Pierre Villiers, who served for a time as Robespierre's secretary, but see the rebuttal by R. Garmy, *Actes du Colloque Robespierre* (Paris: Société des études robespierristes, 1967).

15. Walter, *Robespierre*, 1:53.

16. Ibid., 1:63.

17. Ibid., 1:62.

18. Jean Jacques Rousseau, "Discourse on Political Economy," in *The Social Contract and Discourses*, ed. G. D. H. Cole (London: J. M. Dent, 1947), pp. 242, 244, 246.

19. Quoted in Ward, *Robespierre*, p. 36. See Walter, *Robespierre*, 1:34ff., for a discussion of the problem of dating this document.

20. For details and a full-scale psychological interpretation of Rous-

seau's life, see W. H. Blanchard, *Rousseau and the Spirit of Revolt* (Ann Arbor: University of Michigan Press, 1967), and Lester G. Crocker, *Jean-Jacques Rousseau*, 2 vols. (New York: Macmillan, 1968–1973).

21. See ibid. for details.

22. Quoted in Rudé, *Robespierre*, pp. 79–80.

23. Fred Weinstein and Gerald Platt, *The Wish To Be Free* (Berkeley and Los Angeles: University of California Press, 1969), pp. 127–128.

24. To go into the ascetic and libidinal qualities of Rousseau here would be too great a task. His book *Emile*, trans. Barbara Foxley (London: J. M. Dent, 1969), however, would be a good place to start in such an analysis.

25. Weinstein and Platt, *The Wish To Be Free*, p. 130.

26. Ibid., p. 117. Robespierre's follower, St. Just, also expressed this desire in his remarks. He wrote that "obliged to isolate himself from the world and from himself, man drops his anchor in the future and presses to his heart the posterity which bears no blame for the evils of the present. . . . I have left all weakness behind me" (quoted in ibid., p. 118). For St. Just, see Eugene Newton Curtis, *Saint-Just. Colleague of Robespierre* (New York: Columbia University Press, 1935).

27. On one simple ground, Robespierre had an advantage over all his competitors. He devoted his entire time and life to the Revolution once it had begun.

28. Quoted in Gallo, *Robespierre the Incorruptible*, pp. 229, 301.

CHAPTER 7

1. Jeremy Bentham, *An Introduction to the Principles of Morals and Legislation* (New York: Hafner Publishing Co., 1948), p. 9.

2. Ibid., pp. 15–16.

3. Max Weber, *The Protestant Ethic and the Spirit of Capitalism*, trans. Talcott Parsons (New York: Scribner's, 1958), p. 176.

4. Ibid., p. 260.

5. Ibid., p. 263.

6. Quoted in Alexander Bain, *James Mill. A Biography* (New York: Augustus M. Kelley, 1967), p. 397.

7. Ibid., pp. 422–423.

8. John Stuart Mill, *Autobiography* (New York: Liberal Arts Press, 1957), p. 33.

9. Quoted in Bain, *James Mill*.

10. For a much more complete picture, see Bruce Mazlish, *James and John Stuart Mill: Father and Son in the Nineteenth Century* (New York: Basic Books, 1975).

11. Vladimir C. Nahirny, "The Russian Intelligentsia: From Men of Ideas to Men of Convictions," *Comparative Studies in Society and History* 4 (1961–1962):403–435. This is a most stimulating article, with many points of contact with our general thesis; it deserves to be read as a whole. The quotes concerning Belinsky that follow, unless otherwise indicated, are from this article, pp. 409, 411, 413, 415.

12. Martin Malia, "What Is the Intelligentsia?," in *Revolution: A Reader*, ed. B. Mazlish, A. Kaledin, and D. Ralston (New York: Macmillan, 1971), p. 121.

13. Nahirny, "Russian Intelligentsia," p. 421.

14. Ibid., p. 418.

15. Ibid., p. 425.

16. Ibid., p. 424.

17. Quoted in Franco Venturi, *Roots of Revolution* (New York: Grosset & Dunlap, 1960), p. 157.

18. Nahirny, "Russian Intelligentsia," pp. 427–428.

19. Venturi, *Roots of Revolution*, p. 177.

20. The Vintage paperback edition of *What Is To Be Done?*, trans. Benjamin R. Tucker (New York: Vintage Books, 1961), accentuates this fact. It omits a section containing Chernyshevsky's vision of the ideal socialistic utopia, which can, however, be found in an appendix of the Dutton Everyman translation (New York: Dutton Everyman, 1960), of Dostoevsky's *Notes from Underground*, trans. Ralph E. Matlaw, where Dostoevsky attacks it. For these details, and an excellent analysis of Chernyshevsky's significance, see Joseph Frank, "N. G. Chernyshevsky: A Russian Utopia," *The Southern Review* 3, no. 1 (Winter 1967):68–84. Nevertheless, the general point—that the novel is more about an ideal character than an ideal society—still holds.

21. Chernyshevsky, *What Is To Be Done?*, pp. 236–237.

22. Ralph E. Matlaw, ed., *Belinsky, Chernyshevsky, and Dobrolyubov. Selected Criticism* (New York: E. P. Dutton, 1962), p. 120.

23. Chernyshevsky, *What Is To Be Done?*, p. 238. Frank, "N. G. Chernyshevsky," p. 79, offers an interesting explanation of how the "free love" doctrines of the new men and women were reconciled with their ascetic personal lives. "All this [the ascetic practices]," Frank remarks, "is to prove that while the radicals are asking for the political and sexual emancipation of women, and for 'the full enjoyment of life,' they are not doing so 'for the gratification of our personal passions, not for ourselves personally, but for humanity in general.'"

24. Chernyshevsky, *What Is To Be Done?*, p. 110.

25. Ibid., pp. 81–82.

26. Isaiah Berlin, Introduction to Venturi, *Roots of Revolution*, p. xxiii.

27. Chernyshevsky, *What Is To Be Done?*, p. 261.

28. As Frank, "N. G. Chernyshevsky," pp. 72–73, puts it, "Utilitarians had appeared in literature before, most notably in Dickens' novels, under the guise of hypocritical villains wrapping their opportunism in a cloud of Benthamite terminology. But it remained for a Russian—and, even more oddly, for a Russian Utopian Socialist!—to make English Utilitarianism the credo of his heroes, and to attempt to portray its beneficial effect on their lives."

29. Quoted in Venturi, *Roots of Revolution*, pp. 365–366. Later in life, Bakunin seemed to have second thoughts about the virtues of such a revolutionary character. He wrote to a friend in 1870, warning him now against receiving Nechaev, whom he had first recommended warmly: "It may seem strange to you that we advise you to turn away a man to whom we have given letters of recommendation addressed to you and written in the warmest terms. But those letters date from the month of May; and since then we have been obliged to admit the existence of matters so grave that they have forced us to break all our relations with N. . . . True that N is one of the most active and energetic men I have ever met. When it is a question of serving what he calls the cause, he does not hesitate; nothing stops him, and he is as merciless with himself as with all the others. This is the prin-

cipal quality which attracted me, and which impelled me to seek an alliance with him for a good while . . . but the methods he uses are detestable. . . . The tepid sympathies of men who are devoted to the revolutionary cause only in part, and who, besides this cause, have other human interests such as love, friendship, family, social relations—these sympathies are not, in his eyes, a sufficient foundation and in the name of the cause he will try to get a hold on you completely without your knowledge . . . when, at a general meeting, we accused him of this [spying, stealing, etc.], he had the nerve to say—'Well, yes, that's our system. We consider as our enemies those who are not with us *completely* and we have the duty to deceive and to compromise them.' . . . All personal ties, all friendship, all [gap in text] are considered by them as an evil, which they have the right to destroy because all this constitutes a force which, being outside the secret organization, diminishes the sole force of this latter. . . . His only excuse is his fanaticism! He is terribly ambitious without knowing it, because he has ended by identifying the cause of the revolution with himself—but he is not an egoist in the usual sense of the word because he risks his life terribly, and leads the existence of a martyr full of privations and incredible activity . . ." (quoted in Joseph Frank, "Dostoevsky's Realism," *Encounter* [March 1973]: 32–33). As we can see, even at the end Bakunin is still impressed by Nechaev's lack of "egoism"—though Bakunin unwillingly recognizes it for what it is, and then denies that recognition—and his character as a "martyr."

CHAPTER 8

1. Maxim Gorky, *Lenin* (Edinburgh: University Texts, 1967), p. 13. Indeed, one can say that Lenin was the first "antihero," thus exposing another paradox, for it was Lenin who prepared the way in the Soviet Union for Stalin and the "cult of personality," though rejecting it for himself.

2. Nikolay Valentinov, *Encounters with Lenin*, trans. Paul Rasta and Brian Pearce (London: Oxford University Press, 1968).

3. Adam B. Ulam, *The Bolsheviks* (New York: Collier Books, 1968), p. 332.

4. Clara Zetkin, *Reminiscences of Lenin* (New York: International Publishers, 1934), p. 45. Cf. the translation in another edition of this book, Clara Zetkin, *My Recollections of Lenin* (Moscow, 1956), pp. 58–59.

5. Nadezhda K. Krupskaya, *Memories of Lenin*, trans. E. Verney (New York: International Publishers, 1930), p. 98.

6. Quoted in E. Victor Wolfenstein, *The Revolutionary Personality: Lenin, Trotsky, Gandhi* (Princeton, N.J.: Princeton University Press, 1967), pp. 184–185.

7. According to Robert C. Tucker, in *Stalin as Revolutionary, 1879–1929* (New York: W. W. Norton, 1973), p. 22, it was an 1897 pamphlet, "The Tasks of the Russian Social Democrats," written in Siberia, that was the first of his writings to appear under the name of Lenin; there is some obscurity as to the whole issue. In any case, it is only after the break with Plekhanov that Lenin becomes the customary pseudonym of V. I. Ulyanov.

8. Quoted in Ulam, *Bolsheviks*, p. 195.

9. Krupskaya, *Memories of Lenin*, p. 86; cf. ibid., p. 175.

10. V. I. Lenin, *What Is To Be Done?* (Moscow: Foreign Languages Publishing House, 1950), p. 290.

11. Krupskaya, *Memories of Lenin,* pp. 42–43. Some Russian scholars, such as Richard Pipes, insist this statement is to be interpreted in merely ideological terms. I remain unconvinced, and believe that one must take seriously Pipes' own statement that "The origins of Lenin's political theory have to be sought at least as much in psychology as in ideas" ("The Origins of Bolshevism: The Intellectual Evolution of Young Lenin," in *Revolutionary Russia: A Symposium,* ed. Richard Pipes [Garden City, N.Y.: Doubleday, 1969], p. 26).

12. Krupskaya also informs us that "Vladimir Ilyich told me of his brother's activity as a naturalist. The last summer that he came home, he had been preparing a dissertation on worms, and was working all the time at the microscope. In order to get as much light as possible, he rose at daybreak and immediately set to work. 'No, my brother wouldn't make a revolutionary, I thought then,' Vladimir Ilyich recounted; 'a revolutionary cannot devote so much time to the study of worms.' He soon saw how he was mistaken [we would question this]. The fate of his brother undoubtedly profoundly influenced Vladimir Ilyich" (Krupskaya, *Memories of Lenin,* p. 5).

13. Quoted in Ulam, *Bolsheviks,* p. 113.

14. Isaac Deutscher, *Lenin's Childhood* (London: Oxford University Press, 1970), p. 22.

15. Ibid., p. 10.

16. Stefan T. Possony, *Lenin: The Compulsive Revolutionary* (Chicago: Henry Regnery, 1964), p. 5. In general, this book must be used with great caution.

17. Zetkin, *Reminiscences of Lenin,* p. 48.

18. In another, covert, sense, of course, the revolutionary marriage, with its subordination of love to utilitarian ends—in this case, revolution—does duplicate the Victorian marriage with its differing, but equally utilitarian, aim. Cf. Ronald V. Sampson, *The Psychology of Power* (New York: Pantheon Books, 1966).

19. Valentinov, *Encounters with Lenin,* p. 141.

20. Krupskaya, *Memories of Lenin,* p. 155.

21. N. G. Chernyshevsky, *What Is To Be Done?,* trans. Benjamin R. Tucker (New York: Vintage Books, 1961), Introduction, p. xiv.

22. Valentinov, *Encounters with Lenin,* p. 57.

23. See Louis Fischer, *The Life of Lenin* (New York: Harper & Row, 1964), p. 22.

24. Robert H. McNeal, "Women in the Russian Radical Movement," *Journal of Social History* (Winter 1971–1972):143–163, advances the thesis that the reason for the unusual number of female participants in Russian radicalism is to be found in "national factors" peculiar to Russia, manifesting itself in the narodnik tradition rather than in the social democratic movement. The educated nobility, according to McNeal, unable to uplift the "people" directly, turned to the next available oppressed class: women. Thus the female liberation question was joined to the peasant question. Guilty, privileged nobles embraced a form of "heroic self-denial," of "asceticism," while living and working in the movement with nubile young women. As McNeal says, "This self-denial might seem an especially fitting way to expunge the guilt of the class that took advantage of its

serf-girls" (p. 148). In fact, of course, with few exceptions all the women in the Russian radical movement were noble women! (Krupskaya, for example, was of this class.) Relations between these "new people" were Chernyshevsky-like and McNeal makes an interesting point when he remarks that the purpose of these "ascetic" unions was "Certainly not the delivery of revolutionary babies, for the radical women do not appear to have become mothers very often" (p. 153).

25. Krupskaya, quoted in Fischer, *Life of Lenin*, p. 76.

26. See ibid. for a full account (see p. 79 for the lover's quarrel). Balabanoff's comment is in Angelica Balabanoff, *Impressions of Lenin*, trans. Isotta Cesari (Ann Arbor, Mich.: University of Michigan Press, 1964), p. 14.

27. Valentinov, *Encounters with Lenin*, p. 56–57.

28. Fischer, *Life of Lenin*, p. 69.

29. Wolfenstein, *Revolutionary Personality*, p. 252.

30. Fischer, *Life of Lenin*, p. 194. Needless to say, the imagery of the revolution emerging from the womb of capitalism and going through birth pangs was readily to hand in the writings of Marx and Engels. Nevertheless, the Revolution as Lenin's "child" is original with him, though it obviously has been prepared by the earlier usage.

31. Leon Trotsky, *Lenin* (New York: Minton, Balch & Co., 1925), p. 215. Trotsky knew whereof he spoke, for in general the loss of a great leader is perceived as the loss of a father. See, for example, Martha Wolfenstein and Gilbert Kliman, eds., *Children and the Death of a President* (Garden City, N.Y.: Doubleday, 1966).

32. Ulam, *Bolsheviks*, pp. 424–430, 520. Cf. Moshe Lewin, *Lenin's Last Struggle*, trans. A. M. Sheridan Smith (New York: Pantheon, 1968), where the emphasis, however, is put on Lenin's final political message.

33. Peter Struve, "My Contacts and Conflicts with Lenin," *The Slavic Review*, April 1934, p. 591.

34. Wolfenstein, *Revolutionary Personality*, p. 233.

35. Valentinov, *Encounters with Lenin*, pp. 42, 228–229.

36. Anatoly Vasilievich Lunacharsky, *Revolutionary Silhouettes*, trans. Michael Glenny (New York: Hill & Wang, 1967), p. 43. Other translations of Lunacharsky's remark use the term "magnetism" (*ocharovanie*) instead of fascination.

37. Gorky, *Lenin*, p. 68.

38. Krzhizhanovsky quoted in Fischer, *Life of Lenin*, p. 56; Gorky, *Lenin*, p. 14; and Trotsky, *Lenin*, p. 41. If one believes Geoffrey Gorer, Russia was uniquely situated to appreciate the full force of Lenin's eyes. According to Gorer, "The Psychology of Great Russians," in *The People of Great Russia. A Psychological Study*, by Geoffrey Gorer and John Rickman (New York: W. W. Norton, 1962), p. 133, Russian swaddling allows the child to move only with his eyes; his eyes "possess" objects, since his hands cannot. Exchanges of glances become particularly meaningful. Numerous love songs, for example, are devoted to the general subject, and "Dark Eyes" is a typical Russian favorite. The power of Lenin's eyes, if Gorer were correct, would receive powerful reinforcement from Russian culture and psyche itself; the hypnotist, so to speak, had a subject who was already predisposed. (The example of Rasputin also comes to mind in this context; can one see much of Russia's recent history as being mirrored in the eyes of two such disparate types as Rasputin and Lenin?)

39. Valentinov, *Encounters with Lenin*, pp. 13, 40, 102.

40. Ibid., p. 184.

41. Bertram D. Wolfe, "Leninism," in *Marxism in the Modern World*, ed. Milorad M. Drachkovitch (Stanford, Calif.: Stanford University Press, 1965), p. 54.

42. Theodore H. Von Laue, *Why Lenin? Why Stalin?* (Philadelphia and New York: J. B. Lippincott, 1964), p. 108.

43. Valentinov, *Encounters with Lenin*, p. 128.

44. Ulam, *Bolsheviks*, pp. 420, 428.

45. Quoted in René Fulop-Muller, *Lenin and Gandhi* (London: G. P. Putnam's Sons, 1927), p. 41.

46. Balabanoff, *Impressions of Lenin*, p. 146.

47. Ulam, *Bolsheviks*, p. 156.

48. Trotsky, *Lenin*, p. 48.

49. Pipes, *Revolutionary Russia*, p. 51.

50. Balabanoff, *Impressions of Lenin*, p. 82.

51. Ulam, *Bolsheviks*, p. 574.

52. Valentinov, *Encounters with Lenin*, pp. 140–141.

53. Possony, *Lenin*, p. 382.

54. Cf. Wolfe, "Leninism," p. 53. (We might also make the comparison to Cromwell.)

55. Fischer, *Life of Lenin*, p. 61.

56. Ibid., p. 215.

57. Ulam, *Bolsheviks*, p. 438. A comparison with both the puritan and the Chinese Communist armies is in order here.

58. N. Lenin, *The Letters of Lenin*, trans. and ed. Elizabeth Hill and Doris Mudie (New York: Harcourt, Brace, 1937), p. 27.

59. Valentinov, *Encounters with Lenin*, pp. 101–102.

60. Leonard Schapiro, "Lenin After Fifty Years," in *Lenin. The Man, the Theorist, the Leader. A Reappraisal*, ed. Leonard Schapiro and Peter Reddaway (London: Pall Mall Press, 1967), p. 8.

61. Bertram D. Wolfe, *The Bridge and the Abyss* (New York: Praeger, 1967), p. 64.

62. Gorky, *Lenin*, p. 36.

63. Ibid., p. 19.

64. Balabanoff, *Impressions of Lenin*, p. 6.

65. Lunacharsky, *Revolutionary Silhouettes*, p. 39.

66. Balabanoff, *Impressions of Lenin*, pp. 10–11. A comparison with Rousseau's comment in Chapter 2, p. 17, seems in order here.

67. Quoted in Peter Reddaway, "Literature, the Arts and the Personality of Lenin," in Schapiro and Reddaway, *Lenin. The Man, the Theorist, the Leader*, p. 53. See the classic analysis of the use of words as anal aggression in Erik H. Erikson, *Young Man Luther* (New York: W. W. Norton, 1958).

68. Trotsky, *Lenin*, p. 193.

69. Valentinov, *Encounters with Lenin*, p. 147.

70. Krupskaya, *Memories of Lenin*, p. 127.

71. Zetkin, *Reminiscences of Lenin*, p. 113.

72. Valentinov, *Encounters with Lenin*, p. 40.

73. Trotsky, *Lenin*, p. 191.

74. Valentinov, *Encounters with Lenin*, p. 42.

75. Krupskaya, *Memories of Lenin*, p. 62.

76. Valentinov, *Encounters with Lenin*, p. 150.
77. Krupskaya, *Memories of Lenin*, p. 84.
78. Quoted in Fischer, *Life of Lenin*, p. 108.
79. Lenin, *Letters*, p. 43.
80. Pipes, "Origins of Bolshevism," p. 45.
81. Krupskaya, *Memories of Lenin*, p. 90.
82. Gorky, *Lenin*, p. 27.
83. Krupskaya, *Memories of Lenin*, p. 89.
84. Quoted in Possony, *Lenin*, p. 331.
85. Quoted in ibid., p. 516.
86. Reddaway, "Literature," p. 62.
87. Ibid., p. 54.
88. Quoted in Wolfenstein, *Revolutionary Personality*, p. 35.
89. Valentinov, *Encounters with Lenin*, p. 43.
90. Ibid., p. 45.
91. Quoted in Reddaway, "Literature," p. 55.
92. Quoted in Fulop-Muller, *Lenin and Gandhi*, pp. 36–37.
93. Quoted in Wolfenstein, *Revolutionary Personality*, p. 185.
94. Gorky, *Lenin*, p. 45.
95. Ibid., p. 43.
96. Ibid. Cf. Hannah Arendt, *Eichmann on Trial* (New York: Viking Press, 1963), and Peter Loewenberg, "The Unsuccessful Adolescence of Heinrich Himmler," *American Historical Review* 76, no. 3 (June 1971).
97. Bertram D. Wolfe, *Three Who Made a Revolution* (Boston: Beacon Press, 1955), p. 42.
98. For an example of how complicated any actual Oedipus complex is, and how intertwined with the period and culture in which an individual may experience it, see Bruce Mazlish, *James and John Stuart Mill. Father and Son in the Nineteenth Century* (New York: Basic Books, 1975).
99. *What Is To Be Done?* was also a favorite novel of Lenin's brother Alexander, as well as of Lenin's later mentor, Plekhanov. As Lenin told V. Vorovsky in 1904 about his 1887–1888 experience, "I read from cover to cover Chernyshevsky's magnificent essays on aesthetics, art and literature, and the revolutionary figure of Belinsky became clear to me. . . . I was conquered by Chernyshevsky's encyclopedic knowledge, the clarity of his revolutionary views, and his unyielding polemical talent" (quoted in Reddaway, "Literature," p. 40). As for *What Is To Be Done?*, Lenin described it as having caused a revolution in his thought.
100. Valentinov, *Encounters with Lenin*, pp. 50–51.
101. Quoted in Wolfenstein, *Revolutionary Personality*, p. 165.
102. Chernyshevsky, *What Is To Be Done?*, p. 81.
103. Trotsky, *Lenin*, p. 27.
104. Ivan Goncharov, *Oblomov*, trans. Ann Dunnigan (New York: New American Library, 1963), p. 182.
105. Ibid., p. 189. However, for this quote I have used the translation in Fred Weinsten and Gerald Platt, *The Wish To Be Free* (Berkeley and Los Angeles: University of California Press, 1970), p. 209.
106. Fulop-Muller, *Lenin and Gandhi*, p. 20. It is interesting to note that in the early nineteenth century, Jeremy Bentham's brother Samuel spent some time in Russia working as an engineer and administrator. A sustained effort to deal with the utilitarian thread in Russian intellectual history is badly needed. Fortunately, Professor Ian Christie of the Uni-

versity of London is at work on Samuel Bentham's experiences in Russia.

107. Note Deutscher's comment about Lenin's home town: "Almost to the end of the century, Simbirsk had no telegraph, no telephone, and no railway connection with the rest of the world" (*Lenin's Childhood*, p. 16).

108. Ulam, *Bolsheviks*, pp. 145, 294.

109. H. G. Wells, *Russia in the Shadows* (London: Hodder & Stoughton, n.d. [1920?]), pp. 35–36.

110. Fulop-Muller, *Lenin and Gandhi*, p. 18.

111. Fischer, *Life of Lenin*, p. 258.

112. Theodore H. Von Laue, "Imperial Russia at the Turn of the Century: The Cultural Slope and the Revolution from Without," *Comparative Studies in Society and History* 3 (1960–1961):353–367.

113. Valentinov, *Encounters with Lenin*, pp. 152ff.

114. Quoted in Wolfe, *Three Who Made a Revolution*, p. 159.

115. Quoted in Alfred G. Meyer, *Leninism* (New York: Praeger, 1963), p. 204.

116. Krupskaya, *Memories of Lenin*, p. 35.

117. Valentinov, *Encounters with Lenin*, p. 80.

118. Quoted in Reddaway, "Literature," p. 62.

119. Wolfe, *The Bridge and the Abyss*, pp. 154, 156.

120. Quoted in Weinstein and Platt, *The Wish To Be Free*, p. 306. Cf. Chapter 7 of the present book.

121. Krupskaya, *Memories of Lenin*, p. 82.

122. Ulam, *Bolsheviks*, p. 232.

123. Vladimir C. Nahirny, "Some Observations on Ideological Groups," *American Journal of Sociology* 67 (1961–1962):400.

124. Cf. Fischer, *Life of Lenin*, p. 79, and Valentinov, *Encounters with Lenin*, p. 61.

125. Valentinov, *Encounters with Lenin*, p. 43.

126. Quoted in Tucker, "Lenin as Revolutionary Hero," p. 23.

127. Cf. Pipes, "Origins of Bolshevism," p. 51.

128. Valentinov, *Encounters with Lenin*, p. 130.

CHAPTER 9

1. James Reston, Boston *Globe*, August 27, 1971, p. 2; Maurice Meisner, "Utopian Goals and Ascetic Values in Chinese Communist Ideology," *Journal of Asian Studies* 28, no. 1 (November 1968):101–110; and Benjamin Schwartz, "The Reign of Virtue: Some Broad Perspectives on Leader and Party in the Cultural Revolution," *China Quarterly* 35 (July-September 1968):14.

2. As an illustration of the nuances of asceticism as it manifests itself in different cultures and religions, we can mention the connection between meditation and self-denial in the Chinese tradition. Emi Siao tells how Mao and some companions shared a pavilion one summer on top of a mountain: "They went without breakfast and supper. . . . Their diet consisted largely of fresh broad beans. Of course, there was an idea of economizing since none of them had much money. They went to the hilltop to meditate in the morning and then came down to bathe in a cold pond or in the river. . . . They believed in the steady practising of this 'austerity

training' programme" (Mao Tse-tung. His Childhood and Youth [Bombay: People's Publishing House, 1953], p. 41). Here, of course, meditation is linked to "austerity training," although the link is not a necessary one. What Mao eventually did was to detach his "austerity training" from meditation, to deny the contemplativity of the latter in the name of cultivation of actual hostility, and to place austerity and hostility in the service of the revolution. As another example of the different attitudes of different religions to aspects of asceticism, in this case to a seeming sadistic quality, we may note André Malraux's comment that "The basis of the West was individualism; an individualism which was at the same time the crucifix and the atomic reactor. I had earlier come across the uneasiness of Buddhists in face of the crucifix ('Why do they worship a man being tortured?')" (Anti-Memoirs [New York: Bantam Books, 1970], p. 287). If one thinks of the penitential strain in Christianity, one can see that what is torture for the Buddhist is asceticism for the Christian believer. Clearly, the variations in the theme of "classical," i.e., religious, asceticism are legion.

3. Quoted in Richard H. Solomon, Mao's Revolution and the Chinese Political Culture (Berkeley and Los Angeles: University of California Press, 1971), p. 293.

4. Stuart Schram, "What Makes Mao a Maoist," New York Times Magazine, March 28, 1971, pp. 8, 23.

5. Stuart R. Schram, "Mao: The Man and His Doctrines," in Revolution: A Reader, ed. Bruce Mazlish, Arthur Kaledin, and David Ralston (New York: Macmillan, 1971), p. 293.

6. Cf. Chapter 8, p. 149.

7. For a profound analysis of Mao's thought underlying the cultural revolution, see Frederick Wakeman, Jr., History and Will. Philosophical Perspectives of Mao Tse-tung's Thought (Berkeley: University of California Press, 1973).

8. Cf. Francis L. K. Hsu, Americans and Chinese (Garden City, N.Y.: Doubleday, 1970), p. 392, for evidence that the role of land distribution was less than it is usually thought to be.

9. Lucian W. Pye, The Spirit of Chinese Politics (Cambridge, Mass.: M.I.T. Press, 1968), p. xviii.

10. Solomon, Mao's Revolution, passim.

11. Pye, Spirit of Chinese Politics, p. 102.

12. I am aware, and should share this awareness with the reader, of the criticisms in various reviews of Solomon's book, some of which are severe. For example, in Journal of Asian Studies 31, no. 1 (November 1972): 101–105, Thomas A. Metzger says that, though "the concepts of authoritarianism and dependency do seem to point to some major behavioral tendencies in traditional China . . . yet . . . onesided . . . he [Solomon] ignores neo-Confucian aspects of the tradition, such as the knight-errant ideal, which influenced many Chinese including Mao." Metzger adds that it is "impossible to accept his position that traditional attitudes toward authority precluded legitimate protest," and believes it a "mistaken impression that Confucianism equates familial and political ethics . . . polity involved a different relation between leader and followers (no father stood in danger of losing Heaven's mandate)." In the same issue, F. W. Mote is even more severe. He takes Solomon to task for gross misconceptions and oversimplification of the "Confucian Great Tradition," which Solomon erroneously

treats as "monolithic and unchanging." Ezra Vogel, in *China Quarterly* 49 (January-March 1972):157–160, criticizes some of Solomon's methodology and states that the jump from Confucian classics to Mao, from peasants of all time to present-day fishermen (some of Solomon's respondents), and from Taiwanese (Solomon's interviewees) to mainlanders is too great. In addition, Vogel reminds us that Solomon has had no chance to investigate the family situation under Communism, thus basing half of his comparison on flimsy data. Benjamin Schwartz, in his review of Solomon's book in *Journal of Interdisciplinary History* 4, no. 3 (Winter 1973): 569–580, while admitting the truth of some of Solomon's propositions, also criticizes Solomon's view of Chinese (and Western) culture as reducible to one strand, and attacks his simplistic view of concepts such as "autonomy" and "authoritarianism," used by Solomon as if they were clear constants rather than shifting, ambiguous terms. For Schwartz, "the relationship between patterns of child-rearing and the emergence of ideas of individual autonomy may be far more complex than anything suggested in this book." So, too, "There is a singular failure on Solomon's part to distinguish that which may be universally human in his respondents' reactions from that which is peculiarly Chinese." In spite of these criticisms (and Solomon, of course, might argue as to their correctness), used with caution, and limited to our particular purposes, the Solomon book is most helpful and suggestive (all of the critics, except Mote, agree that the book has some virtues). Whatever its exaggerations and one-sidedness, Solomon's work has highlighted certain important aspects of Chinese political culture, unexamined elsewhere in such psychological detail. (For purposes of comparison, however, Hsu's *Americans and Chinese* is also indispensable.) I have found it legitimate, therefore, indeed requisite, to use Solomon's book in setting a context for Mao's own thought and behavior, as related to issues of revolutionary asceticism.

13. The May 4th movement suggests that this break with tradition was a "generational" experience for a number of young people.

14. Cf. Solomon, *Mao's Revolution*, p. 51.

15. Ibid., p. 515.

16. As my own book was being prepared for press, a manuscript copy of the book, *Mao Tse-tung: The Man in the Leader* (Basic Books, 1976), by my colleague and friend, Lucien Pye (who had previously favored me with a reading of an earlier version of this present chapter), came to my hand. I recommend the reader to turn here for a fascinating full-scale treatment of the depths and complexities of Mao. Pye, incidentally, tends to deprecate the role of the Oedipus complex in Mao's personal and political life, and to emphasize a pre-oedipal attachment to the mother. In my view, however, the two explanations need not be in conflict, but may go hand in hand, dealing as they do with different stages in the individual's life.

17. Jerome Ch'ên, *Mao and the Chinese Revolution* (New York: Oxford University Press, 1967), pp. 6, 20.

18. Edgar Snow, *Red Star Over China* (New York: Grove Press, 1961) (references in the text, with page numbers in parentheses, are to this edition). Some of the problems encountered by the psychohistorian in using autobiographical materials are discussed by Erik H. Erikson, "On the Nature of Psycho-Historical Evidence: In Search of Gandhi," *Daedalus* 97, no. 3 (Summer 1968):695–730, and Bruce Mazlish, "Autobiography

and Psychoanalysis," *Encounter* 35, no. 4 (October 1970):28–37. More specifically, as my friend Roxanne Witke points out, one would need to ask: "To what extent were Mao's experiences unique? How much was he a man of his generation? A man, or child, of his class, which was famous for raging, recriminating fathers and dominated mothers?"

19. In general, Chinese culture set itself in opposition to introspection (cf. Pye, *Spirit of Chinese Politics*, p. 149, and Hsu, *Americans and Chinese*, p. 24). While there are autobiographies, increasingly so under the impact of Western culture, and indeed forming a definite trend in the May 4th movement, they are usually not as revealing of self as Mao's.

20. Pye, *Spirit of Chinese Politics*, p. 122, makes the point that Mao may have exaggerated the "richness" of his father in order to justify his unfilial behavior. For Communists, of course, to be rich was to be a member of an evil class.

21. Erik H. Erikson, *Young Man Luther* (New York: W. W. Norton, 1958).

22. Ch'ên, *Mao and the Chinese Revolution*, p. 21.

23. Siao-Yu, *Mao Tse-tung and I Were Beggars* (Syracuse, N.Y.: Syracuse University Press, 1959), p. 6. Cf. Erik H. Erikson's analysis in *Childhood and Society* (New York: W. W. Norton, 1963) of Hitler's memory of a similar period in his life.

24. According to Siao, *Mao Tse-tung*, p. 6, "Mao Tse-tung was extremely devoted to his mother and remained all along her obedient, loving son. The many virtues she personified have had a good deal of influence on his later life."

25. Personal communication.

26. Solomon, *Mao's Revolution*, p. 36. Solomon, however, makes the interesting suggestion that it is the daughter who was the "Oedipus" of the Chinese family. She, in fact, is sent off by her family, with bound feet (the meaning of Oedipus is "wounded feet," i.e., his feet were pierced by the shepherd who was to leave him on the mountainside), and is perceived as disruptive of stable political life.

27. Vogel, "Review," p. 159.

28. Siao-Yu, *Mao Tse-tung and I Were Beggars*, p. 11, remarks about Mao's relation to his father, "It was always a question of money, and he [Mao Tse-tung] felt very despondent."

29. As Pye (*Mao Tse-tung: The Man in the Leader*) and others point out, however, Mao in fact continued to exhibit both markedly feminine and masculine traits in the rest of his life. What I am suggesting, of course, is that the feminine traits were highly threatening to him, therefore requiring a conscious effort at rejection.

30. Professor Leo Lee of Princeton University suggests that Mao later, as an "outsider" intellectual in Peking, reemphasized tough, military figures for his inspiration, becoming ever more and more antiintellectual. The identification problem in all of this is of great complexity; we can be sure, however, that it is rooted in Mao's original relations to his parents, though by no means fully explained on these grounds, since later experiences and persons also enter into the picture. In any case, the flavor of Mao's antiintellectualism comes through vividly in such statements as: "Since ancient times, those who create new ideas and new academic schools of thought have always been young people without much learning. It is reported that penicillin was invented by a launderer in a dryer's shop. Benjamin Franklin

of America discovered electricity. Beginning as a newspaper boy, he subsequently became a biographer, politician and scientist. Naturally one can learn something in school, and I do not mean to close down the schools. What I mean is that it is not absolutely necessary to go to school" (Speech at Chengtu Conference, March 22, 1958, quoted in the New York Times, March 1, 1970, p. 26).

31. Pye, Spirit of Chinese Politics, p. 121.

32. Our interpretation is strengthened if we remember that the Manchu officials' refusal to feed the starving people echoes Mao's accusation against his father of not feeding him enough.

33. Cf. Stuart Schram, Mao Tse-tung (Baltimore, Md.: Penguin Books, 1966), p. 54.

34. Leo Lee also informs me that changing schools was a common phenomenon of that generation, and Mao's personal odyssey must be seen in that context.

35. Emi Siao, Mao Tse-tung, p. 36, suggests that Mao mixed up some of his readings in his memory. According to Emi Siao, Mao read John Stuart Mill's System of Logic and Spencer's Study of Sociology.

36. Although Snow spells the name Yang Chen-chi, Schram spells it Yang Ch'ang-chi (Mao Tse-tung, p. 58); I follow the latter spelling.

37. Siao-Yu, Mao Tse-tung and I Were Beggars, pp. 41, 240.

38. If Siao-Yu is to be believed, Mao had an even earlier love, a girl named Tao Szu-yung, with whom he opened a cultural bookstore in Changsha. However, Siao claims, "They had very different ideas and later they separated on friendly terms." She was "much older than K'ai-hui, his second love" (ibid., pp. 43–44).

39. Snow, for example (p. 281), tells of another Chinese Communist, much like Mao, P'eng Teh-huai, who in 1926 married a middle-school girl who was a member of the Socialist Youth. Separated in 1928 by the Revolution, P'eng, in 1936, had not seen her since.

40. Malraux, Anti-Memoirs, p. 464. Siao-Yu hints darkly that Mao abandoned her to the Kuomintang while pursuing his own ambitions (Mao Tse-tung and I Were Beggars, p. 45), but this does not seem to accord with the other evidence we have.

41. Malraux tells us that the third wife "was the heroine of the Long March: wounded fourteen times. He divorced her (divorce is rare in the Chinese party); today she is governor of a province. Finally he married Chiang Ch'ing, a Shanghai film star who found her way to Yunan through the lines to serve the party. She directed the army theatre" (Anti-Memoirs, p. 465).

42. Schram, Mao Tse-tung, pp. 228–229.

43. Jacques Marcuse, "The Love Affair of Comrade Wang," New York Times Magazine, November 8, 1964, p. 41.

44. Stuart R. Schram, The Political Thought of Mao Tse-tung (New York: Praeger, 1963), pp. 94–102.

45. Anna Freud, The Ego and the Mechanisms of Defense (New York: International Universities Press, 1965), p. 181.

46. Schram, The Political Thought of Mao Tse-tung, p. 15.

47. Ibid., p. 16.

48. Mao's personal experience must constantly be set in its generational frame, for 1919 marked a watershed in both political and personal development for many of his contemporaries as well.

49. Mao does not mention it, but according to Emi Siao, "Among the articles involved in the regulations [of the Society] were those prohibiting gambling, visiting brothels, and loafing" (*Mao Tse-tung*, p. 57).

50. Robert Jay Lifton, *Revolutionary Immortality: Mao Tse-tung and the Chinese Cultural Revolution* (New York: Random House, 1968).

51. For the confusion about whether or not Mao did attend this meeting, see Ch'ên, *Mao and the Chinese Revolution*, pp. 85–86.

52. Robert Jay Lifton, *Throught Reform and the Psychology of Totalism* (New York: W. W. Norton, 1961), p. 369.

53. Schram, *Political Thought*, p. 30. For a factual account of some of these occurrences, see Ch'ên, *Mao and the Chinese Revolution*, chap. 5.

54. E. J. Hobsbawm, *Primitive Rebels* (New York: W. W. Norton, 1965).

55. There is great ambiguity as to what happened to Mao's children. See, for example, Ch'ên, *Mao and the Chinese Revolution*, pp. 86–87, and Malraux, *Anti-Memoirs*, p. 455.

56. Snow, *Red Star Over China*, pp. 78, 72, 74; Schram, *Political Thought*, p. 213.

57. Lifton, *Thought Reform*, p. 13.

58. Ibid., pp. 383, 385.

59. Quoted in Lifton, *Revolutionary Immortality*, p. 39.

60. Hsu, *Americans and Chinese*, p. 10. Cf. Pye, *Spirit of Chinese Politics*, p. 94.

61. Siao-Yu, *Mao Tse-tung and I Were Beggars*, p. 154.

62. Hsu, *Americans and Chinese*, p. 81. The persistence and tenacity of the old family pattern is suggested, however, by a *New York Times* report of October 27, 1968, which says among other things that "Peking officially discourages traditional attachments between parents and children, but members of Communist China's first families have established close public and private ties. . . . Recent reports . . . disclose that the first families are extending their power and influence through their children. Daughters of both the Chinese Communist leader, Mao Tse-tung, and his chief aide, Lin Piao, whose wives are already significant political figures, have emerged as influential personalities in journalism. Mr. Mao's daughter, Hsiao Li, is chief editor of *Chieh Fàng Chun Pao*, the publication of the armed forces, while Mr. Lin's daughter, Lin Tou-tou, writes for . . . the air force journal" (p. 10).

63. Hsu, *Americans and Chinese*, pp. 57–58.

64. Siao-Yu, *Mao Tse-tung and I Were Beggars*, p. 194.

65. Pye, *Spirit of Chinese Politics*, p. 26, claims that the Chinese have "a deep sense of insecurity over unstructured and ambiguous social relations—which leaves them with an insatiable need for total control or predictability in human relations."

CHAPTER 10

1. "Followers" is an amorphous term as we remarked earlier (see pp. 40). It can refer to immediate disciples and to general, mass supporters. Moreover, among the mass supporters, different groups may follow a particular leader for very different reasons, both emotionally and politically. For our purposes, we have used "followers" in a vague way—to do other-

wise would have required another book—and tried to indicate certain
functions the revolutionary ascetic fills for their common psychic needs.
For a critical treatment of this particular problem, however, see Fred Weinstein and Gerald M. Platt, *Psychoanalytic Sociology* (Baltimore: Johns
Hopkins University Press, 1973), passim.

2. See, for example, Gregory Rocklin, *Man's Aggression* (Boston: Gam-
bit, 1973). To put it another way, libidinal theory is only one part of
psychoanalysis, and analysis in terms of object relations, internalization,
narcissism, etc., may be, in many cases, more realistic and rewarding for
the psychohistorian. Our intention here, however, has been to pursue to its
ultimate revelations the hints offered in Freud's notion of the "leader
with few libidinal ties," while recognizing its limitations.

3. Barrington Moore, Jr., "Revolution in America?" *New York Review of
Books*, January 30, 1969, pp. 6–12.

4. For Reich, see Paul A. Robinson, *The Freudian Left* (New York:
Harper & Row, 1969); for Brown, *Life Against Death* (Middletown, Conn.:
Wesleyan University Press, 1959).

5. Daniel Cohn-Bendit and Gabriel Cohn-Bendit, *Obsolete Communism:
The Left-Wing Alternative*, trans. Arnold Pomerans (New York: McGraw-
Hill, 1968).

6. Quoted in Julius Lester, review of *Soledad Brother* (New York:
Coward-McCann, 1970) by George Jackson, *New York Times Book
Review*, November 22, 1970, pp. 10–14.

7. Lester, *Ibid.*, p. 14.

INDEX

INDEX

Abbott, W. C., 67–68, 69

Adolescence: asceticism in, 32, 33; intellectualization in, 33, 34

Aestheticism, revolutionary, 14, 216–219

"Affaire Deteuf," 81

Aggression: 214; Chinese attitude toward, 162; encouragement of, 210; Puritan perception of, 64–65

Ahimsa, 65

Akimov, Vladimir Maknovets, 115, 155

Alexander III (Tsar), 117, 142

Ambivalence: of Lenin, 113, 136–140, 147; of Mao, 158, 160

Anality, 59n; and capitalism, 58–59; and Lenin, 132, 134

Anarchism, 191–192

Anger: of Cromwell, 68, 70; of Lenin, 131, 136–137; of Mao, 168–169, 172

Anxiety: Puritan, 64; of Robespierre, 81

Armand, Inessa, 121–123, 139, 146, 154

Asceticism, 4, 214; in adolescence, 32–34; advantages of, 42; Chinese tradition of, 158; Christian compared with Hindu, 48; defined, 29, 30; democratic, 55; described, 41; and doctrine of election, *see* asceticism, elite; elite, 52, 53, 55, 73; Freud on, 6n; and masochism, 31, 32; of Lenin, 111–156, *passim*; of Mao, 172, 207; of Mill, 96; as model for followers, 38–39; occasional release from,

54; and Puritanism, 29–30, 61; religious and guilt, 47–49; revolutionary, 5, 6, 34, 206–207, 218–220; of Robespierre, 78, 82, 83, 89; and sadism, 31; and selflessness, 41–42; and utilitarianism, 94; worldly, 29, 61

Ashley, Maurice, 68, 70

Authority: Mao's problems with, 206

Autobiography, 165n, 166

Autumn Crop Uprising, 202

Axelrod, Pavel Borisovich, 136

Babeuf, François Emile, 82

Bain, Alexander, 96–97

Bakunin, Mikhail Aleksandrovich, 99, 106, 107n

Balabanoff, Angelica, 112, 122, 133–134

Baptist sects, 54–55

Barras, Paul, 24

Baxter, Richard: *Christian Directory*, 95

Beard, Thomas, 67, 68

Beethoven, Ludwig von, 6, 139, 140

Belinsky, Vissarion G., 97, 98, 99, 100, 101, 102

Bentham, Jeremy, 93, 94, 105; *Introduction to the Principles of Morals and Legislation*, 94; as revolutionary ascetic, 96, 97

Bentham, Samuel (brother), 148n

Bergasse, Nicolas, 25

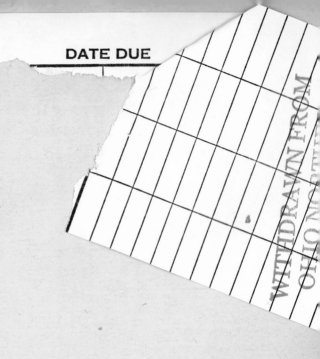
Catalog

If you are interested in a list of fine Paperback
books, covering a wide range of subjects
and interests, send your name and address,
requesting your free catalog, to:

McGraw-Hill Paperbacks
1221 Avenue of Americas
New York, N.Y. 10020